Wh

Carolee Duckworth and Brian Lane have written, for the serious independent traveler, the first in their European Travel Series of comprehensive guides, certain to be a valuable resource for initial planning and take-along on one's journey.

Your Great Trip To France, in an easy-carry, easy-reference format, deals step-by-step with such important topics as: Envisioning Your Trip; Guides on the Side; Master & Use the Train System; Your Trip Overview; Travel in the Spring or Fall; Castles & Gardens; Chateaux of the Loire; William the Conqueror's Caen; Arromanches & the D-Day Beaches; Art Markets, Gardens & Palaces; How to Pack Like a Pro; Play It Safe While Traveling and What to Take With You.

As the text of *Your Great Trip To France* tells the traveler: "If any or all of this strikes a chord, this is your book. You will not be traveling in a group. But you will not be alone out there on your own either...It will be our job and our mission to provide you with guidance so that you know exactly *what* to do, *why* you would want to do it, and *how* to do it every step of the way."

Glenda Loftin, Columnist & World Traveler

"Voila! Without leaving my home I feel like I've had a "Great Trip to France." Carolee and Brian do an outstanding job of blending advice, insights, suggestions and personal stories while walking the reader through an exciting journey. Bon Voyage – oui, oui!

Dr. Ed Bice, III: PEAK Performance Expert

An honest and thoughtful primer for those avoiding structured tours or who do not wish to travel abroad with a large group of Americans. The authors cater to the DIY crowd who have the confidence to experience travel adventure on their own terms.

Enough practical tips, suggested destinations, cultural context, and logistical information are presented to provide the prospective traveler with the everyday information needed to relax and enjoy the experience of living in France for the duration of their visit. The book is as much focused on the dynamics of interpersonal relations between travel companions as it is a travel guide. The advice offered in the "Travel Style" chapter alone would benefit any traveler to any destination.

From budgeting expenses for your French adventure to selecting and folding your clothing for packing, and reserving a table at a Parisian bistro, this travel guide is full of information you will use. Suggestions are offered to help you decide which of your credit and debit cards to take, trip planning calendars, where to visit outside of metropolitan Paris, hotels, museums, and train connects with memorable vistas that form the stress-free memory of your great trip to France.

This book is more of a guide for self-actualization while traveling than a listing of hotels, restaurants, and historical facts. This is accomplished by providing common everyday knowledge needed to relieve much of the stress of negotiating *quotidian* activities like buying train and tram tickets, interacting with waiters, exchanging money, avoiding pickpockets and scams, selecting museums to visit, ordering wine, and avoiding conflicts with travel companions. Lots of useful information.

Richard Budet, Business Solution Architect & World Traveler

Just the right amount of delightful local color experiences, and so many practical details to make you feel confident that you, too, can make this trip on your own, with the book as a most reliable, user-friendly "travel companion" in tow.

Dr. Marie Langworthy, Author & World Traveler

Your Great Trip to France is a valuable guide, giving great advise and tips for your travel experience to France. Carolee and Brian paint a picture to make you feel as if you are already there enjoying the many things France has to offer. You will catch yourself smiling as you read about their experiences, and will soon be on your way there, if you choose, with the detailed saving and planning advice they have prepared.

Karen Rought, Entrepreneur & Future Traveler

Your Great Trip to France:

Loire Châteaux, Mont Saint-Michel, Normandy & Paris

Carolee Duckworth & Brian Lane

ISBN-10: 978-0984513635

ISBN-13: 0984513639

YourGreatTrip.com

Published in the United States by New Cabady Press

Index included.

Library of Congress Cataloging-in-Publication Data

Duckworth, Carolee, and Lane, Brian

> Your great trip to France: Loire Chateaux, Mont Saint-Michel, Normandy & Paris/Carolee Duckworth and Brian Lane. New Cabady Press.

ISBN 978-0-984-51363-5 (paperback)

1. Travel—France. 2. France—Description and travel. 3. France—Guidebooks. I. Title. II. Title: Your great trip to France: Loire Chateaux, Mont Saint-Michel, Normandy & Paris.

    914.4   DC 707

Cover design by Debra Lane

ISBN-10: 978-0-984-51363-5

ISBN-13: 098-4-51363-9

About the Authors

Carolee Duckworth is a passionate traveler and trip designer, specializing in immersive, independent travel in France, Italy, Europe, Canada, and the USA. Having shifted from a 40-year career as an educator, she is now entirely focused on a lifestyle of travel design, research and writing. She is enthusiastic about  bringing the unique travel style and approach, developed jointly with her son, Brian, to maximize reader's fun and sense of fulfillment and to help them get the very most out of their travel experiences, wherever their journey leads them.

Brian Lane began traveling internationally at age 8, caught the "travel bug" early, and has never looked back. Having traveled independently in Europe, Asia, South America, Canada and the USA, he has refined his own approach to traveling, and developed an earnest desire to share those insights and techniques with others to help  build their confidence and empower them to strike out on their own, armed with the help of a solid plan. He is passionate about bringing readers the very best technology, safety, time and money-saving travel tips and techniques to make solid preparations in advance and not get caught off-guard by problems that can arise from poor planning. He strives to provide everything they will need to have a smooth travel experience and focus on their extraordinary adventure.

For more books by these authors, please visit their Author Central Page: amzn.to/26R7yaN.

Download Your Bonus Content

To access your free *Reader Resource Content*, go to: *http://YourGreatTriptoFrance.com/CustomizeYourTrip/*.

Here you will be able to download, customize and print your *2-Week Trip Calendar*, *Itinerary*, *Day Pages*, *Budget*, and *Packing Checklist*. Download them now so you can start to customize your own trip as you go through the book! You also will have access to customizable documents for two 1-Week trips, should your travel time be more limited.

In addition, you will find the authors' *trip photo gallery, short videos detailing a variety of how-to tips (including a ninja travel tactic that will make setting up your overseas communications drop dead simple, while potentially saving 100€ on your SIM card and cell phone connection service), as well as additional future travel resources that we will continue to add over time.*

Note: For a shortened link, use *http://bit.ly/1pZ9T1y*.

TABLE OF CONTENTS

Preface

There are hundreds of travel books out there, many of them very detailed and useful. These are excellent resources for learning everything possible in any given country or location. They are encyclopedic in their scope, and factual in their presentation. So what makes this book different and special?

Maybe you are eager to travel abroad independently, but overwhelmed by the encyclopedia of possibilities. You need to know more than what is possible; you need a plan. You would prefer to know in advance precisely what you will be doing, and how, for a number of reasons. First you may want to know what your trip will be like so that you can look forward to it—anticipation is always a large part of the enjoyment. Also you want to know exactly how much your trip will cost, and what trade-offs and choices you will need to make to get the most out of your travel budget.

But, although you need and want to have a plan, you have outgrown prescripted and preorganized bus tour travel, or you never liked it in the first place. You may have been abroad before, but on a group tour that ended up in a disappointing blur by the time it was over. Or you may have struck out on your own, but became frustrated that you were missing out for lack of a clear idea of what you were doing.

These less than optimum experiences even may have discouraged you from future traveling. Still, at some point, you may hope to discover a different style of travel that is more immersive and engaging. Even though you know what type of travel does *not* meet your expectations and ideals, the vision and possibility of what travel can be may still intrigue you.

If any or all of this strikes a chord, this is your book. You will not be traveling in a group. But you will not be alone out there on your own either. And so the quality of your experience will significantly surpass that of any group or ad hoc trip you've taken in the past.

Our mission is to provide you with guidance so that you know exactly *what* to do, *why* you want to do it, and *how* to do it, every step of the way. We are well prepared to be your guides because we have traveled extensively ourselves, and have taken the trip laid out in detail in the chapters ahead.

As you read this book, you will begin to envision your trip in vivid detail. You will be guided through the process of making the arrangements, preparing yourself well for a successful journey, and embarking on a kind of travel that will immerse and absorb you so completely, that you will return home already planning where you would like to travel next. You will feel inspired, well-guided, confident, empowered and ready to set off on your own travel odyssey.

In Chapter 1 you will be guided through the process of *imagining and dreaming* about your great independent trip, and understanding fully how it will be different from any group travel you've experienced in the past. This will be followed in Chapter 2 by a *descriptive trip overview* that will enable you to envision your trip vividly as a whole, and to walk through the itinerary in brief of each day's activities and experiences. By the end of this chapter, you will begin to feel excited about your upcoming trip. Chapter 3 will lay out *travel principles and tips* that will bring to your trip an entirely different level of connection and engagement, based on considerable freedom of choice and a hierarchy of options to keep your trip balanced and fun.

Then in Chapter 4 to Chapter 8, you will read the detailed version of each day of your trip, and what reservations to make before you set out. These descriptions and directions will form the basis for your customized *"Day Pages,"* adapted to your own trip details. You will take these along each day when you set out in order to have with you everything you will need to make that day work as planned... or as changed or amended when that suits you better, for whatever reason.

Your *Day Pages* will become your day-by-day lifeline, supplying at a glance everything you will need for the day, all readily available when you need it. Trains and train times. Addresses and opening hours for places you will be visiting. Phone numbers or locations for transportation to get you there. Reservation numbers for restaurants so you can call ahead to ensure a good table. Locations of interesting shops and markets. Small walking maps so that you will become better oriented with each passing day.

In Chapter 9, you will be guided through the tasks to make all your arrangements, with a *timeline and countdown* to ensure you have covered every base, and know exactly what to do and when. Chapter 10 will help you to prepare yourself well to make your trip a *great* trip.

"Great Trip" travel is a life-changing gift to give to yourself. So let's be off... Bon voyage...

Carolee Duckworth & Brian Lane

SECTION I:

YOUR TRIP

CHAPTER 1:
Imagine & Dream

"The world is a book and those who do not travel read only one page."
Augustine of Hippo

Join us on a remarkable 2-week trip to France, rich in experiences you will remember forever…experiences that will have an impact on you and your approach to life. This will be a "trip of a lifetime." History to walk around in. Phenomenal food. Parks and cafés. People-watching opportunities. Eating outdoors, with views of cathedrals, or rivers, or châteaux, or the tides coming in. Villages and old towns, some walled, some tiny, some medieval, some situated within a larger city, some perched on hilltops. Children in the squares, laughing as they ride the town Merry-go-Round. Fountains and gardens, with benches for pausing. Outdoor markets. Charming shops. Unexpected encounters. Vivid memories.

With this book as your guide, prepare yourself for a new experience in international travel.

Introducing Your "Guides on the Side"

First to introduce ourselves… We are Carolee Duckworth and Brian Lane, mother and son travel enthusiasts, who have experienced firsthand many "great trips." The style of travel we have planned here for you has grown out of hundreds of days of first-hand experience, some remarkable, some nerve shattering, some life-changing, and some laugh worthy.

Between us, we have experienced a snowmobile ride on a frozen lake north of the Arctic Circle on Christmas morning… The puzzlement of getting over, under, around, or through a wall of mountains blocking our way to the French Riviera, where we were staying for the next few days… Plus countless winding medieval village streets. And even a glorious stay in rooms atop a castle tower overlooking vast expanses of gardens, which turned out to be totally delightful once Brian managed to carry our luggage up the 40 narrow and worn stone steps to the top of the turret. One of our most memorable stays was in a former palazzo, where in order to get into our apartment, Brian was invited, in rapid and demonstrative Italian, to kick in the huge, ancient door that was stuck.

We have tried many styles of travel, ranging from guided group trips to taking off by car on our own for weeks at a time, driving through France. What we want to pass on to you is a style of travel that we can assure you far surpasses either traveling as part of a "group herd" or the opposite extreme of traveling lost and alone.

Group-guided tours came to mean, in our minds, a study in missed opportunity. Granted, as part of a group, you do know where to go and what to do at every moment. But what you are missing are just those specific types of activities and experiences that were your entire reason for taking the trip in the first place. Memorable, immersive experiences that could have and should have been defining moments of your trip, are sacrificed to the pace and style inherent to group travel, and the practical limitation that the only activities and venues possible are those that can accommodate a group of 30.

As you race past outdoor tables, where you long to pause for a café crème or a glass of wine while you take in the surroundings… As you converse mainly with your fellow group members, and rarely with the locals… As you watch dejectedly while what *you* would like to do dangles temptingly out of reach, subverted by the needs and demands of 30 other travelers… As you charge through a dizzying checklist based on "see it, take your picture, and move on"… Throughout these missed opportunities, you, like us, may come to recognize that you will need to *return* later in order to have the experience of actually *being* here.

At the opposite extreme, driving around on your own, in a country where you have only a rudimentary understanding of the language, results in feeling lost and BEING lost much of the time. This causes all sorts of anxiety. Not knowing where you are or what you are doing. Wondering whether or not you will ever find your way back to your "home base." Abandoning your rental car at one end of the city to find your way on foot and then return to move it. Not understanding the graphic and text on the airport sign, and overshooting the airport when you return to Paris to catch your plane home.

Two defining past travel experiences stand out, one for each of us. For Brian this moment of truth goes back to his first European trip, visiting Scotland with his grandparents at age eight. When he returned home and was asked: "What did you learn on your trip?" he replied, earnestly: "I

16

learned that in the cathedrals, the rest rooms are on the left and the gift shop is on the right." The stories and mysteries—the wonders of the enthralling country in which he had been traveling—had been lost for him. He had experienced no connections—no mind-opening moments. What could and should have been an enriching life experience for him had been reduced to a predictable formula for shopping and restroom visits.

For Carolee, the defining moment occurred on a trip called "*Spring Tulips of Holland.*" As a garden lover, she was eager to immerse herself in the culture of tulips and flower markets. And since she was spending her own hard-earned money to experience this beauty firsthand, she had high expectations. Driving through Amsterdam, the ultimate moment finally arrived as the bus paused at an intersection and the guide pointed out the location of the famous *Amsterdam Flower Market.* Carolee prepared to get off the bus to spend the next several hours absorbed in the colors and scents of all those lovely Spring flowers.

But, unbelievably, the bus door did not open. When the light changed, and the bus started to pull off, Carolee called out, "Stop the bus! I want to get off here!" Others joined her plea, begging to exit the bus too. But the bus moved on, rushing to the next "sight" on the list. No time had been allocated for us to immerse ourselves in all those glorious tulips we had crossed the Atlantic to see.

The travel landscape has now changed for both Carolee and Brian. Once they made the shift from group travel, as well as from the opposite extreme of traveling around adrift and lost in a rental car, they designed a style of independent travel that ensures a "great trip" every time. And they have never looked back. They now have a passion for travel that defines and inspires their every waking moment.

As your, "guides on the side," Carolee and Brian have provided you with a well-designed trip blueprint. Now they invite you to enjoy this remarkable *Great Trip to France*—a trip where you will know what to do, yet be free to discover, explore, immerse yourselves, learn, and otherwise to have "the full experience." *Following the guidance of this book, you will truly experience the country you are visiting… the culture of that country… the local people and their approach to life, which is, most certainly, distinct and different from yours. You will learn new things about yourself… And redefine and change your life patterns… And come to appreciate a broader view.*

As you join Carolee and Brian as your "Trip-in-a-Book" guides, you will experience for yourself this whole *other* immersive, connected, experiential mode of travel. You will have opportunities to absorb and embrace the culture, revel in encounters with the locals and their way of life, explore and satisfy your curiosity about history, and expand beyond your own known universe, seeing the world with new eyes.

With this book as your "invisible" guide—there when you need it and out of your way when you don't—you will be forever freed from that dreaded command to "get back to the bus on time."

Through this book, you will be inspired and guided, and otherwise will build your own confidence to step out the door and into your own travel odyssey, off to see the world.

Purpose, Mission & Philosophy of Travel

The mission of this book is to give you a full and independent trip, with all the details and possibilities laid out in advance... a blueprint. Although your trip will be well planned, you will be free to shape its pace and focus as you like, but with confidence, awareness and the capability to make it all work.

Your trip will immerse you, engage you, and enrich you. You will have an amazing experience and lots of fun...and possibly even make some friends with the locals along the way.

You will bring home lasting memories of the sights, the sounds, the feel, the sense, the tastes, and the ambience, because you will have ample time and opportunity to experience these fully. And you will bring home treasures that will recall your trip to mind whenever you use or look at them... And stories to share with family and friends... And ideas that stimulate you to think in broader ways.

Our Desiderata of Travel

We believe that ultimate travel is not just a trip to "see sights," but a life-changing journey that is to be fully experienced and remembered. Ultimate travel is made in untethered freedom that builds confidence and enables you to immerse yourself in a place, its culture, its history, its people, its sights, sounds, senses and energy. It is balanced...not overwhelming. It is engaging...not superficial. It opens the way to encounters with the locals and does not disconnect you from the people in whose homeland you are a guest. It is not dictated by the constraints of traveling in a group or controlled by rigorous and inflexible time limits. It is glorious and enthralling. It is never to be forgotten.

A Travel Connections Story

On a lovely evening in Paris, after a long day of museums and walking, Carolee and her husband, Barry, climbed aboard a boat bar docked along the Seine across from Notre Dame. They took a table, ordered a carafe of wine, and breathed in the beauty and the calm, studying the Notre Dame gargoyles and flying buttresses from their seats, and watching the boats cruise by on the river.

This turned out to be such a lovely spot, they decided to order appetizers as an excuse to stay awhile longer. Eventually musicians began to set up on the small stage directly across from their table. When the music started, it was clear this was no time to leave, so they ordered more wine and more appetizers, and decided to call this dinner. The band was amazing, particularly the keyboard player who played with total abandon, fingers flying.

A smiling Frenchman, who had been sitting at a table toward the far end of the boat, stood up and walked over, introducing himself politely in French, and asking if he could join Carolee and Barry at their front-row center table. Carolee, who speaks some French, responded with "Oui, certainement" ("Yes, certainly!").

The Frenchman explained, still in French, that this phenomenal keyboard player was his keyboard teacher, thus his interest in sitting up close where he could watch. He lamented that he would never play as brilliantly as his instructor.

Carolee countered: "C'est parce qu'il a quatre mains." That's because he has four hands! The Frenchman burst out laughing, and agreed that that could explain it.

Throughout these exchanges back and forth, Barry, who speaks very little French, sat smiling and nodding, but saying nothing. When the Frenchman looked inquisitively in Barry's direction, Carolee explained that her husband spoke little French, but had fully mastered one sentence. This intrigued the Frenchman, who of course wanted to know what this sentence was. So Carolee queued Barry, "Say your sentence, Darling."

Barry, with his sentence always ready, belted out: "Il fait très beau aujourd'hui!" It's a very beautiful day today! The Frenchman laughed and affectionately threw his arm around Barry's shoulder.

Later the Frenchman invited Carolee and Barry to stay with him and his family the next time they came to Paris. This is the type of priceless connection that becomes indelibly imprinted in memory.

And So... Learn About Your New Travel Style

So this is going to be a wonderful trip – *your* wonderful trip. France will unfold before you, and you will have full experiences that you will remember forever. Let's focus next on the style of your trip... the big picture.

CHAPTER 2:
Travel Style

The great trip that has been set out for you here will empower you with a clear understanding of what you are doing and how to do it, as well as provide you with the tools to make it all possible. Your trip will be unrushed, with many choices, filled with experiences and opportunities to connect with the locals. You will be taking a trip that is, in a word, unforgettable... A trip of a lifetime...

Your travel confidence will grow as you go, knowing that you will:

1. Travel independently, but with a plan.

2. Make modifications to adapt your trip to your own liking.

3. Master and use the train system.

4. Arrive and "be there."

5. Make optimum use of local transportation.

6. Have the full experience.

7. Enjoy yourself completely and thrive.

8. Connect with the locals.

9. Balance the budget.

10. Take treasures and memories home.

Your Trip Will Be Independent But Well Planned

You will be traveling to places that are so remarkable, and seeing things that are so interesting, you will immediately begin to reap the benefits of traveling independently. Before you leave, you will adapt your trip to your own preferences, interests, style and pace. And you will have the flexibility of altering your timing according to your interests... to pause and fully experience what strikes you.

This book provides you with a complete trip blueprint, based on in-depth research, as well as experience. So you will have a good idea of what your options are before you arrive. And you will be able to avoid the frustration of missing out on things you really would have liked to do or see had you only known about them in time.

Anticipate and Plan

Lack of preparation can add to stress levels on any trip, especially a trip to a foreign country like France, where people speak a different language, and you may have limited access to the internet while you are traveling. Doing some preliminary groundwork before you leave home will make a tremendous difference in how smoothly your trip goes, and how much fun you have along the way.

As an example, when you visit the Louvre for the first time, you likely will be overwhelmed by its vastness, with over 35,000 pieces on display. Visiting the entire museum is simply out of the question. The day plan for Day 14 (in Chapter 8) provides you with a pathway for your Louvre visit. You may opt to further plan your visit on the Louvre website (*http://www.louvre.fr/en*) to decide which wings, historical periods, mediums and styles of art interest you most, and then make sure to view the works at the top of your list before you run out of time and energy.

Adapt Your Trip to Your Liking

Your trip Day Pages will provide you with a full schedule, and lots of specifics. But what if you discover that tomorrow is *Market Day*? Or you hear enchanting pan flute music drifting down the shopping street and emerge onto the square to find live performers playing in the sun beside a café that faces a lovely old church?

What if you spot a shop that sells *Santons*—those remarkably detailed artisan-created figurines, popular for collecting, that portray all the chief characters in the village including the baker, the "goose girl," the old couple, the crazy man, and the ladies of Provence, as well as Mary, Joseph, baby Jesus, the shepherds and the Wise men? Or when you encounter a wine-tasting tour in the candle-lit catacombs of a former abbey?

When these and other golden opportunities present themselves, you are free to, even encouraged to, deviate from the plan, alter your path, and otherwise seize the moment, then rearrange as needed. Take advantage of happy coincidences that occur. Experience *Market Day*. Listen while the pan flute music soothes your soul. Pause in the *Santon* shop to pick out a few figures that strike your fancy—maybe the woman carrying a basket of lavender or the little drummer boy. When you happen upon the old abbey that offers wine tasting in its crypt, pay the few Euros for your tasting cup, and pick up a form to record your descriptions and scores of the wines you taste, placing asterisks beside your favorites. Then walk through the catacombs, pausing in front of the wine barrels to pour yourself samples by the light of the candle.

As you shift your plans for the day to get the most from unforeseen opportunities, you may need to do some rearranging of what you had planned, according to what is most important to you. But you will always have your original itinerary as a guide to help you avoid missing out on any of the "must see" items at the top of your list.

And as you make choices, and reprioritize how you spend your time on *this* trip, remember that, if this trip awakens your thirst for adventure, as it did ours, you likely will return here again in years to come. So you will have other chances to do what you miss doing this time.

Master & Use the Train System

You will be traveling by train, so you will face none of the heady challenges of independent travel by car. Instead, you will have the luxury of relaxing as you pass through the vibrant landscapes, possibly even drifting into a contented nap to reenergize yourself for your next venture. Using the excellent European rail system will help you bypass many of the daunting, even overwhelming, trials you otherwise would be forced to face the moment you set foot in France.

Given that you already will have your fair share of challenges on this trip, eliminating the additional tribulations of driving will be a marvelous gift to give yourself so that you can enjoy your trip, not just survive it. *A firm suggestion. Do not consider traveling by rental car instead of by train. Please! And do not compromise by substituting a group bus trip. No cars! No buses!*

Since you will not be driving in France, you will not experience the complete confusion of the "autoroute," or the spot-on energy it requires to drive in France, where tailgating is a given, and where you will always be in the way, with highly impatient drivers riding your bumper. You will not be confounded figuring out how to buy gas from unpeopled gas stations, with pumps that are mysteriously labeled "Plomb" and "Sans Plomb," not to mention the mind-boggling prices per *liter* (about 1/4 gallon).

You will not face the absolute requirement for a full-time navigator, with a GPS and two maps at the ready at all times, one for the whole of France and one for the immediate region, continuously plotting your path in connect-the-dot fashion from one "round pointe" (traffic circle) to the next. Each traffic circle becomes its own multiple-choice test, with the distinct likelihood that you will get it wrong, and end up speeding off in the wrong direction to who knows where.

And have we mentioned that even when you think you may for once know where you are going, there is a good chance you will come upon a sign that simply declares "Rue Barrée." Road barred. And, no, there will not necessarily be a "Detour" arrow pointing you in the direction you need to go instead. Then there's the challenge of parking. Even when you do manage to find one of those rare parking spots, you then will need to work through the puzzle of parking rules and procedures that vary town by town.

And, oh, by the way, how good are you at reading French? Will you understand the road signs, the street signs, the system of blocked pedestrian streets, enough to function? Will you be successful finding a way to park your car on the street or in a parking garage, and correctly pay for parking? Will you find yourself looping endlessly on and off the Autoroute, trying to get headed in the right direction, then repeatedly misreading and missing your exit? Will you be stymied completely when you encounter a sign declaring that the road ahead is closed—"rue barrée"—with no detour signs to clue you in on which way to go instead?

Enough of all this! Since you will be taking trains from location to location, you will "miss" these and other potentially daunting challenges. Instead, you will sit in your comfortable train seat, sipping coffee and enjoying a chocolate croissant, while you watch the countryside go by—the tidy farms and fields, the villages perched on hillsides, the quaint railway stations. Which plan sounds better to you—REALLY?

Arrive and "Be There"

Instead of swooping through, then moving on, a style of travel that prohibits you from actually *arriving* anywhere, you will have the time you need to learn the charms and significance of each place you visit. You will take the time to experience its lifestyle and hear its stories. By staying longer in each of your "home bases," you also will have rich opportunities to venture out on day trips that will give you a broader sense of the cultural bounty of the region.

There is always an all-important trade-off between trying to take in more places and taking more time in each place. What you will gain from having more time in fewer places is that you will have the luxury of settling in and making yourself at home. You will experience more when you decrease the frantic flitting around and actually arrive. As with many things in life, less is more!

To *arrive and be there,* you will:

1.   Orient yourself and "make yourself at home."
2.   "Live" there, however briefly.

Orient Yourself and "Make Yourself at Home"

On group trips, , although you will have a guide, you likely will feel lost much of the time. As you play "follow the leader," you will forego any opportunities to learn and find your own way. You may not even know where you have been after you have been there. At the other extreme of making up your trip as you go, you again will often feel lost, but because you *are* lost.

On this, your *Great Trip,* you will not feel lost. And you will most certainly know where you have been after you've been there. In each new location, you will begin your time there with a walkabout to get oriented, using this book to guide you. If there is a river, lake or ocean, you will use them to establish your own sense of direction.

Starting with your immediate neighborhood, then branching out to surrounding areas, you will discover where "your" bakery is, as well as "your" delicatessen, wine shop, fresh market, pharmacy and ATM. You will know "your" closest stops for public transportation. And you will identify an appealing spot to meet up with your travel companion(s) when you venture off to spend time independently. This meeting spot may be a café in the square or on a bench beside the fountain, or any such spot where waiting will be its own entertainment. Once you are oriented, you will know where you are and where to go next. Then you will be able to expand on your knowledge, and begin to feel comfortable and confident moving about and exploring your new "home away from home."

You will carry with you a good map, and so will feel assured that if you do happen to wander beyond the bounds of the areas you know, you will be able to reorient yourself in short order. Also, each day as you venture out, you will have along with you "Day Pages" with all the information, addresses, phone numbers and thumbnail maps you need to navigate your day comfortably. On the rare occasions when, despite your maps and Day Pages, you somehow do find yourself completely lost, you will know to resort to "Plan B"—asking a local for help, which often leads to an interesting encounter.

Or, if all else fails, and you feel over your head at any point, you always will be able to extricate yourself by simply hailing a taxi to take you back to more familiar territory. Always take along a written copy of the address where you are staying and enough cash to get you back to your flat, should you need to.

By using this approach to finding your way, you will surprise yourself at how quickly you will feel confident walking out to your bakery for fresh croissants in the morning, then stopping by "your market" to gather up items for your picnic in the park beside the river. And you *will* actually know where the river is!

"Live" There, However Briefly

When traveling with a group, you will, by necessity, be staying in larger hotels, often in areas that are thickly populated by tourists. And you will be limited to areas that can be reached by a huge bus. So, wherever you go, you will "hover" there, not "live" there.

In contrast, during *Your Great Trip*, you will be free to book accommodations that make for their own memorable experiences, situated in prime locations. A room in a charmingly restored 17th century manor house, with a French balcony from which you can watch sunsets over the Loire, and a connected turret room that looks out on the castle across the street... A restored abbey... The tower of a ruined castle perched high above the river... A small hotel near the Seine, across from Notre Dame.

For breakfast you will walk down the stairs of the 17th century townhouse to the elegant dining room, or up the stairs to the rooftop terrace, with a view of the river. Or you will step out onto your little balcony to breakfast on the bread and cheese, salami and fruit you gathered yesterday at the Saturday Market.

And so the place you stay will become an essential part of the full experience of your trip. Your location will put you at the heart of what you have come to see and experience. You will walk out the door to old town, or to the river, or next to the chateaux. In a word, when you walk out the door, you already will "be there."

Make Optimum Use of Local Transportation

Once you arrive by train in each of your home-bases and orient yourself, you will immediately tackle the challenge of becoming adept at the transportation system unique to that location, then use it at will from that point on. As well as carrying you where you need to go, these local modes of transportation can be rich experiences, and part of the pleasure.

In Amboise, you will speed across the countryside by taxi, wind in your hair through the open windows, experiencing firsthand the dauntless French approach to driving through the mazes of fields and vineyards, curves and circles, and the narrow streets of the villages.

In Paris, you will travel mainly by *Batobus* (boat bus) along the Seine, cruising under stunning bridges, enjoying unobstructed views of the many famous sights that border the riverfront to your left and right. Quickly you will learn the sequence of the bridges, as well as the stops along the route... *Notre Dame. Hotel de Ville. Louvre. Champs-Élysées. Tour Eiffel. D'Orsay. Sainte-Germain.*

When you do occasionally venture away from the Seine, you will travel by Metro. Or possibly you will take a jaunt on one of the readily available Vélib' city bikes, gliding up and down streets at a faster clip, able to cross from one end of Paris to the other at will, with the option of stopping where and when you like. This will enable you to channel your energies, and save your feet, so you can see and experience more during the precious time here before you run out of steam for the day.

These various local modes of transport will add their own value to the richness of your trip. *Getting there will be part of the fun.*

Have the Full Experience

As you read about, then plan, your *Great Trip*, you will immediately begin to experience it in your mind's eye. Anticipation is a significant part of the pleasure of *Great Trip* travel.

Well before you actually board the plane, imagine yourself on your way. As you set up places to stay and book your planes and trains... As you read the *Day Pages* ahead (in Chapters 4–8) that will walk you through your upcoming trip day by day and bring it to life... As you adjust these *Day Pages*, customizing them to the particulars of your own trip plan...

27

Throughout the process, let the experiencing begin in your imaginings.

When you actually do set off on your trip, be prepared to take an active role, "seize the day," and otherwise reap the full experience. To accomplish this, deliberately carry out the actions and methods, and embody the attitudes, of a *Great Trip* traveler. These include:

1. Seek out experiences that excite you and your interests.
2. Activate your senses.
3. Shift your habits to increase your range of experience.

Seek Out Experiences that Excite You

Because you will be in control of your own trip, you will be able to act upon it—to ensure that it will be a full and enjoyable experience for you. Prepare to take charge of your trip, participate in it actively, and otherwise make this trip work for you.

Each and every great trip has its own somewhat different focus and quality, based on the unique interests and enthusiasms of individual travelers. If you are a music lover, insert more music opportunities as you go—organ concerts in cathedrals, string ensembles in ancient churches, jazz groups on boat bars, singers in piano bars, sitting atop pianos, belting out love songs.

If you are a history enthusiast, learn as much as you can in advance of your trip, as well as during it. Explore the historical significance of what you are seeing—the towns, the châteaux, the monuments, the historical figures, whose stories abound. So too, if you love architecture... Or art... Or sculpture... Or all of the above...

Activate Your Senses. Look Up, Look Down

You will be surrounded throughout your trip with a feast for the senses. This will not be the time to meander around with eyes glazed over and your mind on other things, or glued to your Facebook feed. Become an active *noticer* of your surroundings. *Above all, be where you are.*

There will be no need to rush. Everything you are doing throughout the days of your trip will "count" as "doing it." You won't need to race off to get anywhere else fast, because you already will be there. This *is* what you have come to see. Even as you walk toward an essential museum on your list, you will pass through the "living museum" that surrounds you everywhere you turn.

Look up at the tops of buildings to spot the decorative carvings and gargoyles. Look into shop windows at the colorful and stylish displays, then look at the medieval buildings in which the shops are housed.

Pause to notice both the natural and the man-made, the people and the things. Watch the children riding the carousel. Observe the couples talking intently in the cafés, while sipping wine and attacking an oyster feast served on a three-tiered tower of ice. You may decide to enjoy your own oyster feast later. Find a bench from which you can watch the fascinating flow of humanity. Stand on bridges as boats glide beneath you.

Peek into the bakeries in the morning to see and smell the fresh bread, crusty and tempting, spilling from the shelves. Look in again when you walk by later to see those same shelves, now stripped bare. Spot the flowers. The fountains. The curiosities. The unexpected.

In a word, give yourself permission in advance to slow down or even to STOP! Treat your trip as a stroll, not a race or a marathon! If your mind begins to drift, bring it back to your surroundings. And remind your travel partner to do the same. Your only task at the moment is to BE here.

Because there will be so much to be seen, there also will be much to be missed. Make it your plan, and your objective, to take it *all* in.

Shift Your Habits to Increase Your Range of Experience

You know what your established habits are—your comfort zones. You may be tempted to cling to your habits throughout your trip. But this will decrease significantly the fullness of your experience, and you will emerge untouched and unchanged at the end of it. Make every effort to reach beyond your habits. If you're going to do what you've always done, traveling is a very expensive way to do that. However, if you are ready to break free of former habits, and have some fun in the process, you will be repaid royally.

Yes, you normally eat cereal for breakfast, with a banana and a single piece of dry toast. And, yes, you like to have a chicken sandwich for lunch, or maybe a ham and cheese. Generally you may see shopping as a chore to be gotten out of the way. So you stride past anything unrelated to your mission, make your selections, purchase what you need, then get out as quickly as possible. Wherever it is that you need to go, you may be in the habit of taking the shortest route to get you there, so you can get it over with and return home. And, as a rule, you may end each day reading or watching television, then take a quick shower, and get to bed early.

So now here you are in France. First of all, you will find that you will not have ready access to your favorite box cereal for breakfast. But if you are willing to let this go, you will discover something much better—a typical French breakfast of breads and cheeses, salami and yogurt, café crème and fruit. Even the McDonald's in France offers the option of a proper French breakfast—three pastries, including a croissant and a chocolate croissant, with great coffee. So, just for now, decide to forgo your tried-and-true, and experience breakfast the French way.

If you are partial to a ham and cheese sandwich for lunch, you will be happy to discover that, yes, you can enjoy one here. But it will be deliciously toasted, and it will be called a "croque monsieur" (translation: a "crunchy for the master"). Yummm!!!

And please, at least temporarily, alter your attitude toward shopping. Instead of viewing shopping as a chore to get through quickly, regard it as an opportunity to explore. When an occasion to shop presents itself, approach it with curiosity, or even enthusiasm.

There may be nothing in particular that you need or want to purchase. Nonetheless, just wander the shops as "living museums," where everything on display is also for sale. Look for the unusual. Admire the handwork— the tapestries and embroidery, the lacework and carvings. Study closely the old maps, and the local booklets that offer a different perspective from your own. Even the illustrated children's books, with legends and stories that may be unfamiliar to you, will be interesting to peruse. And, should you discover a treasure you would like to take along, all the better.

Despite the fact that your general evening habit is to stay in and go to bed early, break free and venture back out after dark. Take an afternoon rest, or a "power nap" to prepare yourself to "stay up with the grown-ups."

As evening falls, you will enter a new and illuminated world. Bridges will be aglow. The château on the hill will hover majestically above you, resplendent with spotlights. The locals will come out to stroll along the river. Cafés will come alive. Music will drift out into the streets. Catch a glimpse of this night world. These will be memories for life!

Enjoy Yourself Completely and Thrive

To make *your* vacation unforgettable, find ways to protect your fun and enjoyment and to avoid falling unwittingly into traps that are potentially energy-sapping. Such hazards are particularly perilous for travelers who have been conditioned by habits and attitudes learned from past marathon experiences on group trips, or from traveling as best they could on their own.

With a little pre-planning, and by observing a few simple keys to being a more balanced traveler, you will have better experiences and more fun, and be assured of a great trip every time you travel. These keys include:

1. Maintain a comfortable pace.
2. Avoid traveling with the crowds.
3. Keep your trip relaxed and fun.
4. Work at being a good travel partner

Maintain a Comfortable Pace

Often travelers try to pack in as much as they possibly can, thinking that by doing so they will get more value for their money and have a more enriching experience. While this may seem to make sense intellectually, it can be a recipe for disaster. It's easy to get so caught up in the excitement of trying to do everything, that you end up feeling rushed and exhausted by the overly-aggressive pace you have imposed on yourself. Ultimately, such errors in pacing can make the enjoyment go out of the trip, or even cause you to get sick. And this you do not want.

Group trips often try to pack too much into a limited amount of time, leaving travelers feeling rushed and frustrated—aware that they are missing out. Constantly racing from place to place, herded about by travel guides who have seen all this dozens of times before, the trip flashes by so quickly it all becomes a blur by the time they return home.

While you are on your *Great Trip*, traveling independently with this book as your guide, you will be in control of the pace of your trip. When you need more time, take it. When you spot something marvelous, stop and enjoy it. Lounge on the steps outside d'Orsay, listening to the marvelous pianist playing his full-sized piano on the sidewalk. Hang out watching the sidewalk artist beside the Pompidou Center as he completes his chalk drawing masterpiece. If you discover an organ concert in progress in Notre Dame, take the time to listen to it for as long as you like.

When you are out and about, there's no need to push yourself too hard. Give yourself permission to slow down, to take "power pauses" to recharge your batteries, and to experience things that pop up along the way. Sometimes "less is more."

Often you will be walking... at your own pace, pausing where you wish. On your strolls through the elegant *Tuileries Gardens*, with its vibrant colors and striking sculptures, you will reach a large pond surrounded by inviting chairs, where Parisians gather to sit and bask in the sun. And you will have the freedom to find yourself a chair and join them before you climb the hill to stand in awe surrounded by the misty loveliness of Monet's waterlily murals in *l'Orangerie*.

If you have a yen to linger over a coffee, or a glass of wine in a café... If you feel that you're at the end of your rope and need to sit awhile on a park bench to regain your energies, while watching the parade of people passing by... Even if you've just had enough for the day... Set your own pace. When it suits you, especially on the day after a strenuous travel day, allow yourself the luxury of a slow morning. Ease into your day as you would on a Saturday at home, after a hard week at work.

Remember, this is *your* vacation, to be spent as you like. There is no need to set new records of how many museums and attractions you can see in one day. Traveling is not about doing everything you possibly can. It's about relaxing, unwinding and having great experiences.

Avoid Traveling with the Crowds

When you travel with a group, every place you go will be crowded because you *are* a crowd. By definition, traveling in the company of 30 others produces a constant reality of "hurry up and wait." You will suffer through long, tiresome lines for hotel check-in, to purchase tickets for sights, and to use the restroom. At restaurants, you will be one of 30 people placing your dinner orders at the same time, then awaiting the arrival of your drinks and food, and later your check.

On your *Great Trip* you will be in crowd-avoidance mode, moving against the crowds, not with them. Wherever you encounter swarms of people, and see that the lines are building up, you will have the flexibility to go somewhere else instead, then come back later when the crowds disband.

So you will be able to admire Monet's pond lilies, or Van Gogh's self-portrait, or the model of da Vinci's rotating bridge, without throngs of people blocking your view. And you will be first in line for ice cream in da Vinci's park. In Paris you will have in your pocket the "magic" Museum Pass that will allow you to skip the lines at museums. And you will have advance tickets to avoid the lines at the Eiffel Tower.

While you visit the châteaux of the Loire Valley, you will have the time freedom to fully explore these phenomenal and historical palaces, inside and out. If there are crowds blocking the door to Chenonceau, you will be able to shift the order of your visit to take in the gardens first and delay your entry to the palace itself until after the masses have dispersed. You will have time to wander the gardens, as well as to visit the ballroom and royal chambers. And, if you so choose, you will be free to pause for lunch right there, sitting at an outdoor table, with a view of the castle.

When you visit Mont Saint-Michel, again you will enjoy the considerable benefits of traveling against the crowd, moving about in a pattern that separates you from the throngs. Since you will be staying overnight on the Mont, by the time the masses arrive and flow like a torrent through the gates, you already will have climbed up to the Abbey at the top. When the hordes complete their climb to reach the entrance to the Abbey, you will be making your way back down by way of the ramparts.

As the throngs flood the restaurants on the Mont for lunch at noon, racing to bolt down a meal in time to get back to their buses, you will be at liberty to snack on the cheese and crackers you gathered earlier, and wait to dine later, after the streets have emptied and you have the Mont more to yourself. So you will dine at a window table as you watch the spectacle of the tides advancing across the sands at the speed of galloping horses, until the sea surrounds the Mont and renders it an island again.

Keep Your Trip Relaxed and Fun

Have you ever been on a vacation that turned out to be more stressful than your normal work and life at home? Let's face it, traveling anywhere can be remarkably challenging, whether it be visiting relatives nearby, making your way to a national park you've always wanted to see, or embarking on a grand adventure overseas. You find yourself plucked out of your comfort zone and in unfamiliar territory. But travel doesn't need to add to your stress level, raise your blood pressure, or make you run for antacid tablets.

Here are a few tips that can help make traveling more balanced, relaxing and fun.

1. Design in your creature comforts
2. Go easy on yourself
3. Balance your activities

Design in Your Creature Comforts

Being away from home doesn't mean that you have to "rough it" as you would if you were backpacking in the mountains. Before leaving on your trip, consider what comforts of home you'd like to bring with you to help soften the impact of travel. Ultimately, you will be the one carrying your own suitcase, so think carefully about which items on your "comfort" list are sufficiently necessary to merit the additional weight in your luggage.

These choices will be largely personal, so add or subtract from this comfort list:

☐ refillable water bottle,
☐ small umbrella or rain jacket,
☐ sweater or light wrap,
☐ second reliably comfortable pair of shoes,
☐ across-body shoulder bag or daypack,
☐ sunhat and sunglasses,
☐ medical kit items like Band-Aids, anti-diarrheal, antihistamine, painkillers, antibacterial creams, and cough drops,
☐ tissues, lotion and sun block,
☐ collapsible shopping bag,
☐ nightlight,
☐ music source and a small Bluetooth speaker,
☐ laptop, notebook, or tablet.

Just think of some of the small items that make your life a little bit easier at home, and put them on your creature comforts list. More about this in Chapter 10.

Go Easy on Yourself

Anytime you travel and step out of your comfort zone, the number of things that can "challenge" you dramatically increases. Cut yourself some slack when traveling. There's no reason to get upset when things that are normally simple, and a matter of routine, trip you up and get in your way.

For example, when traveling in a foreign country like France where you don't speak the language, even finding a restroom can be a challenge. The food is not what you're used to, and asking simple questions with unfamiliar phrases from a book can feel daunting and embarrassing. Even going to the pharmacy to buy basic essentials can be an ordeal, with unfamiliar brands, not to mention that everything is in French.

Allow yourself some extra time to "flounder" a bit. Quickly get over any initial shyness you have about asking for help whenever you need it. These "permissions" can make a huge difference in how smoothly your travel days will go. And you will be surprised at how quickly the French people will make every effort to assist you once you overcome your hesitations about asking for help.

If you let the intriguing uniqueness of the French culture and lifestyle be part of the adventure of your trip, you'll find yourself eliminating stressors, having a lot more fun, and making friends along the way.

Maintain a Balance of Activities

Since this is your trip, you get to decide where you will focus your attention for activities. However, as a general rule, you will have the best experience if you maintain variety in what you do. Too much of anything can get tiring. More does not necessarily mean "better," even for activities that are immensely interesting to you.

As an example, two castles a day, for three days in a row, is definitely out of balance. If you attempt this pace, the charm and the magic, the history and the amazement, will be lost. Stop at four! By the time you reach your fifth castle, you will be on "château overload," dragging yourself through the motions, and thus "wasting" a castle. It will be much better to save some castles for another year, and intersperse other types of activities into your castle days to break things up a bit.

Your *Trip Day Pages* will provide you the bones of a balanced set of activities to keep your daily adventures fresh and exciting. These *Day Pages* will be your starting point to help make sure that you won't get burned out on any one type of activity. Make adaptations to your trip based on your own particular interests, adding more of the types of activities that you will particularly enjoy. And don't forget to keep your travel partner's interests in mind when you do. One way to ensure that neither you nor your travel partner tires of a single type of activity, is to take turns deciding what comes next for the day.

Work At Being a Good Travel Partner

Traveling with another person can be a challenge. As easy as it may be to be around friends, spouses and significant others for long periods of time at home, there is a difference when you enter the closer confines of a shared trip. At home, you both have a degree of control over your environment, with time apart and space for breathing room. When you travel outside your comfort zones, problems can occur.

When things don't go your way, and circumstances are beyond your control, both you and your travel partner may find this unsettling. Those who have a high need to stay in charge can find themselves shaken to their core. Your inherent "fight or flight" protective instincts can kick in when you are pushed too far, causing you or your normally cheery traveling companion to become an agitated and over-reactive sourpuss.

When this leads to reciprocation, unproductive arguments may follow that can really put a dampener on your day. And if this sort of adrenaline-soaked emotional conflict happens over multiple days, the trip can cease to be fun. In order to avoid interpersonal meltdowns, here are a few best behavior tips for *Great Trip* travel:

1. Practice a problem solving mindset.

2. Openly communicate and avoid conflict.

3. Be willing to compromise; be flexible and adaptable.

4. Be transparent about how to handle trip budgeting and responsibilities.

5. Give each other space.

6. Approach everything with a sense of humor.

7. Sense when fatigue might be the culprit.

Practice a Problem Solving Mindset

Actively work toward finding ways to cooperate and collaborate with your travel companion, facing challenges you're confronted with together. Keeping a productive, problem solving outlook, and working from the same page, as a team, can help you overcome just about anything that comes your way.

Unexpected events are a given when traveling. Your perfect plans will get derailed somehow, forcing you to take a detour. It's your mindset, and how you approach handling these bumps in the road, that will make all the difference in the world to ensuring that you have a *Great Trip*.

Openly Communicate and Avoid Conflict

When you and your travel companion are confronted with challenging situations along the way, this can cause stress and lead to disagreeable behavior. Don't let this happen. Agree in advance that you will communicate openly and constructively, so that when potential conflicts do arise, you will calmly discuss your issues or concerns.

Be diligent about listening as well as speaking. You may be a born equivocator, poised and ready to eloquently lay out your case before the jury. But your skills of oration won't serve a constructive purpose if you royally annoy your travel companion and disrupt the flow of fun.

Try to recognize your own trigger points when you start to react. Then STOP. Take a deep breath. Count to 10. And think carefully before you say anything. This is a big one. Be on sensory alert and disarm situations before they turn into arguments. To quote Ben Cameron, a consummate diplomat, "Smile when you say that."

On the other hand, when you discover something interesting, or funny along the way, be quick to share it with your travel companion. One thing that can make travel so exciting and fun is to swap stories about what you liked best from your most recent experiences. If you have the time, you may even take each other back to see your special discoveries. Nothing can solidify a relationship faster, or feels nicer than to have your ideas validated by another person.

Be Willing to Compromise, Be Flexible and Adapt

Along the same vein, as you encounter unforeseen obstacles or so-called "opportunities" on your trip, be adaptable and compromising in how you handle them. When you're forced to change your plans and make quick decisions on the fly, you and your travel companion will need to address these issues together, remain flexible, take your inconveniences in stride, and cheerfully adapt to your newfound circumstances.

Part of that flexibility means a willingness to compromise early, be considerate, and actively work to see things from the other's point of view.

37

By putting yourself in someone else's shoes, you will avoid "stepping on toes" and thus maintain your flow of fun.

Don't see eye to eye with your travel companion about the afternoon activity? Before you draw your line in the sand, and get ready for an all-out battle, ask your travel partner what it is about the activity that excites her and is important to her. Then share the same information with her about your activity ideas. By simply taking the time to share why each of your ideas is important to you, you may discover that one of you has a better, or a more heartfelt, reason. This can make agreeing to the other's way of thinking much easier to accept. Or you may opt to move in two separate directions and to meet up later, with both of you happy to have had the chance to do something that was important to you.

Can't check into your hotel yet? Arrange for the hotel to hold your bags, and venture out to find a bistro for a cup of coffee, or a glass of wine, or lunch. Unplug for a while, and take the opportunity to plan and anticipate—to look around you and see where you are—before you leap into what you had intended to do next.

Missed your train for the day's planned activity? Consider what else could be swapped to still make it all work. Then find a comfortable table where you can wait it out while writing a few postcards, or posting to your blog, or going through your photos, or simply chilling while you watch the people around you. Is it raining on a day you were planning an outdoor activity? Again, see if you can swap *Day Pages* around, replacing today's outdoor activity with an indoor activity. Being willing to "go with the flow" when things don't go as planned can set you apart as a great travel companion and prevent interruptions in your trip fun.

When my mother and I were on our way to visit a château one day while car traveling in France pre-GPS, we were stymied by a sign that simply said "Rue Barrée," and blocked our route along the road we needed to follow to the spot where we could cross the river.

Since we could not go straight, our only real options were to turn right, up a steep hill, or to turn around. We opted to head up the hill, in hopes of finding a way to drive around the blocked section of road, then head back toward the river to continue on to our destination. In our rerouting, we stumbled upon signs for a Roman aqueduct. Neither of us had seen a Roman aqueduct up close, so we postponed our original plans and set off to visit the aqueduct before working our way back on track toward our original destination. For some reason, both of us found this digression to be amusing, and somewhat exciting. Sometimes obstacles can be opportunities in disguise. You just need to keep your eyes and your options open— and, if possible, retain your sense of where the river is.

Be Transparent About How You Will Handle Expenses and Responsibilities

Money concerns have a way of creating undue stress. Defuse what could become a problem in the middle of your trip by addressing it early. Plan ahead how you will split paying for things on your trip—hotels, meals, incidentals, train tickets. Will you create a group pot of money for daily expenses, or alternate paying back and forth? If you save the receipts and split things later, agree to settle up before you return home.

Even if you are using a joint travel account, early clarity about money matters will prevent any festering dissatisfactions as the trip progresses.

Likewise, being clear about how you split different responsibilities can prevent one person from feeling that they will be left to handle the majority of the work along the way. Getting the day pack ready. Packing the picnic. Reading through today's *Day Pages*. Studying maps. Speaking in French with the locals when you both are too tired to think. Being the runner in the morning to grab fresh baked goods and coffee.

Find ways to balance the workload. Splitting up tasks and taking on different roles can make your travels happier, and more rewarding for both you and your travel companion. A trip is no time to take to the sidelines.

Give Each Other Space

Because you will have cell phones to stay in touch with your travel partner, don't be afraid to head different directions from time to time to give each other space. It's tough to be attached at the hip 24/7 for extended periods of time if you're used to being more independent.

This strategy will give you both a needed break from each other and likely allow each of you to do an activity that does not particularly interest the other person. One of you might spend some extra time shopping while the other heads off to see an additional museum. When you do come back together, don't forget to share the highlights of what you liked best about your individual exploits. That always seems to lead to fun stories and adds to the excitement about your next adventures, both individually and together.

Approach Everything with a Sense of Humor

Whether traveling for recreation, self-discovery, or just to escape and get away from it all, making the most of the time you have away from home is important, regardless of snafus that pop up along the way. If you keep in mind a few simple tricks you'll remain in a healthier head space and be able to view any obstacles with rose-colored glasses and maintain a good sense of humor. You'll become an expert at finding ways to better enjoy yourself, despite the situation at hand.

We've already talked about expecting the unexpected and being flexible when things don't go your way. But remember, too—don't sweat the small stuff. If your maid forgets to replace your shampoo or towels... Or your waiter forgets to bring the butter for your bread, or doesn't refill your water glass as fast as you might like... It really isn't worth turning a small hiccup into the "theme" of your trip. Be patient, kind and quick to forgive, while politely asking them to correct the situation rather than becoming confrontational. It's not worth interrupting your "flow of fun" and your positive state for something so trivial.

Remember to smile often. Smiling is universal, transcending all language barriers... something that everyone around the world understands. Laughing and smiling are contagious, brightening everyone's day and causing others to feel better too. A smile or a laugh can lighten the mood in any situation, make you seem more approachable, and ease your interactions with others. Smiling also will make you more appealing to be around and will draw other people to you.

Even when you force yourself to smile when you don't feel like it, this releases neurotransmitters called endorphins that cause you to feel happier and less stressed. Crazy as this may seem, even "faking" a smile helps you shake off a funk and changes your mood. Keep this in mind whenever tensions start to heat up with other people. And since the goal of a *Great Trip* is to have a fantastic experience, smiling more often will help keep the atmosphere fun!

Connect with the Locals

To have the time and opportunity for memorable experiences and encounters during your own *Great Trip*, you will stay in each place for at least three days, with four days each in Amboise, Bayeux and Paris. So you will actually "be where you are" and connect with the locals.

In this bounty of time, you will not only learn your way around each locale, but also come to know and experience what is remarkable and special about it. In Amboise you will dine across from the castle wall, interacting with the attentive servers who will expertly create for you a superb dining experience. You will experience *Market Day* beside the river, seeking assistance from the vendors in the stalls as you select a pretty scarf or a leather wallet. In Blois, you will join the locals in the courtyard café in front of the *House of Magic* for a front row view when the hour strikes and the six-headed hydra bursts its head and claws out of the windows, bringing gasps and giggles from the children.

In Paris, you will relax on a boat bar along the Seine, or a piano bar in the Latin Quarter, enjoying live music with the locals. You will pause to watch as sidewalk artists sketch portraits in Montmartre, or as break dancers perform impossible tricks near the fountains at Pompidou Center.

Four essentials to your *experiencing and connecting* are:

1. Immerse yourself in the cultural milieu.

2. Optimize encounters.

3. Interact, question, process and relate.

4. Make connections along the way.

Immerse Yourself in the Cultural Milieu

France preserves a way of life that embraces history, as well as "joie de vivre" (joy of life). You will stroll through streets that will take you back through time... an authentic living museum that will carry you into the heart of history. And you will experience the European approach to life, where it is mandatory that the work week stops after 35 hours, and that standard vacation time is 6 weeks a year. And where even the concept of "fast food" is an anathema to a good and healthy life.

In France, you will enter a world where friends and lovers meet at day's end at the outdoor cafés for a drink and animated conversation... Where there is always time to stroll along the river... Or to pause on a bridge as night falls and the lights come on... Or to find a table in a local bar to listen to jazz...

Food and wine are extremely important to the French lifestyle. So you will dine like the locals, taking the time to relish food that has been carefully and artistically prepared—fresh and interesting, and ultimately memorable. And you will experience the pleasures of outdoor dining—one of the key elements of the European lifestyle—joining all those happily conversing people sitting under umbrellas at outdoor tables savoring delectable 3-course meals. Or dine at that small but charming bistro on the corner, run by a husband and wife team, with only eight cozy tables, gaily covered in bright red, hand-woven tablecloths.

Your meal will be served by a French waiter, who is thoughtful and savvy about the nuances of good food and wine, and eager to be consulted as you jointly plan your dining experience. And as you seek your waiter's expert "recommendations" about what would be your best choices, and discuss your upcoming meal, you will possibly experience a moment of connection with a local. And this will add significantly to your overall enjoyment of your stay.

Optimize Encounters, Occurrences and Events

Since you will be the ones in charge of the pace of your trip, you will have the latitude to optimize all your encounters, occurrences and events. When you enter St. Chapelle to marvel at the exquisite stained glass windows, you may decide to optimize this experience by combining sight with sound while attending a chamber music concert here later that evening. As you shop for wine in the "Cave" (pronounced caah-ve) built into the wall of *Amboise Castle*, you will have the option of requesting a tasting first, for the combined pleasures of learning about the wines of the region and engaging in a lively interaction with the charming shopkeepers.

To optimize your experiences, ask yourself questions. "Is there a better spot from which we could watch the sunset?" "Is there another café from which we could better experience the parade of humanity crossing the square?" "Would we rather sit outside?" "Is it time to take a break for a glass of wine or an ice cream?" "Could we learn more of the stories of this château by requesting the audio tour?" "Could I engage this attentive shop keeper in my task of finding a lovely and special gift for my beloved mother-in-law?"

As you stand someplace beautiful looking "over there," think about going "over there" to look back. If you can see the river from the château, then you can see the château from the river. And from either perspective, you may enjoy a possibly even more stunning display at night.

Give yourself permission to do one thing at a time and experience it fully before you move on to something else. When you are wandering through museums, focus your attention on one display or piece of art or sculpture at a time, and give it its moment. You cannot look at and read about everything. So focus on examining a dozen or so objects closely and reading the details about them. This is probably all your mind will be able to hold at one time before you take a break. Possibly, at day's end, share with your travel companion five things you found most interesting that day, and ask that they share back.

Perhaps most important, know when to stop. Hopefully stop *before* you tire of *it*, however wonderful *it* is. Plan to come back later after a break, when you are rested and ready for more.

Interact, Question, Process and Relate

Again, in the spirit of taking charge of your own experiences, and ensuring that they are as rich, meaningful and enjoyable as possible, decide in advance of your trip that you will seek out ways to be observant, inquisitive and interactive with the locals, even if these are not normal elements of your behavior. Be intentionally open to learning, pursuing opportunities, and taking time to digest as you go.

As you walk about surrounded by the history, the architecture, the art, ask questions in your own mind. When was this cathedral built, and how? What would have been the challenges of accomplishing this project at that point in history? How much would it have cost, and how would these costs have compared to the standard earnings of the times?

Put yourself into the life and times that surround you, and imagine yourself there. Discuss your thoughts, observations, and questions with your travel companions. For the duration of this trip, understand that you have entered a "living classroom," as well as a "living museum." Pursue the rich and lively experiences and encounters that will be yours for the taking.

Observe and participate in the "spirit" of the places in which you find yourself. In the cathedrals, let your spirit soar as you look up at the brilliant colors of the stained glass windows, and soak in the peace. While

43

wandering the open air markets, join in the sense of exuberance as you search for a special treasure to take home with you to activate your memories of this point in time whenever you wear or use it.

As you listen to the jazz group in the piano bar, or the drummer performing on the street, let yourself feel the music as well as hear it. Smile as you watch the bright-eyed children struggle to select from the magical array of carousel animals which ones they wish to ride, while secretly making your own choice. Allow the experiences of your trip to feed your spirit as well as your body and mind.

Make Connections Along the Way

Group travel, by definition, encapsulates and insulates you from having the quintessential European experience—the people first, quality of life, "joie de vivre" that makes Europe so distinctive. Enclosed in the cumbersome, road-hogging, climate-controlled capsule of your bus, you are separated from the local people whose towns and villages, culture and lifestyles, you have come to experience.

In contrast, your *Great Trip* will most definitely give you a sense of connection with the local people. And you will find that the local people will respond to you, even befriend you, and certainly be ready, even eager, to help you. Their shyness about speaking what they perceive to be their "bad English" will be overcome by your willingness to struggle along with your "bad French."

A Travel Connections Story

In a shop on a pedestrian street in Avignon, Carolee was trying on two coats in the same style, one grey and the other red. Noticing that a stylishly-dressed French woman was watching her with interest, Carolee asked for her opinion about which coat would be the better choice. "Qu'est que vous pensez? Le gris ou le rouge?" The French woman responded emphatically, "le rouge!!" and smiled encouragingly.

Several days later, Carolee was walking toward the door of an elegant restaurant after enjoying a sumptuous holiday dinner. One of the other diners leapt up to embrace her, joyfully crying out: "La femme avec le manteau rouge!" The woman with the red coat! Then affectionate holiday greetings were exchanged.

So much for the mistaken notion that the French are cold and unapproachable. To the contrary! Experiencing connections like these with the locals will be among the true treasures you will bring home from your *Great Trip*.

Balance the Budget

As you imagine some of the glorious splurges you will be enjoying as part of the "full experience" of your *Great Trip*, you are probably beginning to view with alarm the dollar signs (or Euro signs!) that seem to be mounting up to a frightening level. A room in a hotel located right on Mont Saint-Michel? An apartment within a 3-minute walk to Notre Dame? These locations sound expensive. And then what about this lunch in the restaurant of the former grand hotel at d'Orsay? And possibly the dinner atop the Eiffel Tower?

These and other extravagances may be sounding off alarms in your mind asking: "How much is all of this going to cost?" and "Will we break the bank during the first week of our trip?"

Be assured that the *Great Trip* style of travel does take cost into consideration. To balance your budget, splurges will be counterbalanced by economies. And even these economies will actually add to your overall fun and enjoyment of your trip. Conversely, economies will be counterbalanced by splurges. All of this will work together to make your trip even more memorable, and certainly more affordable.

Four essential trip strategies to keep your budget in balance are:

1. Balance splurges with economies.

2. Alternate restaurant dining with market shopping.

3. Engage in "creative sharing."

Balance Splurges with Economies

As you select where you will stay during your *Great Trip*, there will be some definite splurges. But each of these splurges will be balanced by economies that will help keep your costs within reason and your budget under control. You will splurge to stay in the well-located plaza-view room, preferably with a balcony, even when there are smaller and less expensive options available at the same hotel. And, if at all possible, you will stay

45

inside the ancient gates of *Mont Saint-Michel* in order to have the Mont to yourself when the crowds leave.

To balance out these higher cost accommodations, you will need to book less costly choices in other locations. Or you will implement balancing economies such as gathering together your own breakfast of croissants and cheese, coffee and oranges, to be enjoyed in peace from that balcony or your plaza-view room, or sitting on a bench across from the market, or while speeding along on the train.

So the additional 40 euros you may end up spending on your splurge room will be balanced out by the 40 euros you will save by eating breakfasts of your own design, sitting in a beautiful place, without needing to put on your shoes.

Other balancing will come from strategies like eating royally at lunch, when prices are lower, and less expensively at dinner. And since you are in France, there will be few, if any, bad wines. You will be able to order house wines by the "pichet" (pitcher), or pick up bottles at the market, at shockingly modest sums.

Alternate Restaurant Dining with Shopping the Markets

You will learn where *your* market is as you orient yourself to each of your destinations. And you will be traveling with a full "picnic-ary," including a cork screw and plastic wine glasses, as well as plastic plates, metal utensils and cloth napkins. So you will be ready to shift into picnic mode at a moment's notice, to save money, or to enjoy a glorious outdoor setting on a beautiful day, or even just to take a break from all the dining out.

So if you splurge on lunch at a restaurant, you will have the option of putting together a more casual dinner. Or if you opt to picnic for lunch, you then will have the budget latitude to feast at an outdoor table for dinner. Aside from money considerations, the goal will be to achieve balance so that meals in restaurants continue to be treats. Picnics on your own will give you needed respite, both financially and personally.

Engage in "Creative Sharing"

When traveling in France, "creative sharing" is the answer to many questions, both budgetary and caloric. Given the French love affair with food, it is possible to spend outlandish amounts of money on restaurant dining, with an equivalently impressive weight gain.

As much as you may want to avoid this extreme, the opposite version of going overboard would be to institute total self-control, spend little on dining, and gain no weight. But this would entail a tragic sacrifice of potential enjoyment and experience.

Instead, engage in "creative sharing." You do want to experience the food, but hopefully without overeating, and certainly without breaking the bank. To use this method, one of you orders the full "Menu"—appetizer plus entrée plus dessert—while the other orders just one course—an appetizer or soup or salad or entrée. Then you share all of the above, dine magnificently, yet avoid sticker shock when you request "l'addition" (the check). By practicing "creative sharing" at lunch and/or dinner, you will avoid overeating or breaking the bank, and also minimize wasted food.

Plan Transport & Admission Strategies

Additional economies to balance the budget will derive from knowing which options for transport and museum admissions to purchase and use in each location. In Blois, you will purchase a combined discounted ticket for entry to *Blois Castle* and the *House of Magic*, plus a magic show.

You will receive a discount, and also be able to skip the lines, by purchasing a combo ticket for the *Arromanches 360 Museum* and the *Caen Memorial Museum*. And in Caen you will purchase a two-day transportation pass that will allow you free access to all buses and trolleys throughout your visits.

In Paris, you will purchase a two-day pass on the Batobus and be able to hop on and hop off the boat at will, providing you with both transportation and also an orientation to this unique city, with stunning views.

In Paris you also will purchase a 4-day museum pass. This card will allow you to jump the lines, and enter museums immediately. It also will remove the barrier of deciding museum by museum whether or not to pay the admission fees. You will feel free to stop in and visit even when you have very little time.

Take Treasures and Memories Home

As you experience your *Great Trip*, you will find parts of it to bring home, because "time away should be time remembered." There will be many encounters, stories, experiences and sights from your trip that will come home with you as vivid memories. You will find treasures along your way.

And take photos. And as you experience the lifestyle of the French, you may find you want to capture some of that too and keep it as part of your own lifestyle after you return home.

You will be able to purchase treasures as you discover them, without worries about overloading your luggage. Accumulated treasures will be no problem for you, because whenever you go beyond the limitations of what you are able or willing to carry, you will use the technique of "mailing home the weight."

By giving yourself "permission" to mail home a box each week, you will be saved from overload, as well as from steep airline fees for overweight luggage. And all of this will be accomplished without the need to impose limits on your freedom to add treasures as you travel.

Mailing boxes home is a simple process, and well worth the effort and cost. As you mail home treasures, send back any stacks of papers from days gone by—*Day Pages*, maps, brochures, booklets, books, receipts—as well as any items you brought from home but find you aren't using. So as your trip progresses, your "burdens" will grow lighter, not heavier.

As well as treasures, you may discover lifestyle changes to bring home from your trip. Have you loved eating outside at tables covered by Provençal tablecloths in vivid Crayola yellows, reds, purples, greens and blues? Then bring home cloths, placemats and napkins, and set up your own café on your front porch.

Have you savored those café crèmes at breakfast, or the carafe of wine with dinner? Then bring (or mail) home the large cups to hold coffee with milk, and perhaps a lovely carafe with glasses for wine. Then make these a part of your daily life after you return home.

Perhaps you will select some favorite places during this trip to which you will wish to return, once or many times. As you choose where to come back to, and what you will add when you come "next time," this *Great Trip* will become your launching pad for future adventures.

And So... Now on to Envision Your Trip

To begin this journey, let's move on to envisioning your great trip in your mind, start to finish. Take a comfortable seat and read on, beginning with the "armchair version" of your trip to paint the picture of what your trip will be like.

CHAPTER 3:
Envision Your Trip

Your roadmap starts from the broad view of your trip. Picture yourself on a plane to Paris... Settle back and take the armchair version, journeying in your mind's eye to vividly envision your trip as a whole, including a brief overview of each day's activities and experiences.

Later, in Chapters 4–9, you will read through the detailed *Day Pages*, to be adapted as you make your own arrangements, substituting your own specific accommodations, train schedules and other particulars. Then, during your trip, as you set out each day, you will carry with you the set of *Day Pages* for that day in order to have with you everything you need to make that day work smoothly.

Your Trip Overview

Your adventure begins as you fly overnight to Paris, arriving early the next morning at the hectic Charles de Gaulle (CDG) airport, where everyone around you will suddenly and confoundingly be speaking in French. You will only pass through Paris at this point and board the train to the small town of Amboise in the Loire Valley—*Valley of the Kings*. You will return to Paris later, to spend four enchanting nights falling in love with this glorious *City of Lights*.

After taking the shuttle from the CDG arrivals terminal to the TGV ("Train à Grand Vitesse"—"train of great speed") station at the airport, you will board the fast train to travel in just over two hours to Amboise, where you will reside for the next four days, surrounded by a city shaped by the Renaissance. Arriving at the little train station in Amboise, then crossing the bridge (on foot or by taxi) over the Loire toward the castle that looms above a row of river-front mansions, you will begin to sense that you have walked back into history. Although what lies before you is very, very old, the world you will be entering will be all new to you, rich in discoveries and possibilities.

After four days in Amboise, you will travel, again by train, to the coast of Normandy, and the remarkable ancient abbey of *Mont Saint Michel*, a UNESCO world heritage site perched on a rock, surrounded by water when the tides come in. There you will stay three nights, one night near the train station and two nights on the Mont itself.

You then will make your way to Bayeux, near the Normandy coast, for four nights, where the stories of conquest and liberation span the 11th to the 20th century—from William the Conqueror to the D-Day landings.

Finally you will complete the loop, arriving back in Paris for four nights, where you will experience the grand boulevards and bridges, the awe-inspiring art and architecture, and all the many timeless attractions that make this the city most people put near the top of their bucket lists.

You Will Travel in the Spring or Fall

Plan to take your trip in the Spring or Fall, NOT the summer, if possible. Since you will want to spend as much time as possible outdoors while you are in France, the optimum time to travel is when the weather is mild and sunny. April will work, but May would be even better. If you opt to travel in the Fall, plan on September or October.

Once summer arrives, and temperatures rise, you will fully experience the discomfort of every additional degree. Do not assume air conditioning as a given in French hotels, restaurants, shops, or even museums. Climate control in Europe is not as ubiquitous as it is in the United States. And it's difficult to relax and enjoy a great meal in a restaurant when the inside temperature is even hotter than it is outside. Europeans are seemingly indifferent to summer heat, considering it acceptable just to suffer through the hottest weeks of the year in order to avoid installing air-conditioning units. And heat or no heat, the French continue to linger in outdoor cafés.

During your trip, you will want to spend most of your time outside, experiencing the European approach of taking your time as you dine, while engaging in animated discussion and captivating people-watching. And you will be doing lots of walking. This means that encountering hot weather during your trip will likely become a problem. You could end up as Brian did during one stay in Paris when our scheduling crossed the line into the heat of early summer. Running ahead to meet Réné, our guide for a 4-hour walking tour of Paris' Marais district, Brian had difficulty keeping a straight face as he offered René his drenched hand, with sweat dripping off his nose and chin. Oh misery!

The French have good reasons to forego air conditioning, given the vintages of the buildings they visit, inhabit and revere. In such buildings, installing AC may be forbidden. Even when it is allowed, such installations involve difficult and expensive retrofits, and likely would detract from the architecture. Given a choice between preserving the architecture and increasing personal comfort, the architecture generally wins out.

In addition to the scarcity of air-conditioning, another negative of summer travel is that some of the sights, restaurants and shops are closed in August. This is when the locals take their own holidays. Keep in mind that many of the best places to eat and experience the local specialties are family-run businesses. When the family leaves for vacation, they just lock the door and put up a sign indicating that they'll be back in a month.

Despite these reasons to aim for spring or fall travel, you may for some reason be forced to travel during the summer months. If so, there will be some advantages. Although smaller businesses may be closed, most major attractions and museums will still be open. And there may be fewer people around, since many of the locals will be gone. Just be certain to stay in places that have air-conditioning.

If you will be traveling in the summer, check for special events that will be taking place during your stay. During the summer, for example, Paris closes off several streets and brings in tons of sand to establish a beach along the Seine, complete with palm trees.

In Amboise during summer months, King François and Leonardo da Vinci "appear" in person on the castle grounds to host just the type of sound-and-light extravaganza François would have commissioned da Vinci to produce for him back in the 1500s. Even peaceful Bayeux holds a medieval festival in the summer, complete with feasts and a Medieval Ball, with people parading through the streets in medieval costumes.

Your Trip at a Glance

As you travel and immerse yourself in these four locales, Amboise, Mont Saint-Michel, Bayeux and Paris, your trip will offer a variety of rich experiences, with a balance of history and culture…"sights" as well as encounters with locals… museums and castles as well as local events.

51

15-Day Trip Overview	
Amboise & the Loire Valley	4 days
Mont Saint-Michel	3 days
Bayeux & Normandy	4 days
Paris	4 days

Your trip-at-a-glance will be presented in summary here. Full details for each day will follow in Chapter 4 to Chapter 9, providing you with a complete set of *Day Pages*—specific daily plans that have been qualified and verified as interesting, balanced experiences.

The detailed plans for each day are very specific, and include recommendations for walks, restaurants, activities and transport. These day plans are based on our own personal experiences as well as on reviews posted by other travelers. By giving you a clear path to follow, we hope that you will enjoy the best experience possible during your limited time in each locale.

But remember that you can always deviate from these plans, making any modifications that better suit your own tastes, interests and style of travel. Less? More? Slower? Faster? More art? More music? These are and will always remain your own choices. This is, after all, *your* trip. For now, read through these brief summaries of each day and begin to envision your trip.

Day 1   Arrive CDG airport. Train to *Amboise*. Orienteering walk about. Dinner outdoors, across from castle.

Day 2   Amboise Market. *Amboise Castle*. Da Vinci's last home, *Clos Lucé*. Dinner outdoors, across from castle.

Day 3   *Chenonceau Castle*, Gardens & Wax Museum. *Mini-Châteaux Park*. Dinner outdoors.

Day 4   *Chambord Château* (optional). *House of Magic. Blois Castle.*

Day 5   Train to *Pontorson*. Stay near the station at a peaceful retreat with gardens. Night views of *Mont Saint-Michel*.

Day 6   Move to the Mont and visit the Abbey. Window-seat dinner overlooking the Bay.

Day 7   Morning rampart walk. Browse four little museums. Shop for treasures. *Piano Bar* jazz.

Day 8	Train to *Bayeux*. Orienteering walk about. *Bayeux Tapestries*. Bayeux's Dinner across from *Notre Dame Cathedral* at night.
Day 9	Train to *Caen*. Sunday Market. *William the Conqueror's Castle. Normandy Museum.* Old town lunch & shopping.
Day 10	To *Arromanches. 360° Theater* and *D-Day Museum. Omaha Beach*, monument and museum. "Home" to Bayeux.
Day 11	To *Caen. Holocaust Museum* exhibits and movies. Caen old town. Back to *Bayeux* for river walk & dinner.
Day 12	To *Paris* & arrive. Orienteering walk about. *Notre Dame*. Flower Market. Sainte-Chapelle. Night cruise.
Day 13	Batobus to d'*Orsay*. Walk St. Germain to the *Cluny. Luxemburg Gardens. Pantheon. Shakespeare & Company.* Evening in the Latin Quarter.
Day 14	*Louvre. Tuileries Gardens* & *L'Orangerie. Champs-Élysées. Arc de Triomphe. Tour Eiffel.* Dinner. Boat bar jazz.
Day 15	*Maubert Market. Montmartre* artists & Sacré-Coeur Basilica. Vintage shop the *Marais. Pompidou Fountains & Center.* Dinner outdoors.

Day 1 (Saturday): To Amboise

Today you will arrive in Paris after an overnight flight, and immediately board the train on your way to tiny Amboise, in the legendary Loire Valley. When you have arrived and checked into your manor house accommodations at the base of the castle wall, you may opt for a shower and a "power nap" after your long night on the plane.

Once you are refreshed, take a walk-about in town, and locate the river. As you stroll along the pedestrian street to the church on the hill, then turn out toward the river, you soon will begin to know your way around. And you will have a chance to spot *your* wine shop, *your* deli, *your* bakery and fresh market... *your* restaurants, gift shops, phone shop and pharmacy. You quickly will be familiar and comfortable with charming Amboise, your "home" for the next four days.

Your walk-about will end at the "Cave" beneath Amboise Castle, where you will have a chance to sample a few of the extraordinary wines for which France is known. Crisp, dry Rosés. Velvety reds. Delightful whites. Take advantage of this opportunity to make a cultural connection. Discuss the wines with the smiling women in the Cave before you make your choice, and discover the warmth and genuineness of the French people.

You will already have made reservations at a charming restaurant across from the castle. Here you will dine outside, under the stars, and imagine the times when kings lived atop the wall across the street from where you sit.

Day 2 (Sunday): In Amboise

If today is *Market Day* (Friday or Sunday), you will start your day by experiencing a French outdoor market, smelling the flowers, buying samples of cheese and sausage, selecting a scarf or locally-made pottery. If there is no market today, check to determine when you might be able to fit this in later during your visit to Amboise.

Then climb to *Amboise Castle*, perched high above the town, with stunning views down to the river. As you walk up the ramp to the castle, note the shops to your left along the ramp and plan to return later to explore them. In the courtyard of the castle, you will see the small chapel where King François buried Da Vinci. After walking out to the rampart wall to look down across the river, explore what remains of the castle and gardens. Pause to study the 3-D castle model that illustrates the size of the castle when it was in its full glory.

As you leave the castle to make your way to *Clos Lucé*, da Vinci's final home, you will wind down a horse-and-carriage ramp inside the fat tower to the pedestrian street where you ate dinner last night. Pause to spot the 15th century graffiti carved into the tower walls.

Turning left as you exit the base of the tower, climb the hill to da Vinci's home. King François sponsored da Vinci's move here from Italy, and supported him for the rest of his life. In return, da Vinci brought the Mona Lisa as a gift to the King, carrying it over the Alps on his arduous journey to France.

While walking up the steep street to *Clos Lucé*, take in the Troglodyte (cave) dwellings along the way, now renovated for modern-day living. At *Clos Lucé*, observe how the master artist and inventor lived, and view his inventions, made real through video animations and models of some of his most remarkable creations. Take a stroll in the park that surrounds the artist's home, pausing for ice cream or a glass of wine at one of the cafés, either in the park or in the rose garden courtyard of the château. Then head back down into town for some free time, followed by another sumptuous meal, dining outside across from the castle wall.

Day 3 (Monday): Visit Chenonceau Château

Today you will taxi off to the incomparable *Chenonceau Château*, the castle that Catherine de Medici, Henri II's wife, snatched away from her husband's mistress, Diane de Poitiers, immediately after Henri died. Here history will come to life, starting with the life-sized wax figures of Henri and his two paramours.

Walk through the château doors to visit the chapel, reception rooms, ballroom and bed chambers, and imagine how it would have been to live here. Then stroll through the two lovely gardens, Diane's to the left of the château along the river's edge and Catherine's to the right. Everywhere you look, you will see evidence of the jealous competition between the wife and the mistress. Two gardens. Two balconies. Two lavish bedrooms. The mistress built a bridge. So the wife built a 2-story ballroom atop the bridge. The mistress had tiles installed with her initial "D" intertwined with Henri's "H." So later the wife had these tiles modified, changing the "D" (for Diane) to a "C" (for Catherine). Whatever Diane did, Catherine was determined to do better.

After lunch outside the château, you will move on to *Mini-Châteaux Park*, or, if you are tired, return to Amboise. At *Mini-Châteaux,* you will walk through a landscape of realistic 1:25-scale models of 45 of the most remarkable châteaux in the Loire region. Just for fun, select which three of these you would have lived in had you been a Renaissance royal.

Day 4 (Tuesday): Day Trip to Chambord & Blois Castles

This morning, you will leave by train for the 15-minute ride to Blois, the "other" home castle of the same kings who occupied Amboise Castle. From Blois, you will take the bus or a taxi out to Chambord castle to spend the morning in this 440-bedroom hunting lodge, with 84 staircases and 365 fireplaces, one for each day of the year.

After you've had your fill of wandering the rooms of the château, shaking your head in disbelief, and climbing the double helix staircase (thought to be designed by Leonardo da Vinci himself) to peer out from the rooftop terrace across the 13,440 acres of hunting grounds (about the size of Paris), you will lunch outdoors in front of the château .

Back in Blois, you will visit the *House of Magic*, a palatial former home that faces the Blois Château. This building now houses a 6-headed hydra, as well as a magicians' theater and an intriguing museum honoring Jean Robert-Houdin. Robert-Houdin (a hyphenated name that combined his own and his wife's last names) was a watchmaker who turned magician after he accidentally received a set of books about magic that piqued what for him had been a lifelong interest.

Robert-Houdin was the first recognized "serious" magician, and the inventor of modern magic and conjuring. Escape artist Ehrich Weiss was so impressed by Robert-Houdin that he adopted his own stage name, Harry Houdini, in Robert-Houdin's honor.

After you have experienced the magic museum, and visited the gift shop to purchase magic tricks to take home, you will make a brief visit to Blois Castle. The audio guide to accompany your castle visit will recount in vivid detail stories of the intrigues and murders the castle has seen, some by blade, some by poison. Can you spell "M-E-D-I-C-I"?

While walking back to the train station, remember to look back up at the looming castle and pause for photos. Then "home again" to Amboise for one last dinner at your favorite of the restaurants beneath the castle wall.

Day 5 (Wednesday): Head Toward Mont Saint-Michel

Today you will travel by train to Pontorson, the station closest to the phenomenal Mont Saint-Michel. Your day's travel will take you from the Loire Valley to the Atlantic Coast of France, where Brittany and Normandy connect. You will spend your first night in Pontorson, in a peaceful small hotel near the train station, with gardens and a bar terrace, and within walking distance of this tiny town's main street.

After dinner, take a 10-minute taxi ride to a terrace bar across from Mont Saint-Michel to sit and soak in the stunning night views of this mirage rising up from the sea. Tomorrow you will mount the Mont.

Day 6 (Thursday): Mount the Mont & Take Up Residence

This morning you will enter the gates and climb the Mont, arriving early enough to beat the densest crowds. Before you cross the peninsula to the Mont, pause at the visitor center to gather maps and stop in the shops to gather together picnic supplies for lunch. Then board the shuttle, walk through the gates, and climb up and up the *Grand Rue* to locate your hotel and deposit your bags.

After quickly orienting yourself, continue walking up the *Grand Rue* to the *Grand Staircase*, then up to the Abbey. You will be passing by, for now, all the intriguing shops along the way. But keep going. You will have ample time for shopping later. Do make one brief stop at the *Terrasse Poulard* to make dinner reservations at a window table for later in the evening after the crowds have departed. Communicate clearly that you hope to view the phenomenon of the tides, and the hostess will do everything she can to accommodate your wishes.

Hopefully you will reach the Abbey well ahead of the masses, so you will be able to complete your visit before they get there. By the time the hordes make it to the top, you will be ready to work your way back down toward the garden area at the foot of the Abbey. Lunch will be a picnic, or possibly an omelet, sandwich or crêpe at a brasserie out near the ramparts. All the while, congratulate yourself for moving in the opposite direction to the crowds.

As the throngs continue to swarm the *Grand Rue*, walk back down along the ramparts, with views out to either sea or sand, depending on the state of the tides at the moment. Later, as the *Grand Rue* begins to empty out, you will have ample time to return to the shops before your dinner at the *Terrasse Poulard*, at a window-table, with a view of the procession of the tides, moving swiftly in to surround the Mont.

This evening, if you have the energy, walk out through the gates to look back up at the Mont, spectacularly illuminated against the sky.

Day 7 (Friday): Experience Life on the Mont

Your morning will begin with a meandering visit to the shops before the crowds arrive. These shops may, at first glance, appear to be touristy, but many of them are much more, once you walk in. There are many treasures to be found. By the time the masses arrive, you will be ready to escape the *Grande Rue* and make brief, interesting visits to the Mont's four small but earnest museums. Here you will see the history, legends, and intrigue of the Mont, as well as ship models, an Archeoscope (WHAT is an Archeoscope?), ancient weapons, and instruments of torture.

Lunch will be a picnic in one of the garden areas, or sitting outside at *Vielle Auberge* along the ramparts near Boucle Tower, again to dodge the noontime crowds, and enjoy the ambiance of the Mont. By dinnertime, the hordes will have departed, and you will have the Mont almost to yourself. Feast at a restaurant of your choice, with a view out to sea. Then, as night falls, find a cozy seat at the *Piano Bar* of the *Mere Poulard* to listen to jazz.

Day 8 (Saturday): Set off for Bayeux

Today you will travel by train to Bayeux, near the coast of Normandy, where conquerors and liberators braved the precipitous cliffs—William the Conqueror in the 11th century and the Allied troops in the 20th.

After you arrive in captivating Bayeux, you will begin your walk about town, pausing at the *Saturday Weekly Market* (7:30 am–2:30 pm) at Place Saint-Patrice, then stopping for lunch at *La Fringale*, on the pedestrian street, *rue St. Jean*. After lunch, continue your orienteering, locating the river and otherwise learning your way around your new "home base."

This afternoon, you will visit the *Bayeux Tapestries*, taking time to "read" your way visually through the story of William the Conqueror, revealed in vivid detail, embroidered into an ancient 230-foot tapestry. Then watch the movie and study the scaled models, life-sized armored figures, and other interesting displays that bring the vivid history of this area to life.

This evening you will dine outside, across from Bayeux's *Notre Dame Cathedral*, enjoying its architectural grandeur, brilliantly illuminated at night.

Day 9 (Sunday): William the Conqueror's Caen

You will take a brief train ride to Caen to focus on the Caen of William the Conqueror, taking in the drama of his history as he claimed the British throne, crossed the English Channel, and conquered England.

After a stop at the Sunday Market, and lunch at *Le Bouchon du Vaugueux* in old town Caen, you will begin your orientation to the tales of William by riding full circuit on the *Little Train* (*Le Petit Train*), learning about his style as a ruler, as well as his love story, and hopping off when you return to the castle gate.

Then you will enter the castle walls to wander the ruins and visit the fascinating *Musée Normandie*. After visiting the castle, you will have your choice of one or more afternoon activities—a visit to the *Botanical Gardens*, a walk along the shopping street, *rue St. Pierre*, and/or a stop at the *Musée des Beaux-Arts*.

When you are back "home" in Bayeux, enjoy dinner beside the river at *Le Moulin de la Galette*.

Day 10 (Monday): Visit Arromanches & Omaha Beach

Starting your day with a taxi ride to the cliffs above Arromanches, you will look down and out to sea, surveying what was once a full artificial harbor, with miles of floating pontoon docks. Vast hunks of hollow concrete, each the size of a football field, along with 17 sunken ships, were dragged into position under cover of night to form a breakwater to shield the harbor from the turbulent seas. Some of these chunks remain. This harbor provided the 18,000 tons of daily supplies needed to break the barrier into the Nazi's "fortress Europe," and support the Allied troops as they liberated France, and then took back Europe.

From this elevated vantage point on the cliff, pause to absorb the magnitude of effort that was required to land troops along this coastline in the face of German fire from gun bunkers embedded in the cliffs. You will relive this turning point in history at the *Arromanches 360° Theater* as you view archived footage of actual battles, and later walk down to the *D-Day Museum* to see the fascinating collection of working models that bring this complex operation to life.

You will lunch near the water at *La Marine*, enjoying fresh seafood, with splendid views out to sea, now tranquil where once there were troops and an active harbor.

After lunch, you will travel by taxi to *Saint-Laurant-sur-Mer*, code named "Omaha Beach," one of the landing points taken by the American troops. Here you will visit the 170-acre *American Cemetery*, with graves of 9,386 American soldiers who died at Normandy, and the *Garden of the Missing*, with a wall displaying the names of another 1,557 soldiers whose bodies were never recovered.

From here walk down the path to the beach, then 15 minutes along the beach, to visit the *D-Day Monument* sculptures standing at the water line, and to look back up toward the cliffs, the better to understand what the troops faced as landing boats deposited them into the surf.

After a pause for drinks and a snack at *Restaurant l'Omaha* on the water, and a 5-minute walk inland, you will have the option of visiting the *Musée Mémorial d'Omaha Beach*. At any point, when you have had enough, simply call a taxi to take you back to decompress in peaceful Bayeux.

Dinner will be at *La Rapiere* or *Au Petit Bistrot* in old town Bayeux.

Day 11 (Tuesday): Experience the Caen Holocaust Museum

Your day will start at the Tuesday Weekly Market (7:30 am–2:00 pm) in Bayeux on rue Saint-Jean. Then you again will travel by train to Caen to visit the famous *Caen Memorial,* with its tribute to the Holocaust and the D-Day Landings. This extensive museum, with eclectic and thoughtful exhibits, will provide you with an emotional as well as an informational perspective. The excellent audio tour and movies will complete the experience. You will take the time you need here, probably at least four hours, with a pause midway for lunch.

After the *Memorial,* you will travel by taxi or tram to downtown Caen, stopping off near William the Conqueror's castle to locate an inviting café in old town and decompress from the intensity of your museum experience. Then you will have free time for a bit more shopping along the popular rue St. Pierre and the *Vaugueux Quarter,* with its half-timbered buildings, before you head back to catch the train "home" to Bayeux. Once back in Bayeux, you will have free time to walk along the river or explore the shops on the pedestrian street, *rue St. Jean,* before dining at your favorite choice of Bayeux restaurants.

Day 12 (Wednesday): Now off to Paris

Traveling by train back to Paris, you will complete your loop today, and arrive in time for lunch. The *Left Bank* ("La Rive Gauche") of the Seine— historically known as the artistic part of the city—will be your "home base" for the next four nights. Your apartment will be within a few blocks of the river on the *Left Bank,* or on the smaller of the two islands in the middle of the river, *Ile Saint-Louis.*

After checking in, begin your walk-about to learn your new "neighborhood," locate your shops, and stock up on wine, cheese, bread and deli. Then you will head for the river and cross the bridge to *Ile de la Cité* ("Island of the City"). This larger island was the original seat of Paris, birthplace of Roman river commerce, and the location of the 4th century cathedral that was replaced by the 12th century *Notre-Dame.* As you pass in front of *Notre-Dame,* pause before the entrance to absorb its grandeur and to study the statues of kings above the door. The heads you see now are replacements. The original heads of these sculptures were loped off during the Revolution by a Parisian mob that mistakenly took these to be sculptures of French monarchs, when actually they were the ancient kings of Judea and Israel.

You will return later for a visit inside this magnificent cathedral. But at this point, head straight to lunch at *Brasserie Esmeralda*, hopefully at an outdoor table, with a view of the cathedral buttresses. From your table, look across to the smaller island, *Ile Saint-Louis*, and spot the restaurant where you will be having dinner, *Le Flore en L'Ile*.

After lunch, walk downriver, on the *Right Bank* ("La Rive Droite") side of the island. To orient yourself to the flow of the river, remember that when you face *downriver* the *Left Bank* will be on your left and the *Right Bank* will be on your right. Take in the impressive buildings that border this bank. The *Right Bank* is far more tightly packed with buildings and people, and the buildings are more formal, including the impressive *City Hall* (Hôtel de Ville), and, further downriver, the Louvre.

During your walk you will pass the *Flower Market* (Marché aux Fleurs) on your left, and wander through this colorful maze of flowers and garden shops. You may decide to return here later to spend more time at this beautiful market.

When you reach the end of the island, with views downriver toward the Louvre, walk through the park and back up the other side of the island toward the incomparable *Sainte-Chapelle*. This small chapel is remarkable and unique in all the world, with its exquisite 49-foot tall 13th-century stained glass windows, at their loveliest in late afternoon.

You may stop now to view the windows, or possibly return later for a concert in the chapel. While you are here, purchase your *4-day Museum Pass* at the shop across the street from *Sainte-Chapelle* in order to bypass the lines for the remainder of your stay in Paris.

Ending your full circuit of the island, you will find yourself back in front of *Notre Dame*, this time to venture inside. Note in passing the entrance to the *Crypt Archéologique*, located under the square that fronts *Notre Dame*. You may elect to return here later to view the ancient remains discovered here during excavations in 1965—archaeological layers that reveal 2000 years of history, dating back to the Romans in 52 BC.

As you move in through the doorway of *Notre Dame*, look up to study the pictograph images overhead. Once inside, sit awhile to take it all in. If, by good fortune, the magnificent organ is being played when you arrive, take time to listen. When you are back outside, check out the slow-moving line to decide if you wish to climb up the cathedral tower for a stunning view of Paris and a closer look at the gargoyles. If the line is too long, you may want to return early on another day, before the crowds gather.

Dinner will be at an outdoor table on the little island, *Ile Saint-Louis*, at *Le Flore en L'Ile*. After dinner, take an evening cruise from *Notre Dame* to the *Eiffel Tower* and back, passing under the illuminated bridges, enjoying the spectacle of Paris aglow at night.

Day 13 (Thursday): D'Orsay Impressionism & the Left Bank

After a breakfast feast of the breads, cheese, fruit and coffee you gathered yesterday, and a visit to the Thursday Market at *Place Maubert*, you will head to the river where you will purchase your 2-day Batobus ("boat bus") pass. This will allow you to cruise up and down the river, hopping on and off at any of the eight stops: *Hôtel de Ville*, *Louvre*, *Champs-Élysées*, *Eiffel Tower*, *Musée d'Orsay*, *Saint-Germain-Des-Pres*, *Notre Dame* and *Jardin des Plantes*.

Today your first stop will be at *Musée d'Orsay*, the remarkable art museum housed in the former beaux-arts railway station built for the *1900 Paris Exposition Universelle*. Here you will jump the line using your *Museum Pass*, then head immediately to the impressionist paintings: Renoir, Van Gogh, Monet, Degas, Cézanne, Gauguin. After you have feasted your eyes on paintings, you will shift over to sculptures.

Lunch today will be in the incomparable former dining room of the *Grand Hotel* that was once part of the turn-of-century train station. As an alternative you may choose to lunch at an outside table at *La Frégate*, near the museum and facing the river. After lunch, you will take a walk through Saint-Germain-des-Prés, pausing to window shop for antiques and other treasures. As you walk along *rue de Buci*, you will be following in the footsteps of Pablo Picasso who did his daily shopping here.

Your walk will lead you to the *Cluny Museum*, with exhibits that illuminate three distinct eras of Parisian history. From Roman times, you will see remains from a Roman *Frigidarium* (cold-water bath), and from the Middle Ages, the exquisite *Lady & the Unicorn Tapestries* and medieval stained glass from *Sainte-Chapelle*. From the time of the French Revolution, you will view stone heads that were loped off the sculptures of kings above the doorway of Notre-Dame by the revolutionaries, then discarded and unearthed some 200 years later.

After visiting the Cluny, you will head over to *Luxemburg Gardens*, either on foot or by Vélib' bike, to view the palace designed by Queen Marie de' Medici, second wife of King Henry IV, and patterned after the Pitti Palace and Boboli Gardens in Florence where she was raised. After wandering the gardens, you will take a break on a peaceful bench beside the Medici Fountains. Your walk or bike ride will continue to the vast, ornate, architecturally astounding, Pantheon, modeled after the *Pantheon* in Rome. This is where Voltaire, Émile Zola, Victor Hugo, Marie Curie, Jean-Jacques Rousseau and other French luminaries are buried.

Next you will walk or bike back to the Latin Quarter to *Shakespeare & Company*, where well-known writers have gathered, including Hemingway, Fitzgerald, Gertrude Stein and James Joyce. Stop for a drink at *Café Procope*, meeting place of the 18th century intellectual establishment, including Voltaire, Benjamin Franklin and Thomas Jefferson. Afterwards you will wander the narrow, lively streets of the Latin Quarter. Dinner will be at *Le Jardin du Roy* in the Latin Quarter, followed by jazz at a cozy piano bar.

Day 14 (Friday): Art & Gardens, Arches & Towers

Today you will be back on the Batobus, heading for the *Louvre*, formerly a palace, now a world-class art museum, to spend the morning exploring the incomparable collections of sculpture and paintings, including *Winged Victory* and the *Mona Lisa*, with a short break at *Café Mollien* on a terrace overlooking the pyramid and the *Carrousel Garden*.

Back outside, pause at the *Arc du Carrousel*, the smaller of the two triumphal arches commissioned by Napoleon I to celebrate the victories of his armies. Catch the view from the smaller arch toward the larger arch at the other end of the grand boulevard. Later today you will be looking back this way from the larger arch to the smaller.

Next take a walk through the lovely *Tuileries Gardens*, admiring the designs of flowers and hedges as well as the statuary. When you reach the large octagonal basin surrounded by statues, pause to sit in the sun along with the many Parisians who enjoy this spot. Then make a brief stop at *l'Orangerie*, the former greenhouse for the gardens, now the display space for Monet's famous waterlily murals.

After walking out to the center of *Place de la Concord* for an up-close look at the Egyptian obelisk, popularly called *Cleopatra's Needle*, you will hire a pedal cab to transport you along *Champs-Élysées* to *Pizza Pino* to feast on a late lunch before shopping your way down to the *Arc de Triomphe*. Using the tunnel to venture out to the Arc (climbing to the top is optional), pause to read the inscriptions, to watch the bedlam of traffic, and to look back toward the smaller arch in the Louvre courtyard where you stood earlier.

As you taxi back to the river to catch the *Batobus* to the *Eiffel Tower*, ask your driver to drop you off at the *Petit Palais* to take a peek into the courtyard. This impressive building, and the *Grande Palais* across the street, are remnants left from the 1900 World's Fair. The *Eiffel Tower*, where you will be heading next, was built 11 years earlier for the 1889 World's Fair to celebrate the 100th anniversary of the French Republic.

When you arrive at the Eiffel Tower, pause to stand beneath it studying the intricate lattice work of its four legs, oriented with the four points of the compass. Then use your pre-purchased ticket to take the elevator to the first level and walk across the glass floor peering down, if you dare. Ascend to the second level to circle the perimeter for views in all directions. Then board the elevator to the top, and splurge on a glass of champagne from the *Champagne Bar* tucked into the structure. As you sip champagne, and contemplate the thrilling panorama of Paris stretched out beneath your feet, toast your grand adventure in Paris.

After riding the Batobus "home," sit outside at the *Beaurepaire Café*, or another restaurant of your choosing, and enjoy a relaxed dinner while recapturing the wonders of your day.

Day 15 (Saturday): Montmartre & Marais

Today you will begin your day at *Maubert*, where you will find breakfast, then take the metro or a taxi to the funicular at the base of *Montmartre*. Ride up from *Gare Basse* (Low Station) to *Gare Haute* (High Station), and step off to stand before the resplendent *Sacré-Coeur Basilica*. You will walk over to watch the sidewalk artists in *Place du Tertre*, then stand (or sit) on the basilica steps looking down over Paris and enter the basilica to see the stunning golden dome. Crossing the street, and walking down the steep steps, you will head off to the brightly-colored tables of *l'Eté en Pente Douce* for lunch.

This afternoon take the Metro or a taxi down from *Montmartre* to the Marais neighborhood, where you will explore vintage and other shops while walking toward the fountains beside *Pompidou Center*. These fountains feature the vividly playful sculptures by *Niki de Saint Phalle*. Find a perch beside the fountains to watch the street performers. For dinner, you will sit outside at *Bistro Beaubourg*, a typical French bistro frequented by locals, tucked away on a small street near *Pompidou Center*.

After dinner, walk home, or pick up a Vélib' bike to ride back. If you do chose to bike home, take some additional time to cruise along the bike paths in the direction of the Louvre, then down toward the river, and along the river embankment, before you cross the river to the left bank on the *Pont des Arts,* and head back to your neighborhood.

This evening, stop for one last drink at your favorite boat bar, watching the lights appear along the Seine. This will be your "au revoir" to France *this time.* But "au revoir" means "until I see you again." And, perhaps, you will.

And So... On to Your Trip, Day by Day

Now that you have an overview of your trip, let's move on to mapping out the details, place by place and day by day. These next five chapters will become your full set of "*Day Pages*" to guide you throughout your trip.

SECTION II:
DAY-BY-DAY TRIP PLAN & NOTES

CHAPTER 4:
Enter the Dominion of Kings—Amboise

Your trip begins in the *Valley of the Loire*, also called the *Valley of the Kings*, south of Paris. After flying into Paris, you will immediately board a fast train that will take you, in just over two hours, from the airport to Amboise, a lovely town on the *Loire River*, dominated by a Château.

Amboise will be your home base for four days. From here you will explore this historic area of France, with its overabundance of châteaux (totaling more than 300) that will transport you back in time.

A Little History

With the river to carry stone for building, and thick forests to provide wood, the Loire Valley was an ideal place to build castles. In the Middle Ages, these constructions were defensive fortresses, with thick stone walls and moats, perched high on hills or overlooking rivers.

During the Hundred Years' War, from the mid-1300s to the mid-1400s, England gained control over northern France, including Paris. In 1418, the yet to be crowned *King Charles VII* fled Paris with his court, retreating to the relative safety of the massive defensive fortress of Chinon in the Loire Valley.

Chinon is where *Joan of Arc* famously arrived to incite Charles to move forward in an effort to recover his country from English domination. Charles sent Joan on a relief mission to lift the siege of Orléans. Here she successfully led her troops to end the siege in only nine days. This victory restored French morale, and paved the way for the French to expunge the British from France and crown Charles king.

Once Charles was crowned king, the French royalty could have returned to Paris, and left behind their Loire Valley playgrounds. But instead they chose to continue to rule from the Loire Valley for the next 170 years, building new castles, and adding to their existing ones, to achieve an ever more resplendent lifestyle. As France became safer and more stable, protective fortresses were replaced with more fanciful and decorative pleasure palaces.

When the French kings ruled France from the Loire Valley, they moved about frequently from castle to castle, transporting ever-growing numbers of servants, horses and courtiers, complete with all their resplendent royal fixings—furniture, tapestries, artwork, wardrobes, tableware, and household furnishings. The entourage would dismantle itself and move on, then reestablish itself at the next stop, hanging tapestries and art, and hefting massive elegantly-carved trunks into position to serve as furniture.

While the royals and their court were on site, they quickly consumed all the resources in the area, feasting their way through the local wildlife and crops, while their horses (numbering 1000 by the time of King François I) devoured all the grass. Then it was time to move on. It was not until 1589 that *Henry IV* finally moved the court back to Paris.

The Plan for Your Visit to the Loire Valley

Beginning with the castle in Amboise, your home base for the next four days, you will visit a sequence of castles, all of them stunning, with amazing gardens and intriguing stories. These châteaux will take you back to the rule of *Charles VIII* (king from 1483 to 1498), who occupied Amboise castle, through the rule of the austere *Louis XII* (king from 1498 to 1515), who occupied the castle at Blois.

From there you will move to the extravagant *François I* (king from 1515 to 1547), who occupied castles in Amboise, Blois and Chambord. And then to *François'* second son, *Henri II* (king from 1547 to 1559), who occupied castles in Blois and Chenonceau—one with his wife, and the other with his mistress. As you travel back through time, immersed in the lush landscapes of the Loire Valley, you will gain a sense of the opulent, but scattered, lifestyles of the 15th and 16th century royalty.

Day 0 (Friday): Fly to Paris

Today will be your travel day and night if you are traveling from the US or Canada. If you are traveling from Great Britain or continental Europe, skip Day 0 and make your way to Paris on Day 1. During your flight, drink lots of water to stay hydrated, and take melatonin tablets to help prevent jet lag. At some point during your flight, practice your *Key French Phrases* so that you will be ready for the fresh challenges of the morning. Also, make certain you know the exact location of your passport, train tickets and Euros. And fill out your Customs Card to present on entry. Then watch a movie, eat dinner, with a complementary glass or two of wine, and go to sleep. Tomorrow you will wake up in Paris. And suddenly the new day and your great trip will be upon you.

Your arrival day will be the most challenging day of your trip. Awakening sleep-deprived after four or five short hours of sleep, in a time zone that is between 6 and 9 hours different from yours, everyone around you will be speaking French. Signs will be in French, with prices posted in Euros. Distances will be in kilometers. Time will be expressed based on a 2 -hour clock. You will adjust quickly to all these changes. But the immersion experience will be startling at first.

Within your first 8 hours tomorrow, you will accomplish a great deal... Navigate the airport to the TGV station. Purchase your first sandwiches and drinks, paying with Euros. Find the departure board that lists the gate for your first train, and validate your ticket using the designated "composter" machine. Make your first train change. Arrive at your first "home base," and check into your first accommodations. Orient yourself to your first town. With these challenges behind you, you then should reward yourself with an outside table at a café, order a coffee or a glass of wine, and breathe a sigh of relief and pride, saying "Ahh. We have arrived!"

Day 1 (Saturday): Amboise: Arrive & Walk About

You will arrive at Charles de Gaulle airport, likely at Terminal 1. Your immediate tasks will include:

1. Go through passport control.

2. Gather your luggage from baggage claim and pass through customs.

3. Pick up more Euros at an airport desk, if needed.

4. Catch the shuttle to the airport train station.

If your timing is off for catching the TGV from the airport, take a taxi to *Gare Austerlitz* and travel from there to Amboise. If you are arriving in Paris by Eurostar from Great Britain, or by train from elsewhere in Europe, catch a connecting train to Amboise.

Take the Train to Amboise

You will be taking the train directly from the airport to Amboise, making a change at an interim station. If your plane arrives at Terminal 1, take

CDGVAL Airport Shuttle to *"Aéroport Charles de Gaulle 2–TGV"* in the Terminal 2 complex. Spot the CDGVAL logo in Terminal 1, and follow the signs.

Be careful not to go to the wrong train station, or to get off the shuttle too soon. There are two train stations at Charles de Gaulle. The station you want is the *TGV Station*. Get off the shuttle at the *Terminal 2 TGV* station, between Terminal 2C and 2E.

The order of shuttle stops from *Terminal 1* are confusing, since *Terminal 3*, plus two extra stops at parking garages, precede the stop at *Terminal 2*. You likely will be sleepy, so pay attention here. *Do not get off the CDGVAL shuttle until it reaches Terminal 2.* If you need help finding your way to the TGV station, communicate that you are looking for the TGV (pronounced "Teh Jeh Veh").

Purchase Tickets & Seat Reservations

This TGV reservation is the one train arrangement you may *not* want to make in advance of your trip. By waiting to purchase this ticket at the airport train station, you will eliminate the risk of a flight delay causing you to miss your train and forfeit the money you paid in advance. Be aware that the last morning train to Amboise leaves at 10:16 am. Even if your plane arrives early, and you move quickly through passport control, this will make for a tight connection. The next train to Amboise leaves at 2:09 pm. Check the schedule online to update these times.

If your flight arrives before 9 am, and you are able to move along quickly, you may reach the airport train station in time to purchase a reserved seat on the 10:16 am TGV 5202 to Saint-Pierre-des-Corps, transferring there to a local train that arrives in Amboise at 12:20 pm.

72

Otherwise, aim for the 2:09 pm train, again connecting through Saint-Pierre-des-Corps, and arriving in Amboise at 4:21 pm. The advantage of aiming for the later train is that you will be able to take your time, find an airport restaurant where you can sit down for a *real* breakfast, and be assured that by the time you arrive in Amboise your room will be ready.

2:09PM	3:59PM	1hr	
Paris Airport	St Pierre Des Corps	50min	
			TGV Duplex 5218
TRANSFER: 11 mins			
4:10PM	4:21PM	0hr	
St Pierre Des Corps	Amboise	11min	
			TER 16824

When you arrive at the airport TGV station, you will be able to purchase your tickets to Amboise from one of the many SNCF/TGV kiosks, or from the ticket office in the glass-windowed room. Check that you are in the correct line for SNCF/TGV trains. You do not want the line for the RER trains that would only take you into Paris.

On the first part of your train journey, you will have a reserved seat, and so will need to locate your correct coach and seat when you board. The train from your connecting station to Amboise likely will have open seating.

Important Notes About Your First Train Ride

This will be your first train ride. Follow this *12-Step Train-Travel Routine*, then continue to use it for the remainder of your trip. The first time will be the hardest, then you will begin to feel like a pro.

1. Activate your rail pass

Even if you wait to purchase your seat reservations until you determine which train you will be in time to catch from the airport, you may be using a *Flexipass* or *Saverpass,* discounted for two people traveling together, and possibly also for travelers over 60. The decision about whether or not to purchase a *Flexipass* or *Saverpass,* issued for one or multiple travel days, is a choice you will make before you leave on your trip. More information about *Train Passes* is provided in Chapter 9.

If you do plan to use a pass, you will need to activate it before using it on this first train journey. These passes can be used on whatever specific days of your trip you choose, within a one month period. If you and your travel partner always will be traveling together, the math may work out in favor of a train pass for your long days of train travel.

A 7-day second class pass for two (at time of printing) costs $584, equating to around $41 each per day. For each adult or senior pass-holder, up to two children (aged 4–11) may travel free. The way to determine if a pass will save you money is to take a look at how many of your train days will cost more than $41 per person (or whatever the going rate is at the time you book). You will benefit by using a pass *only* for days that otherwise would cost more than $41 each.

When you first activate your rail pass, *do not rip it out of its cover.* To do so will invalidate it. Be sure to carry your pass in a safe place throughout your trip, and in a spot where you can locate it quickly. A *Flexipass*, depending on how many days it entails, is worth hundreds, or even over a thousand dollars. And if it is lost, it is lost. You will need to repurchase it.

To activate your pass, present it, along with your passport, at the ticket window of your first train station. If you are traveling on a *Saverpass*, both of you must be present at the ticket window when you activate it. The ticket agent (not you!) will fill in the blanks on your pass with your passport number and the first and last days you will be traveling, then stamp it in the validation box. NOTE: Rail passes must be activated within six months of purchase.

Located at the bottom of your *Flexipass* are a set of blank boxes where you will enter the day's date (in ink!) each day you use the pass. Make sure that every day you use your pass, you fill in one of these blanks *before* the conductor comes through your train car checking tickets.

2. Check the "Big Board" to find your track

When you arrive at the train station, locate the *"Big Board"* where all the trains are listed, and find the track number for your train. Make sure you are looking at the *Départs* ("Departures") and not the *Arrivées* ("Arrivals"). Look for your first destination train stop where you will be changing trains, probably *Saint-Pierre-des-Corps.*

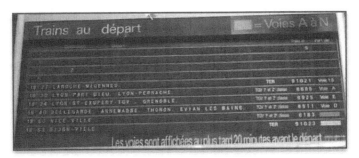

3. Write down your times & stations

Take time to write down all the key information you will need after you have boarded the train. This includes:

1. The exact *name* (in French) of your destination station.
2. The exact *time* you will arrive at your station.
3. The name and arrival time for the station one stop *prior* to yours.

Why is it important to make note of the station *before* yours? Pay careful attention here. Trains in France stay on schedule, and pause only briefly at each station. You will need to know in advance the precise time to get off, and be prepared and ready, with your luggage gathered together, standing by the door, *before* the train stops at your station. Otherwise the train will move on before you can gather your belongings together and get off.

4. Purchase your travel "picnic"

If you have time at the station before your train leaves, watch for a shop where you can purchase sandwiches, drinks and water. When you board, you likely will have a fold-down tray table, or possibly a full table between facing seats. So, as you speed through the countryside, you will be able to have your own little picnic whenever you want.

Shops at larger train stations will have display windows stacked with tasty-looking fresh sandwiches, generally a baguette with your choice of tuna ("thon"), ham ("jambon"), cheese ("fromage"), or tomato with mozzarella ("tomates et de mozzarella"). Watch for "Menu" offers that include a sandwich, drink and desert for a discounted single price. Even smaller train stations that do not have sandwich shops, often do have vending machines with surprisingly viable options.

Recognize that French coffee is an art form, created and purchased one cup at a time. And it is very strong. Your options will include: 1) "café" (a shot of espresso in a tiny cup), 2) "café crème" (espresso with hot milk, in a large cup), 3) "café américain" (filtered coffee) or 4) "cappuccino" (pricier espresso with foamed milk, possibly with whipped cream on top). Other available hot drinks are "un chocolat" (hot chocolate), "un thé" (black tea), "un thé vert" (green tea) or "une tisane" (herbal tea).

You will be paying for your train picnic using euros, probably by breaking one of the €20 notes you obtained before your trip. Be aware that the smallest denomination of euro bill is a €5 note, and both €1 and €2 are coins. So the change you get back from your sandwich purchase likely will provide you with quantities of euro change.

This will be the beginning of carrying around euro change and having it on hand when you need it. Quickly you will come to understand the value of these coins, since *most restrooms likely will require a €1 coin*. And any extra coins will be handy for tipping a street performer, or helping out a beggar.

5.   "Composter" your ticket!

Learn to spot the machines that date stamp ("composter") your train tickets. You must complete this step *before* you board each train in order to avoid expensive fines. Composter machines are brightly colored and are located near the tracks. When you insert your ticket, it will be stamped with the current day's date and will be a *valid* ticket.

Once the train is underway, the conductor will come through your train car checking tickets. Woe be unto the unfortunate soul who has not stamped his/her ticket in advance. But since you will have your properly validated ticket ready to present, you will be fine.

6. Locate your "voie" (track)

Prepare to board your train well before the departure time. Find your track and double check that you have the correct train by looking at the smaller monitor specific to that track.

At larger stations, you will be able to walk directly to your "voie" (pronounced "vwah"), but watch for signs pointing you in the direction of the correct section of the station. Keep your eyes open! If you have trouble finding your track, ask for help. But remember to say "excuse me" ("pardon"), "please" ("s'il vous plait") and "thank you" ("merci"). Good manners are a necessity in France.

At smaller stations, unless your track happens to be adjacent to the station, you will need to reach it by way of tunnels under the tracks. Some smaller stations have elevators down to these tunnels. These elevators may be difficult to spot, blocked from view by lines of people waiting to use them. But they can be a lifesaver after a tiring day. It is always worth politely asking someone to point you to the elevator: "Excusez moi, monsieur/madame. Où se trouve l'ascenseur, s'il vous plait?"

If cannot spot an operating elevator, you will find yourself faced with carrying your luggage down the stairs, through the tunnel to your track, then back up again. As you carry your luggage down and then back up those stairs, you will come to appreciate your pre-trip efforts to pack light!

As your trip progresses, and you purchase "treasures" to take home, lugging all that weight up and down the stairs at train stations will become more difficult. Then you will know for certain that it is time to mail home a box to lighten your load before your next train ride.

7. Find your train car

For all train rides, you will be traveling either 1st or 2nd class. For some legs of your journey, you also will have a reserved seat. Check to make sure you

are entering a car that matches your ticket. First and second class cars have a large numeral **1** or numeral **2** next to the door, as shown here.

If you are boarding a train that does not have reserved seats, enter any car with the correct class number and select a seat. If this train does have reserved seats, you also will need to find your correct *car* and *seat numbers*. You may need to press a metallic or rubberized button to open the door.

It will be much more convenient to walk the platform until you locate your car *before* you board. Running the gauntlet inside the train after boarding at the wrong car can be an extreme challenge. Of course, if you are running late and the train is about to leave, just get on wherever you can before you are left behind.

8. Stow your luggage

You will find places to stow your luggage either at the front or back of the car, or in the overhead rack. Sometimes there is storage space available between or under seats. It is best to place your luggage where you can keep an eye on it during the ride. Keep your luggage together as much as possible to make it easier to watch and to gather together again as you prepare to get off the train.

9. Show your ticket when asked

Soon after the train leaves the station, the conductor will walk through checking tickets. If you are using one of the days on your Flexipass, show the agent your activated pass, with that day's date entered in ink. Also present your seat reservation ticket if one is required for this train. Otherwise just show your date-stamped ticket. The conductor will check that all is in good order, then hand back your tickets. Remember to say "Merci monsieur/madame." Then congratulate yourself! You have successfully navigated the French train system.

You will quickly get used to this well-organized ticketing system, and begin to see how well it works. The requirement that all tickets be stamped, and dates entered on passes, before you board the train is an "honor system" of sorts. You are allowed to board the train unchecked, which allows trains to depart without delay. But if you neglect to stamp your ticket, this is taken as an attempt to cheat the system and ride the train twice using the same ticket. For this reason, the ticket validation system is held to very strictly. Tickets or passes that have not been validated in advance are not tolerated, and result in steep and immediate fines. But so long as you comprehend and honor this efficient and effective ticketing system, you will be well prepared to travel by train without incident or difficulty.

10. Enjoy the passing countryside & your picnic

Now sit back and take in the landscape. French trains are clean and comfortable. The journey can be as enjoyable as the arriving. Pull out your picnic goodies. Follow your progress on your map of France, keeping track of where you are and what you are passing. Spot the small villages on hills, with church steeples rising above the rooftops. Take in the tidy vineyards and fields, where the wine and fresh food you will be relishing throughout your trip are produced.

One word of caution… A train ride can be very soothing. Especially on this first train ride after your long night on an plane, you may find yourself starting to doze. A good practice is to set an alarm on your watch or other device to go off 10 minutes before you are scheduled to arrive at your station so that you don't sleep through your stop. We know from experience that sleeping past your stop can and does happen!

During your journey, pay attention each time you come into or leave a station to note where the station signs are located. Usually you can catch sight of signs in advance of the station, as well as at the station itself. But some station signs are difficult to spot, depending on where your car is located along the length of the train. Get good at sighting them!

Newer trains have monitors or LED displays that show the stops ahead. But older train cars do not have these displays. The best plan is to make an effort to keep track of where you are as you speed along through the French countryside.

11. Prepare in advance to get off at your station
When you reach the station *before* your stop, start to gather together your belongings and move toward the door so you will be ready to get off quickly when the train stops. European trains stop only briefly.

Also, be aware that the doors may not open automatically. So as you stand at the door waiting for the train to stop at your station, look around you and spot the button that opens the door. These buttons look different from one train to another, but you'll be able to locate them fairly easily since you will know to look for them.

As you come into the station, things will happen quickly. Follow this sequence:

- *Spot the Station Sign.* Hopefully you will be able to spot the sign for your stop as your train pulls in. But even if you don't see it, be prepared to get off the train at the designated time. Ask the people standing at the door if you are uncertain.

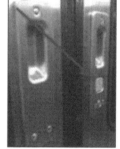

- *Open Sesame.* Push the button to open the door if it doesn't open on its own.

- *Get off the train quickly.* Heft your bags down to the platform and move them and yourself out of the way as quickly as possible to allow others to exit behind you. It helps to have an advance plan of who will be responsible for each item as you exit the train so that nothing will get left onboard when the train pulls off.

- *Pause to get your bearings.* When you have everything (and everyone) gathered around you, pause to look around you and get oriented.

12. Make your way to your connecting train or the exit

Look for the track's exit sign ("Sortie") or just follow the crowd. At smaller stations, you will be carrying your luggage down the steps, under the tracks, and up the other side. Sometimes you will be lucky enough to arrive at the track alongside the station. Or possibly you will spot an elevator ("ascenseur").

Connecting times between trains may be tight, so pay close attention to where you're going and what you're doing. The routine is the same:

- Find the *Departures Board.*

- Find your train and its "voie."

- "Composter" your ticket.

- Find your train car.

- Stow your luggage and find your seat.

Then off you will go again. Already you are starting to get the hang of train travel in France!

Arrive in Amboise

When you arrive in Amboise, you will find yourself at a small, quiet station. Walk inside the station to look around and get familiar with what's there. Then walk out the door toward the street and over to the large city map posted to your left. Orient yourself and *locate the river*. In Amboise, as well as in other places where you will be staying, including Paris, once you *locate the river*, you will be well on your way to getting yourself oriented and being ready and able to navigate your way around.

Locate the train station in the upper left part of the map, and trace the path from there to the river, across the bridge, past the island in the middle of the river, and toward the castle on the other side.

Since generally there will be no taxis waiting outside Amboise station, you will have two choices. One is to call a taxi to come pick you up. A taxi from the station to *Old Town* and the *Château Royal* on the other side of the river will cost under €10. Use the phone number posted outside the station and say: "J'ai besoin d'un taxi de la gare à mon hôtel, s'il vous plaît." These are additional numbers for Amboise taxis:

02-47-57-13-53 or 02-47-57-30-39

Another option is to walk toward the river and cross the bridge to the old city. This will be about a one mile walk, with luggage, but with excellent views of the town, and the Château hovering above it.

81

Whether you travel across the bridge by taxi or by foot, take this opportunity to spot the castle, take in the views, and look down at the island in the middle of the river. You may be coming back to this island one evening during your stay in Amboise for drinks and/or dinner, sitting outdoors, with a view looking back at the illuminated castle.

Find Your Hotel & Check In

For the "full experience," you will be staying *along the Loire River or in Old Town*, at the accommodations you booked months in advance. Since you used the "fly over" map feature on *Booking.com* or *VRBO.com* to see what options were available, you will have selected lodgings that are excellently located, with the ambience to enhance your stay. More about booking your accommodations in Chapter 10.

Some "Full Experience" Places to Stay in Amboise

Chambres d'Hôtes Les Fleurons (20 rue de la Concorde).

In a 17th-century townhouse, in the historic district of Amboise. All guest rooms (4 total) have free Wi-Fi and views of the Château Royal and/or the Loire.

Hotel Le Choiseul (36 Quai Charles Guinot).

Three 18th-century homes joined into 32 rooms with views of grounds or the Loire. *Restaurant* overlooks the river.

Le Manoir Les Minimes (34 Quai Charles Guinot).

Set on the *Loire River* bank. Spacious guest rooms (15 total) have views of Amboise Castle.

Le Clos d'Amboise (27 rue Rabelais).

Housed in a 17th century mansion in the historic quarter, surrounded by gardens, paths, terrace and outdoor pool.

Villa Eve (14 rue de la Concorde;+33-2-47-79-27-44)

Côté Château (26 rue de la concorde).

Set in a townhouse dating back to the 17th century, with kitchenette.

Depending on your time of arrival, your room may or may not be ready. Call ahead to confirm your train information and arrival time to arrange that someone will be available to meet you so that you will at least be able to deposit your luggage. As you check in, use your French first, reverting to English only after you have at least greeted your host in French.

Time to Learn Your Way Around: Orienteering

Amboise is small, and most of what you will be visiting is clustered around the castle. Once you have learned *two "Places" (square), three "Rues" (streets), and the "Quai" (waterfront street) along the river,* you will quickly feel well oriented and at home here.

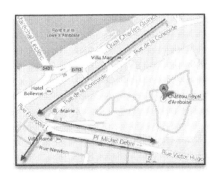

Walk along the road parallel to the river (*rue de la Concorde*), keeping the Château on your left (see point "A" on the map below) and the river to your right. This is the first of your "rues." If you don't see the Château as you walk, *look up!* The Château will be there, looming above you.

Continue to curve to the left, around the wall of the Château, onto *Place Michel Debré*, a square with shops and cafés facing the Château. This is the first of your *"places"* (pronounced "pl-aah-ce").

Pause to take a look up to your left along the castle wall. This is the second of your "rues"—*rue Victor Hugo*—the road you will follow tomorrow when you visit *Clos Lucé*, Leonardo de Vinci's final home. The fat round towers you see along the castle wall enclose wide ramps once used to enter the castle on horseback. During the reign of Charles VIII in the late 1400s, these ramps accommodated the horse and carriage that brought Charles' pregnant wife, Anne of Bretagne, to and from the castle.

Spot the brightly marked entrance to the wine tasting shop, tunneled directly into the base of the castle wall, You will return here after your

walk to request a "degustation" (a wine tasting), trying some of each color— "blanc" (white), "rouge" (red) and "rosé" (rosé)—to determine your favorites. You may select a few bottles to have on hand for future picnics, or to enjoy from your room, watching the sky turn pink over the Loire.

While you are here at Place Michel Debré, make dinner reservations at Chez Bruno. To request an outdoor table at 7 pm (19:00), say: "Nous voulons réserver une table pour deux à l'extérieur à dix-neuf heures, s'il vous plaît."

Meander Down Rue Nationale

As you continue your walk, reverse your steps back along *Place Michel Debré*, with the *Château Royal* now on your right. Turn left onto *rue Nationale*. This is the continuation of *rue de la Concorde*, which changes name at the 15th-century gate under the clock tower. This medieval gate was once part of the city wall through which travelers passed coming to and from Tours. Tours was the hub of economic and administrative activity during the almost two centuries when the French Kings lived in the Loire Valley.

Rue Nationale is now a walking street, lined with shops. No soldiers gallop through on horseback now, but the rustic 1400s medieval buildings are still visible above the shops. Look up at the buildings, as well into the colorful display windows.

Rue Nationale will be your shopping street while you are in Amboise. Take note of your options here. Wine shops. Vegetable and fruit stands. Telephone shops (where you can purchase and activate your French SIM card if you still need to). Gift shops. Patisseries (bakeries) and Boulangeries (delicatessens). ATMs. Look down the side streets too, and make note of all the places to which you would like to return.

Plan to come back later and spend more time on *rue Nationale* to purchase food for future picnics, as well as to replenish your supply of Euros, get your phones working, and start your search for "treasures" to take home.

Pause at Eglise St. Denis

At the end of *Rue Nationale*, you will emerge onto your second "Place"— *Place St. Denis*, with its lovely old church, surrounded by flowers. This is *Eglise St. Denis*, built in the 12th century. As you stand on the church steps, look back toward Château Royale. *Church on one hill, King on the other.*

St. Denis is open all day. Step inside to see the art and the stunning stained glass windows (replaced after the originals were destroyed, probably during the French Revolution).

When you walk inside, do respect the request for quiet. Services are held here on Sunday mornings at 11 am if you wish to come back then.

Walk Over to the River

After seeing the church, walk toward the river and turn to the right on *Quai du Général de Gaulle,* walking back in the direction you came, with the river now on your left. This *Quai* is the last spot on your Amboise orientation learning list. Turn right to arrive back at *Place Michel Debré.*

So, now to review your *three Rues, two Places, and one "Quai."*

- *Rue de la Concorde* to *Place Michel Debré.*

- Left to *rue Victor Hugo* toward *Clos Lucé,* or straight on *rue Nationale* to *Place St. Denis.*

- Over to the river, then back along *Quai du Général de Gaulle,* turning right to arrive back at *Place Michel Debré.*

You now should begin to feel oriented, with a sense of where you are at any point in terms of the Château, the pedestrian street and the river.

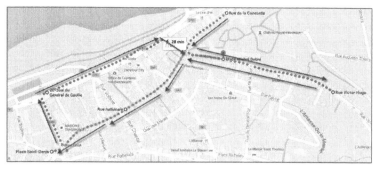

Pause at the TI (Tourist Information Office)

As you walk along the Quai, you will pass the small *Tourist Information Office* (TI). Stop by to pick up brochures and maps. The sign for the TI is tiny, so you will need to watch closely for it.

You may want to consider pre-purchasing your Châteaux tickets for the next few days now to avoid waiting in line. However, if you pre-purchase your tickets for *Chenonceau,* where you will be going the day after tomorrow, make sure they include both the audio guide as well as the museum. Otherwise, wait until you get to the Château.

Enjoy Some Free Time Until Dinner

Well done! You have *arrived*. And you are beginning to know your way around Amboise, your home base for the next four days. Now take some free time to do whatever you want.

Some options include:

- Attend to any remaining phone needs (you know where the phone shop is along *rue Nationale*).

- Find an ATM and get more Euros. NOTE: Most banks have daily limits for withdrawals, so keep yourself well supplied with euros throughout your trip.

- Check out the shops along *rue Nationale* and *Place Michel Debré*. If you don't already own a change purse, consider buying one now to carry around all the euro change you will be receiving.

- Return to the "Cave" (pronounced "kaav") under the Château in *Place Michel Debré* for a wine tasting and to select a few bottles.

- Go back to your room to relax before dinner.

If you decide to shop, start now to estimate price conversions. Or use a currency conversion app on your smart phone. The Euro to dollar conversion rate at time of publishing was €1 = $1.10. To translate roughly from Euros to Dollars:

1. Round off the price.

2. Divide the price by 10.

3. Add this amount to the original rounded off number.

For example:

- A €15 item: 15/10 = $1.50. $15 + $1.50 = $16.50.

- A €35 item: 35/10 = $3.50. $35 + $3.50 = $38.50.

- A €70 item: 70/10 = $7. $70 + $7 = $77.

- A €100 item: 100/10 = $10. $100 + $10= $110.

And so forth. If the exchange rate is different when you travel, just figure out the easiest mental estimation device to apply using the current conversion figures.

Dinner Across from the Château at Chez Bruno

You will have already made your dinner reservations. Now enjoy the delightful experience of sitting at an outside table at *Chez Bruno* ((0)2-47-57-73-49), with the Château across the way, taking in the surroundings and the people. This will be an excellent time to treat yourself to a great meal in celebration of your arrival.

Your feast at *Chez Bruno* could start with delectable *Escargots* (snails in garlic butter) for only €6, followed by *Pavé de Saumon* (salmon, fresh from the Loire) for €10. For désert, possibly the *Crème Brûlée Maison*, adding another €6, for a total of €22 each, plus wine (€14 for a bottle of Rosé Malin). So the final "addition," including wine, would be €58, converting to around $64. "Bon appetite!"

Always Check out Le Menu

Of course here, as at any French restaurant, it is always a good idea to check out "Le Menu," the multi-course options offered that day by the chef. For a single somewhat reduced price, *Le Menu* will include your choice of two or three courses from preset options: Starter (appetizer) + Entrée (main course) or Entrée + Désert (desert), or all three.

Remember the *sharing strategy* for "having the full experience," yet keeping the budget (and calories) under control, as we discussed earlier. One of you could order "Le Menu" and the other order only an Entrée or a Starter. Then share.

About Ordering Wine

And if a bottle of wine seems too pricey, it is always a good value to share a carafe (called a "pichet" in some areas) of house wine. The house wine in France is usually a local wine, chosen to complement the menu. No self-respecting French restaurant would serve a bad house wine. This IS France, after all! Request "un demi-litre (half liter) du *vin rosé*, s'il vous plaît" (or *vin blanc* or *vin rouge*, depending on your taste). For a larger carafe, order "un litre," and for less order "un quart litre" (quarter liter). You will be brought a very nice wine, probably local, at a surprisingly reasonable price.

One more note about the wine. If you like your wine dry, a wonderful discovery in France is that the rosé wines tend to be dry (request "sec" for dry, or "sucre" for sweet). Once you have discovered these wonderful rosés, you may find it difficult to make your way back to the whites and reds.

Courteous Interactions with French Waiters

Good food is a point of pride with the French, and plays a significant role in their quality of life. Servers in restaurants are highly knowledgeable, and take pride and pleasure in sharing their expertise, guiding you to a perfect culinary experience. And they most certainly are not rude! Understanding the culture and courtesies of how waiters and diners interact in France is what will make all the difference between a possibly frustrating and an excellent experience.

Always begin with the niceties of greeting your waiter (in French, please, as mentioned earlier). Then ask in French if they speak English: "Parlez vous anglais?" Although they likely do speak at least a little English, they generally think that they speak it badly. But when you break the ice by attempting to speak at least a little French, they will join with you in the challenge of communicating back and forth in order to answer your questions and together plan your most excellent dining experience.

It is always wise to ask for your waiter's recommendation: *"Quelle est votre recommandation (reh-comb-en-dah-see-on), s'il vous plaît?"* This is a sign of respect for their expertise. Even if you already have narrowed down your choices, point to the two or three options you are considering and ask their opinion. You will have better meals this way. And you will have friendly interactions with your waiters, who will feel respected as the culinary experts that they are.

Be aware, too, that in France it would be considered very rude for a waiter to offer you your check before *you* request it. You are meant to feel welcome to linger over your meal for as long as you wish. When you are ready for your check, the ball is in your court. Catch the attention of your waiter and say *"L'addition s'il vous plait"* and you will receive your check promptly.

How Tipping Works in France

A word to the wise about tipping... Be aware that in France a 15% service fee already has been included, by law, in the menu price of all food and drinks. You may see mention of this, printed at the bottom of some bills or menus, using the words *"service compris."* Service included. The VAT tax is also added automatically, but this does not go to your waiter. The included "service" (pronounced "ser-veece") compensates your waiter for taking care of you throughout the meal, based on his/her job description. Included "service" is not considered to be a *gratuity* or *tip*, which is something *extra* you may wish to add beyond the 15% for "service."

Since 15% has already been included for your waiter, adding another 15%–20% to your bill, as you would do in the States, equates to tipping a total of 30%–35% when combined with the included "service." This is simply *not* done in France. If you wish to give your waiter more than the included 15%, adding 5%–10% as an *extra* gratuity is entirely adequate. You will see no place on your check to write in a *tip*. Tips are generally left in cash, using 1€ and 2€ coins or bills (no small change please).

Consider Where You Are and Adjust Your Expectations

Be aware too that service in a casual bistro, with two waiters handling multiple indoor and outdoor tables, will be at a different level than in a small restaurant. In busy bistros, it is unrealistic to wait for your waiter to check on you to see if you need anything. When you need something, signal your waiter and speak up.

This Evening—Find a Place to Look Out Over the Water

Sunsets over the Loire can be stunning, night after night. Have your camera ready, and plan to pause to enjoy and soak in the beauty from your side of the river. Even better, take the 10-minute walk down to the river and partway across the bridge to look back at the Château, lit up against the sky.

If you have the energy, cross the bridge partway to the island in the middle of the river, and find *Le Shaker Cocktail Lounge* (3 quai François Tissard), where you can sit at an outdoor table for desert or a drink, with the illuminated Château and town before you.

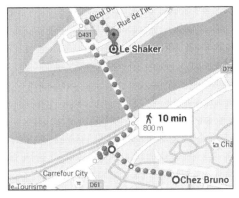

Beyond enjoying the views from *Le Shaker*, there are two additional reasons you may want to expend the extra effort to venture there this first night you are in Amboise. First, since you are freshly arrived from another time zone, your body needs to adapt to your new surroundings. This means resetting your natural time clock by staying up until your normal bedtime, but now based on your new local time zone. To aid in this adjustment, and to minimize jet-lag, you need to spend time outside while the sun is up, and as night falls.

Second, *Le Shaker* may become a favorite spot to return to on future afternoons or evenings. If you are too tired to walk over to *Le Shaker* tonight, plan to check it out another evening you are in town.

91

And So to Sleep...

Tonight your body will be confused by your leap across the Atlantic, not to mention your six (or more) hour change in time zones. It may need a bit of an assist to figure out when it is time to sleep. The nonprescription supplement melatonin that you used on the plane last night, will be very effective in helping your body's natural time clock adjust to your first few nights in France. After that, you will be fine.

Your body generates melatonin naturally to control when you go to sleep and when you wake up. Scientists recognize that when you challenge your body's natural sleep cycle, it is necessary that you supplement your body's natural melatonin production. Taking three milligrams of fast-release melatonin before bedtime for several nights after you arrive in your new time zone will ease your transition, alleviate jet lag, and allow you to start enjoying your trip sooner.

And now, bonne nuit. Tomorrow you will awaken in Amboise, and be on to new discoveries.

CHAPTER 5:
Castles & Gardens: Chateaux of the Loire

Now begin your visits to the Loire châteaux. You will see four of the best and most famous châteaux, and learn their stories: *Amboise, Blois, Chenonceau and Chambord*, the 'home sweet homes" of Kings Charles VIII, Louis XII, François I and Henri II, among others. Four châteaux will be enough for you to visit on this trip. From these, you will gain a good sense of how the Renaissance royalty, and their mistresses, lived.

You will be seeing, in miniature, four additional "best" châteaux, along with many others, at the *Mini Châteaux Park,* including: *Chiverny, Azay-le-Rideau Langeais and Villandry.* For now you will "save" actually visiting these other great châteaux until your next visit to this region. It is best to limit yourself on each trip to no more than four châteaux, then stop while they are still intriguing and impressive. After four, your eyes will begin to glaze over, and the experience will be wasted. There will be a "next time" for you to visit these other royal residences and gardens.

Day 2 (Sunday): Market, Château & Clos Lucé

> **Before You Set Off for the Day**: Make dinner reservations for 7:30 or 8:00 pm at *l'Epicerie* (in *Place Michel Debré*; (0)2-47-57-08-94), at an outdoor table (or request that your hotel do this for you).

Today you will visit two elegant residences, *Amboise Castle* and *Clos Lucé*—one a grand royal castle and the other the royal guest house across the street. The most notable guest to live at *Clos Lucé* was Leonardo da Vinci, who was invited by the young King François I to move there at age 65, and live there for the rest of his life.

Da Vinci arrived after traveling across the Alps, carrying with him the Mona Lisa as a gift for the King. Thus this masterpiece came to reside in France to this day, now housed at the Louvre in Paris, where you will visit it in a few days.

Understanding Breakfast, Lunch (12–2 pm) & Dinner

Meals in France have a predictability to them. Instead of fighting this or becoming frustrated, learn the flow and timings, and adapt. French breakfast is called "petit déjeuner," a small meal, sometimes eaten on the fly, standing at a counter. Lunches and dinners are major and more leisurely events.

Breakfast generally includes something fresh-baked and often sweet. There also may be fruit, yogurt, cheese and thin-sliced ham or salami. Options often include:

- Pain (pronounced "p-aaanh"). Bread.

- Pain au chocolat. Bread with chocolate.

- Pain aux raisins. Bread with raisins.

- Pain au lait. Slightly sweet light bread made with milk.

- Croissant. Always fresh!

- Baguette with jam.

Lunch is a more ample affair that is served between noon and 2 pm. After 2, lunch is "finis," Finished! At this point, many restaurants shut down until time to reopen for dinner. Some French shops and attractions close during lunch, and reopen at 2:30 or 3:00 pm, since everyone, including the staff of the shop or attraction, should be out having lunch during the dedicated lunch hours.

If you miss out on lunch during lunch time, you may go hungry for a few hours. However, you can always stop off for bread, cheese, fruit and wine, and put together an impromptu picnic. Some cafés do stay open, providing a limited menu between lunch and dinner hours.

Dinner is generally a feast, often including three courses, wine, bread and mineral water. The French dinnertime is typically late, around 8 pm, with the earliest seating at around 7:00 to 7:30 pm.

SO… You have several options for how to approach breakfast during your time in France. If breakfast is included with your accommodations, then by all means partake of it. Otherwise, consider gathering your own breakfast of pastries, juice, cheese, fruit & yogurt (or some combination thereof) during your wanderings the day before. In the morning, fix your coffee (using your traveling coffee maker or instant coffee), break out your "Picnic-ery," and set out your array of breakfast items, supplementing them, as needed, from the stash of breakfast bars and peanut butter you brought from home. The money you save from breakfast can be added to the kitty and used toward a remarkable lunch and/or dinner.

Market Day in Amboise!

If today is Market Day in Amboise (Wednesday or Sunday), start your day by visiting the Market. Local markets are great fun! Whenever your trip coincides with a Market Day, make some time to partake.

Find Treasures

Wander the stalls looking for "treasures." Pick up tasty picnic items like fresh-baked bread and pastries, local cheese and olives, sausage and fruit for your picnic later today in the park at *Clos Lucé*. Watch the locals having

fun, out with their families. Ask a vendor to help you select a colorful scarf or a sharp hat, and experience their friendliness, as well as their consummate sense of style. You may even be able to negotiate a small discount if you decide to buy two.

You will quickly begin to notice that shopping is much more engaging and *personal* in France. You're not shopping in chain stores now!

What's a "Treasure"?

You'll know a "treasure" when you spot it. A "treasure" is unique and memorable, and not something designed specifically to appeal to tourists. A refrigerator magnet or a tee shirt is not really a treasure. Is it? A treasure is something you will use and enjoy forever. And whenever you use it or wear it, you will be reminded of your trip, the story of where and how you found it, and your personal encounter with the shopkeeper.

Treasures are distinctively individual. One of you may fall in love with a brightly painted frog prince teapot, and the other with a lovely handcrafted pendant, made from amethysts and rough pearls. Only you will know what your treasures will be.

Here are some sample "finds"…

- Tapestry pieces & pillow covers.

- Brightly colored table clothes, napkins and placemats.

- Soft leather or suede shoes and sandals.

- Unusual hand-crafted jewelry.

- Porcelain, silver, carved or crystal antique items from Market Days.

- Maps showing old country boundaries of Europe and the world.

"Conquer" Amboise Castle

Open 9 am to 6:30 pm, April 1 to June 30

(7:00 pm closing July 1 to August 31)

Admission fee + explanatory leaflet: €10.50

Admission fee + audio visit: €14.50

Confirm these times at: *http://www.chateau-amboise.com*.

This will be your first visit of the day, so plan to arrive fairly early. Pick up the English version of the "Explanatory Leaflet" when you purchase your ticket. Or, for an additional €4, include the excellent "*Audio Visit*" to get the most out of your time here. As you climb the ramp to the expansive terrace, make note of where the gift shop is located. Later, when you are ready to leave, you will use a second exit out through the gift shop to spiral down one of the fat towers to the street below.

At the top of the castle ramp is a large garden and terrace area, with a magnificent view down to the river. To your left is the small chapel where *King François I* buried *Leonardo da Vinci*. After you visit the chapel, cross the terrace to the wall for a kingly view out over the Loire.

A Little History & Royal Intrigue

Flags of both France and Brittany fly along the castle wall, harkening back to the strategic marriage in 1491 between 13-year-old *King Charles VIII* of France and *Anne of Brittany*, who was captured at age 14 and forced to marry him.

This strategic *marriage by abduction* was masterminded by Charles' shrewd sister, *Anne of France*, then acting as regent for the young king, in order for France to gain control of Brittany as *Anne of Brittany's* dowry.

When *Anne of Brittany* was captured and forced to marry Charles, she was already married "by proxy" to the *Holy Roman Emperor Maximilian of Hungary*, whom she had never met. This marriage was another diplomatic ploy, with the contrary strategic goal of blocking French control of Brittany. Unfortunately for Maximillian, he was too busy with his own problems to press his claim to his proxy wife. And so Brittany married France instead of Hungary.

Charles, who had been born and raised at Amboise Château, completely rebuilt it when he became king. He brought to the project his taste for Italian architecture, developed during his three years in Italy (1493–1495) while conquering Pisa, Florence, and Naples. Charles brought in Italian masons, builders, and garden designers to complete these renovations, with the goal of creating the first Italian-styled palace in France.

Charles and Anne had four children, three boys and a girl, three of whom died as infants, and the fourth at age three. The fat round towers of the castle were designed so Anne's horse and carriage could bring her all the way up to Amboise Château when she was pregnant.

Although Charles' father was the notably brilliant Louis XI, the king who brought the silk trade to Tours to recapture the large amounts of currency the French were spending on Italian silk (around 6 million livres a year), Charles himself was not known to be overly bright. He died young at Amboise Castle, aged 28, from bumping his head on a doorway on his way to a tennis match.

Next to be king after Charles was his cousin, Louis XII. Louis orchestrated the annulment of his own long-standing marriage to Charles' handicapped sister, Jeanne, in order to marry Charles's widow, Anne. Again, this was a means to retain control of Brittany. While living in Amboise Castle, Louis XII built his own wing, and also purchased and built a wing at Blois Castle, where you will visit two days from now.

Having no male heir, Louis brought his nephew, François, to live at Amboise castle in order to prepare him as the next king. During an illness in 1505, Louis ordered that the 10-year-old François become engaged to his own 6-year-old daughter, Claude. Again, the intent was for France to retain control of Brittany after Louis died. The marriage between François and Claude took place nine years later in 1514.

And so it went with the chain of politics and intrigue, as royal children were commissioned to play their appointed roles, marrying strategically and on cue, as human puppets in a real-life "game of thrones."

Soon after François was crowned king in 1515, at age 21, he captured the Italian city-state of Milan. While he was in Milan, François met Leonardo da Vinci (painter, sculptor, architect, musician, mathematician, engineer, inventor, anatomist, geologist, cartographer, botanist, and writer), and commissioned da Vinci to design and build him a mechanical lion that walked forward and opened its chest, revealing a cluster of lilies.

The next year, François brought da Vinci to live at Clos Lucé, across the street from his castle, with an annual pension totaling 10,000 scudi (equating to roughly $3,000 then and $135,000 now). This freed the genius inventor to live out his life painting, studying and inventing. The king so enjoyed da Vinci's company, that he made frequent use of the tunnel linking their two abodes. While living in Amboise, Leonardo designed and directed flashy extravaganzas for the king and his court on the castle terrace, complete with illuminations and fireworks.

Leonardo became close friends with the king over the final three years of his life, and died in the king's arms, as you will see in a painting at *Clos Lucé*. François had Leonardo buried in a church on the castle grounds.

François initiated the Renaissance in France, and, with his love of the arts, started the magnificent art collection now on display at the Louvre in Paris. He supported major writers as well as artists, and was extravagantly enthusiastic about building and renovating châteaux. He completed the renovations at Amboise, made major additions to Blois Castle, and built the decadently magnificent Chambord Château. You will be visiting all three of these castles, Amboise, Blois and Chambord, within the next few days. He also transformed the Louvre in Paris from a medieval fortress to a splendid Renaissance castle, and expanded Fontainebleau from a lodge to a palace, with walls covered in frescos painted by Italian masters.

These various building and collecting projects cost a great deal of money. Although François had inherited the kingdom debt-free from the austere Louis, he managed to amass debts totaling over 40 million livres by the time he died—an unfathomable sum of money at that time. He once spent 200,000 livres for a single piece of fabric, a sum equivalent to what Louis paid to purchase Blois Castle.

When François I died, his son, Henri II, was crowned king at age 28, and reigned for 12 years. Henri and his queen, Catherine de' Medici, a member of the ruling family of Florence, Italy, married when they both were fourteen years old, and produced ten children. They lived in Amboise

Castle, and raised their children there.

Henri also was romantically involved with a widow, Diane de Poitiers, who exerted a strong influence over him, and thus over France. You will visit Diane's château, Chenonceau, tomorrow. When Henri died in a jousting tournament, his wife evicted his mistress from Chenonceau and took it for herself.

Henri II was a big spender like his father, François, expanding the royal debt to a staggering total of 48 million livres, four times the royal annual income of 12 million livres.

Following Henri II came three of his sons in quick succession, each of them disastrous as kings. The eldest of these was François II, who married Mary Queen of Scots at age 14 (after a 10-year engagement), and became king at age 15. Amboise Castle was the site of a conspiracy to abduct the young King François, eliminate his advisors, then return the king to power. This plot, motivated by repressive policies toward Protestants that emanated from the king's advisors, ended in a bloodbath, with 1200 Protestants strung up along the town walls in retribution. François II died from an ear infection at age 16, after only seventeen months as king, although some suspected that he actually was poisoned by Protestants. The throne was a hazardous spot to occupy.

Amboise castle was never again a royal favorite. During the French Revolution, the Château was ransacked, then fell into neglect and disrepair. Napoleon demolished a major part of the Château in the early 19th century, including the church where François I buried da Vinci. Only about 20% of the interior buildings of the castle survived and were restored. But the stories of betrothed children and teenage marriages, conspiracies and massacres, wives and mistresses, untimely deaths and suspected murders, live on.

Highlights to Spot at Amboise Castle

Wander the castle and grounds, seeing it through the eyes of its resident kings. As Charles VIII, admire your Gothic-style wing, with its Italian designs and motifs, created by the Italian stone masons and gardeners you engaged to make it look Italian. As Louis XII, take pride in your Renaissance-style wing. As François I, stand on your terrace, and recall the grand extravaganzas arranged for you by Leonardo da Vinci.

While you explore the Château, spot and visit these highlights:

100

- *Saint-Hubert Chapel,* originally built for Anne of Brittany, where Leonardo da Vinci was buried.

- *Salle des Gardes* (guards' room), with a model showing Amboise Castle when it was at its full size.

- *Minimes Tower* and *Heurtault Tower,* the original castle entrances, with spiral ramps wide enough for a horse and carriage. The higher you go, the better the views.

- *Royal apartments,* including Henri II's chamber, the cupbearer's room and the music room.

- *Hall of State,* with vaulted ceilings and beautiful fireplaces.

- Italian-style gardens.

Exit the Castle by Spiraling Down the Heurtault Tower

Instead of walking back down the ramp when you exit, go through the gift shop and down the *Heurtault Tower* to the street below. Watch for carvings on the walls, left by medieval stone-carvers and others…a kind of medieval graffiti, with pictures, scenes, and names… and dates cut into the walls in the 1500s.

Visit Clos Lucé—Da Vinci's Final Home

Manoir du Clos Lucé ("House of Light")

Open 9 am to 7 pm (8 pm July–August).

Entry to château only: €13.50. Château and *Exhibition Hall:* €18.50.

Walk up the road, with the Château on your left, until you reach the entrance to *Clos Lucé* on your right. As you climb the hill, watch for Troglodyte (cave dweller) houses built into the rock. These cave homes housed the poor of bygone ages, as they required no roof and were inexpensive to heat. Now they have been renovated into stylish homes, complete with satellite dishes.

You will be touring:

1. The château itself, where Leonardo da Vinci spent the final years of his life in remarkable luxury for an artist.

101

2. The landscaped park, with full-sized models of some of Leonardo da Vinci's most notable and intriguing inventions.

3. The *Exhibition Hall*, housing copies of da Vinci's art, including a copy of *The Last Supper*, as well as more of his inventions.

These multiple exhibit areas combine to show the "many facets of this most versatile of geniuses." Leonardo da Vinci was four centuries ahead of his time, inventing the concept of the automobile, paddle boat, helicopter, airplane, parachute, tank, machine gun, self-propelled vehicle, swing-bridge, and telephone, among others… And all 200 years before the advent of steam power.

Lunch at La Terrasse or a Picnic in the Park

Enter the park, picking up a copy of the English handout. But start your visit with lunch outside. To reach the courtyard terrace restaurant, *La Terrasse Renaissance Crêperie*, round the left side of the château. The terrace restaurant is planted with "Mona Lisa" roses, and has a splendid view over the town of Amboise and the Royal Château.

Or walk out into the park, filled with models of Leonardo's inventions, and find a bench for a picnic. Pull out your "finds" from this morning's market, or from your shopping yesterday, along with your "picnic-ery" items—plastic wineglasses, plates, napkins, utensils. Then enjoy your feast, starting with a toast to your talented host, Leonardo.

Visit Da Vinci's "Little" Château. How Did He Live?

After lunch, start your tour with Leonardo's château. This is a lovely home—very plush for an artist, with ample space for a laboratory and a workshop where he and his apprentices could paint and invent in luxury.

As you walk through Leonardo's home, pause to take note of some of his philosophical quotes, hung about on the walls. One plaque says: *"Qui peut arrêter la haine sauf l'amour?"* Who can stop hatred without love? Another quote says: *"L'amour triomphe de tout."* Love triumphs over all. And a third says: *"La nature n'enfreint jamais ses propres lois."* Nature never breaks its own laws.

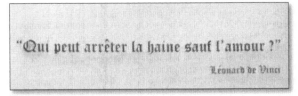

"Qui peut arrêter la haine sauf l'amour ?"
Léonard de Vinci

To quote King François: "There has never been another man born in the world who knew as much as Leonardo, not so much about painting, sculpture and architecture, as that he was a very great philosopher."

Visit the small chapel that was commissioned by King Charles VIII as a haven for his wife, Anne of Brittany, who came here to pray and to escape the clamor of court life while recovering from the tragic deaths of her young children. This tiny chapel was threatened during the revolution. But the resident at the time convinced the revolutionaries that Leonardo would have been on their side, and so it was spared.

Study the busts of Leonardo and François. Look out the window of Leonardo's bedroom at his view of Amboise Castle, where his royal friend lived. Imagine Leonardo relaxing in his music and drawing rooms, hung with tapestries, pondering the mysteries and possibilities of the world, nature and the universe, or entertaining his royal guest. Find the painting of François at da Vinci's deathbed.

After wandering the upper floor of Leonardo's home, descend to the lower level to view the many models and 3D exhibits based on Leonardo's drawings. Study his various designs for bridges, as well as his 16th century versions of the bicycle, airplane, automobile, helicopter, and tank. Watch the videos demonstrating Da Vinci's inventions in action. Read the résumé Leonardo submitted to the Duke of Milan, in which he advertised his skills and services as an inventor of war devices, as well as his considerable talent as an artist, including:

- "I have means, by secret and tortuous mines and ways, made without noise, to reach a designated spot, even if it were needed to pass under a trench or a river."

- "I can carry out sculpture in marble, bronze, or clay, and also I can do in painting whatever may be done, as well as any other, be he who he may."

While you are in the basement, locate the entrance to the secret passageway between *Clos Lucé* and *Amboise Castle* that was once used by François to visit with his exceptional friend for a cozy evening of philosophical discussion.

Plan to Meet Up at La Terrasse

The basement exhibit of Leonardo's inventions empties back out into the rose garden where *La Terrasse Renaissance Crêperie* awaits and invites you to take a well-earned pause. The gift shop is also located off this courtyard. Plan to meet up here when you and your travel partner(s) exit the mansion. This will give you a much needed break, and also will make allowances for the differing speeds at which you may have moved through the exhibits of Leonardo's inventions.

What Was He Thinking??? Fantastic Inventions

Take some time to wander the park and imagine the creativity and genius it took for Leonardo to come up with some of these inventions 500 years ago.

Also visit the *Exhibition Hall*, with many interesting exhibits and models, including a copy of da Vinci's remarkable painting, *The Last Supper*.

Free Time and/or Pre-Dinner Drinks at Le Shaker

Wander back down the hill into town, and take your pick of what to do during this free time before dinner. Shopping? Picking up fresh croissants and fruit for breakfast tomorrow? Walking back over the bridge to *Le Shaker* for before-dinner drinks with a view? A stop back in your room to put your feet up? It's your choice. You know the way.

Dinner at l'Epicerie

You already have made your reservations for dinner at *l'Epicerie*. Now enjoy fully dining at your outdoor table, across from Amboise Castle. Share the highlights of your day, and your thoughts about it all. What have you "taken away" from today? Would you, like François, have chosen Leonardo as a favored friend? What turn would your discussions with him have taken?

Day 3 (Monday): Chenonceau & Mini-Châteaux

> **Before You Set Off for the Day:** Make dinner reservations for 7:30 or 8:00 pm at your favorite restaurant in Amboise. *Chez Bruno*? *L'Epicerie*? *Le Shaker*? Or, for a new experience, try the elegant *Lion d'Or* beside the river (17 Quai Charles Guinot; Phone: (0)2-47-57-00-25).

Today you will be off to see *Chenonceau*, "Château of the Six Women." *Chenonceau* is one of the most beautiful of all the royal playgrounds, and has a varied history, steeped in intrigue, jealousy, celebration and loss.

You will be traveling about by taxi, first to *Chenonceau*, then to *Mini-Châteaux Park*, to see the 1:25-scale models of the most notable of the Loire Châteaux, then back "home" to Amboise.

To Chenonceau in Chenonceaux

> *Chenonceau Château* (http://www.chenonceau.com)
>
> 9 am–7 pm (April & May); 7:30 pm (June); 8 pm (July & August).
>
> *Castle + brochure: €11. Castle + audio visit: €15. Castle, brochure + Wax Museum: €13. Castle + audio visit + Wax Museum: €16.*

Although it would be too expensive to use taxis to visit most châteaux, traveling by taxi to and from Chenonceau from Amboise, a distance of 19 miles, will cost only around €25 each way. Plan to arrive at the château early to beat the crowds.

> *Taxi to Chenonceau: 02 47 57 13 53 or 02 47 57 30 39*

When your taxi drops you off, arrange where you will meet your driver for the return trip, either at the start of the promenade to the Château, or in the small town of Chenonceaux, in front of one of the hotels along the main street, *rue du Bretonneau*. Three possible meeting places in town where you can wait comfortably for your driver, are:

1. *Auberge du Bon Laboureur* (6 rue Bretonneau)

2. *Hotel la Roseraie* (7 rue Bretonneau): Terrace restaurant and bar.

3. *Hostel du Roy* (9 rue Bretonneau): With a lovely terrace.

Purchase a château ticket that includes an audio-guide, as well as entry to the *Wax Museum,* a bargain at only €1 more than the Castle plus audio guide. The wax museum will be your introduction to the "cast of characters" who lived here, including *Diane de Poitier* and *Queen Catherine de Medici.* The audio guide is available in two versions, 45 or 90 minutes. The 90-minute version is more complete, with better stories. You can always fast-forward to the sections that interest you most.

A Little History

Chenonceau was built in 1515 by the tax collector of King François I. It was then seized by the king in 1535 for "unpaid debts to the crown," At François' death in 1547, Chenonceau was passed to his son, Henri II, who offered it as a "gift" to *Diane de Poitiers*, his father's favorite mistress who became Henri's mistress in 1534, when she was 35 and Henri only 16, and already married to Catherine de Medici. Henri also gifted Diane with the crown jewels of France.

At Chenonceau, Diane added a bridge over the river to the opposite bank, and planted an extensive garden along the river. Throughout the château, she installed tiles that intertwined "D" (for "Diane") with "H" (for "Henri").

But then Henri was killed in a jousting tournament, and Diane's status came to an abrupt end. Henri's powerful widow, Catherine de Medici, banished Diane from Chenonceau, and forced her to return the crown jewels.

After evicting Diane, and taking over Chenonceau, Catherine began a total make-over of the château to claim it as her own. Where Diane had built a

bridge, Catherine erected a 2-story ballroom atop the bridge, and hosted extravagant parties, complete with mock "battles" on the river, and the first fireworks displays ever to be seen in France. Where Diane had created lovely gardens, Catherine bettered Diane's gardens with her own more elaborate ones.

When Catherine died in 1589, she bequeathed the château to her daughter-in-law, Queen Louise, wife of Henri and Catherine's bizarre fourth son, Henri III, who was assassinated that same year by a fanatical young Dominican friar who was pretending to deliver a secret message, but instead plunged a knife into the king's abdomen. Queen Louise went into a perpetual state of mourning, enshrouding both herself and the château in black. For the rest of her life, Louise kept herself locked away in the château, in an upstairs bedroom decorated in black tapestries stitched in white feathers, symbols of death and mourning. You will see these as part of your visit to the chateau.

Walk the Tree-lined Avenue & Stop at the Maze

As you approach the château, you will walk down an avenue of magnificent trees. If you wish, take a detour to the left, and test your navigational skills in the *Italian Maze*, rebuilt exactly from Catherine de' Medici's plans. How quickly can you make it through the maze?

As you continue to walk down the lane, the château will suddenly come into view. You may have seen pictures of this magnificent castle before, but gazing upon the real thing for the first time still will take your breath away.

While you are here visiting Chenonceau, you will divide your time among four areas, plus a pause for lunch:

1. The Wax Museum

2. The Châteaux

3. Diane's Garden

4. Catherine's Garden

This exquisite château has up to 6,000 visitors a day. So be strategic about the order in which you see things. Note where people are heading, and go elsewhere. Then double back later when the crowd thins.

If busloads of visitors are walking ahead of you on the avenue, pause to check out the maze and the *Wax Museum* to let the throng get ahead of you. Or move ahead quickly and put yourself well in the lead.

If the château entrance is backed up, head for one of the gardens, then come back later. Plan to eat your lunch at an odd time. Tour groups by the dozen will come and go, racing back to their buses on strict deadlines. But you will be your own time keeper, free to spend more time and select your own pace.

Visit the Wax Museum

As you approach the château, the wax museum will be on your right. This is a modest museum. But it is a good chance to "meet" the cast of characters who inhabited this exquisite château, including Henri and his two women, mistress Diane and wife Catherine, all dressed in the finery of their time.

This little museum will provide you with an overview of the 400-year history of the château, from the Renaissance through the Great Wars. During World War I, the ballroom gallery of the château was used as a hospital ward.

During World War II, this ballroom built on a bridge became a route of escape from Nazi-occupied France to the "free" zone on the opposite bank of the river.

Make Your Grand Entrance Into the Château

Reserving the right to feel as regal as you choose, walk through the château using the audio-guide, preferably the 90-minute version in order to hear all the stories and imagine the lives that were lived here.

As you walk the rooms of the château, spot these highlights:

- The *Keep of Marques*, to the right of the château, a remnant from when Chenonceau was a fortified mill.

- Diane's bedroom, where Catherine had her own portrait installed over the fireplace.

- Queen Catherine's bedroom.

- Diane's balcony and Catherine's balcony.

- Diane's bridge across the river, with Catherine's double-decker ballroom built on top.

- The black bedroom on the 3rd floor, where Henri III's widow, Louise, lived in perpetual mourning after her husband's death.

- The kitchen, with its hidden trap door to unload supplies or provide an escape route to the river below, as need be.

Which is the Best Garden, Diane's or Catherine's?

Diane's garden lies beyond the castle, to the left, along the banks of the *River Cher*, protected from river floods by raised terraces. Two wide paths cross this 12,000 square meter garden, dividing it into eight triangular compartments. The center of the garden is animated by a water-jet that was considered to be a major innovation in its time.

When she banished Diane and took over Chenonceau after King Henri died, Catherine created her own "garden of wonders," with the intention that her garden would "outshine" Diane's garden. Located in the area just below the forecourt and the *Keep of Marques*, Catherine's garden once included an aviary, a menagerie, a sheep barn, a man-made cave and a rock fountain, all set among splendid flowers, rose trees and a majestic alley of 16 orange trees.

These gardens are renewed every spring and summer, replanted with 130,000 flowering plants.

Optional Row Along the River

If you are visiting during July or August, you will have the additional option of hiring a rowboat to float out along the calm waters of the moat and through the arches under the Château ballroom. The rate is €4 for half an hour, for a maximum of four people, to be paid in cash.

Lunch with a View

Eat lunch with a view at the self-service restaurant in the former *Royal Stables*, with seating indoors and on the terrace. Plan to eat either earlier or later than normal hours to avoid the rush at noon.

During lunch, share the highlights of your visit to the château. And place your votes. Which one, Diane or Catherine, do you think wins the battle of the gardens, balconies and bedrooms?

Taxi to Mini Châteaux or Home to Amboise

> *Mini-Châteaux Park*
>
> Open 10 am to 7 pm, May through August.
>
> Entrance fee: €14.

Meet your taxi driver at the appointed place and time, or call as you walk back along the grand promenade entrance to your meeting spot. Taxi from *Chenonceau* to the *Mini-Châteaux Park* on the outskirts of Amboise, and arrange for your taxi to return to pick you up in an hour or an hour and a half.

This is a modest park, but it will introduce you to the larger scope of the main châteaux of the Loire region than you would ever be able to visit during a single trip.

Pick Your Favorite Three Châteaux

Walk among the 1:25-scale models of 45 of the grandest châteaux of the Loire Valley, placed along a miniature *Loire River*, surrounded by mini trees and crossed by a miniature TGV. As you wander, spot the four châteaux you will be visiting: *Amboise. Chenonceau. Blois. Chambord.*

Then compare these four to the other 41, taking in both châteaux and gardens. If you had been one of the château-hopping Renaissance royals, with all of these palaces to choose among, which ones would you have put at the top of your list? Select your top *three* picks. Then think through which 1000+ people you would have invited to join you.

Taxi Back to Amboise & Dinner at Your Favorite Restaurant

As your taxi drives you back into Amboise, you will feel as though you are coming "home." Since you will be eating at one of your favorite restaurants tonight, you will feel like a "regular" there too.

During your free time before dinner, stop in a gift shop to buy postcards of your three favorite châteaux, or a calendar showing 12 of them. Purchase breakfast items to eat on the train tomorrow on your ride to Blois.

Then enjoy your dinner and your evening in Amboise. If there is a special event at Amboise Castle, tonight may be a good night to attend. You now have made Amboise your own.

Day 4 (Tuesday): Châteaux & Magic

> **Before You Set Off for the Day:** Reserve a table on the terrace for lunch at 12:30 pm at *le Grand St. Michel,* at the foot of Chambord Castle (Phone: 2-54-20-31-31). If you plan to eat dinner out tonight, reserve a table now, perhaps at *Chez Bruno, l'Epicerie,* or *Lion d'Or.*

Today you will travel by train to Blois, where you will venture out from town to visit *Chambord,* the largest châteaux you could possibly imagine, with 440 rooms and 365 fireplaces, one for every day of the year. Then you will visit the *House of Magic,* honoring Jean-Eugene Robert-Houdin, for whom escape artist Harry Houdini named himself. Finally you will tour *Blois Châteaux,* scene of multiple poisonings and stabbings.

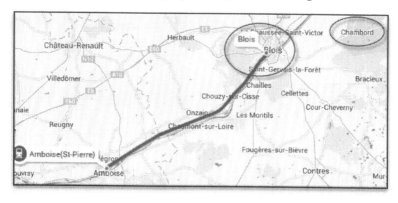

Train to Blois & Arrival

Plan to be at the Amboise train station early, allowing plenty of time to catch the train at 8:07 am. You will arrive in Blois at 8:25, in plenty of time to catch the bus to Chambord.

The path you will be following today, back and forth between Amboise and Blois, is one that was well-worn by Charles and Anne, Louis and Jeanne, François and Claude, and Henri and Catherine… the royal cast of characters of the 15ᵗʰ and 16ᵗʰ century you are coming to know. But you will be traveling much faster, and in greater comfort… And without all that furniture.

Catch the Line 18 TLC Navette Bus to Chambord

As you exit the train station, look to your left to spot where you will catch the *TLC Navette-Châteaux Excursion Bus (Line 18)* to Chambord at *9:10 am*. You may have time for a quick coffee at the *Buffet de la Gare* before you catch your bus. But plan to get to the bus stop early since missing this bus will mean waiting two hours for the next one.

Purchase €6 transport tickets from the bus driver for a full day of travel around the area. While you are on the bus, also buy discounted entry passes for *Chambord*, *Blois Castle* and *House of Magic*—€8 for *Chambord* (regular price: €11), and €8 for a combined pass to *Blois Castle* and *House of Magic* (regular price: €15). This will save you each €10 to add to your lunch budget.

The 9:10 bus will deposit you at *Chambord* at around 10:05 am. Remember to ask your driver for a copy of the bus schedule for your return trip. Or, at the very least, confirm the *2:22 pm* Line 18 pickup time, arriving at Blois Castle at around 3:30 pm. As an initial plan, aim to catch the *2:22 pm* bus back to Blois (for no additional charge). If the bus schedule does not work for you, or you want to save time, call Taxi Radio Blois or KLP Taxi for the return trip (11 miles; around 30€ one way).

> **Taxi Radio Blois**: (0)2-54-78-07-65.
>
> *(http://taxisradioblois.monsite-orange.fr/)*
>
> **KLP Taxi**: Phone: (0)2-54-42-80-84 or (0)6-83-32-23-15
>
> *(http://www.klp-taxi.fr/en/home)*

A Little History of Chambord Castle

Prepare to be impressed! As you catch your first glimpse of *Chambord*, you will be awed and amazed, just as François I would have wanted you to be.

But right after you say "Wow!" your next remark probably will be "Why???"

Everything about this château, the largest in the Loire Valley, is designed to impress. It is definitely "over the top." Why would anyone need or want a château with 440 rooms, 365 fireplaces, 800 sculpted columns, and 84 staircases, plus stables to accommodate 1,200 horses? The surrounding hunting grounds cover 13,440 acres—roughly the size of the city of Paris—bordered by a wall to contain the wild game and make stalking it easier for the hunters.

François I began construction of this opulent "hunting lodge" in 1519, when he was only 25 years old, and in the fourth year of his reign. Wildly extravagant, and eager to proclaim to the world that he was not only *equal to* but *superior to* all other contemporary kings, François built Chambord to demonstrate the extent of his wealth and power, while also featuring his two favorite pastimes—hunting and architecture. Much more just than a castle, *Chambord* was the proof positive of a very young king who was determined to establish himself, and his country, as a world power.

One guest to *Chambord* was a man whom François particularly wanted to impress—his sworn enemy and arch rival, Charles V, Holy Roman Empire and king of Spain, whose empire spanned nearly four million square kilometers across Europe, the Far East and the Americas. François had fallen prisoner to Charles at the Battle of Pavia in 1525, and was held captive in the tower of the Alcazar in Madrid. All work on Chambord came to an abrupt halt.

After two years, François traded his own freedom in exchange for turning over his two sons, François II and Henri II, ages seven and eight, to be held hostage in his place. Some four years after François turned over his sons to the Spanish king, he was able to arrange for their release by agreeing to: 1) abandon his allies, 2) hand over Italy, and 3) pay 2,000,000 gold crowns.

When François returned to France after his imprisonment in Madrid, work resumed on *Chambord*. Over a decade later, in December 1539, François hosted Charles at *Chambord* in order to show off his glorious château, and to establish his stature and power as king of France. Despite the jaw-dropping expense to build it, François ended up spending only a few weeks total at Chambord. Between visits, his magnificent château was left empty of furniture and people.

Tackle Chambord Château

You will have about two hours to visit *Chambord* between when your bus drops you off and your 12:30 pm reservations for lunch at *Restaurant Grand Saint-Michel*. And that will be all the time you will want or need. Visit the best parts first, before you run out of steam. And give yourself permission to stop when you have had enough.

François' design for *Chambord* was a careful balance of Medieval French and Italian Renaissance architecture. The château is built in the shape of a huge cross, like a cathedral, with a distinctive double helix staircase filling the central area. The two stairways of the double helix are wound, one on top of the other, allowing two people to ascend in sight of one another but without ever crossing paths. The marvelous ingenuity of this staircase resembles sketches made by Leonardo da Vinci, and so the design has been attributed to him, although he died a few months before construction of Chambord began.

Look around the reception rooms on the ground floor. Then take different paths on the double helix stairs to the first floor, waving at each other when you pass by.

Royal Lodgings

Start your tour of royal lodgings by visiting the lavish apartment of François I, including his bed chamber, wardrobe and study, and oratory with vaulted ceiling. Continue counter-clockwise through the chambers of Louis XIV and his wife, Maria Teresa, who used the château for hunting. Decide which of these two suites would be your pick if you lived here?

Visit the 2-story chapel. Watch for portraits of François I, nicknamed "Le Roi Grand Nez"—"King Big Nose".

Rooftop Terrace

Take the time to visit the rooftop terrace for an up close look at the château's spires and pinnacles, intermingled lanterns and windows, as well as its 800 columns and 365 chimneys.

From here you also will have awesome views out over the vast hunting grounds.

Museum of the Count of Chambord

When you return to the royal apartment floor, walk through the fascinating *Museum of the Count of Chambord*, with displays about the "king for a week"—Henri of Artois, Count of Chambord.

Henri's father was assassinated before his birth. Henri owned Chambord at the behest of the French Restoration government, but lived in exile from age 10 (1830) and throughout his youth and young adulthood. In 1871, during a Royalist effort to restore the monarchy of France, Henri became King Henri V for seven days. In his eagerness to be crowned king, Henri had even designed his coronation robes, and souvenirs to hand out during the event.

But then Henri made a critical error, declaring that once he became king, he planned to retire the well-loved tricolor flag adopted during the revolution, and reestablish the white fleur-de-lys flag of Henri IV, "as a matter of personal honor." This intention so outraged the populace, that the plan to restore the monarchy was postponed until after Henri's death.

By the time Henri died in 1883, public opinion had shifted, and restoring the monarchy was never attempted again. So France remained a republic, retained its cherished tricolor flag, and has continued as a republic ever since.

The Royal Stables

If you have time remaining before lunch, visit the stables to see the opulent carriages, including one of the last royal carriages made in France. Some of these carriages have never been used.

Lunch with a View at Hotel Restaurant Grand Saint-Michel

You will have already made reservations for a 12:30 pm lunch at *Grand Saint Michel*, at a table on the terrace overlooking the château .

> *Restaurant Grand Saint-Michel.*
>
> Place Saint Louis. (0)2-54-20-31-31

Consider treating yourself by ordering "Le Menu" (appetizer, entrée and dessert for €22.50). Then feast like royalty while gazing back at "your" little castle. To get into the full spirit, plan your next hunting party and which 365 of your closest family and friends you will invite.

Taxi or Bus Back to Blois

TIME TARGET: Aim to catch the 2:22 pm bus back to Blois Castle (check the schedule to confirm the time).

Or call a taxi to save time by following a more direct route and have more time at the *House of Magic.*

> **Taxi Radio Blois**: (0)2-54-78-07-65
>
> **KLP Taxi**: (0)2-54-42-80-84 or (0)6-83-32-23-15

During your ride, imagine yourself "commuting" between your hunting palace, Chambord, and your residential palace, Blois, on a regular basis, accompanied by 3,000 people and 1,000 horses, plus furniture, art, tapestries, dining service and linens to outfit your entire castle.

Amuse and Amaze Yourself in the House of Magic

House of Magic

1 place du Château. (0)2-54-55-26-26

Hours: 10:00 am to 12:30 pm and 2:00 pm to 6:30 pm

You will have already purchased combined tickets for *Blois Château* and the *House of Magic* on the bus to *Chambord*, so you will be able to skip the ticket line. Plan to leave the *House of Magic* by around 4:45 pm. This will give you a little over an hour at Blois château before it closes at 6 pm.

The *House of Magic (Maison de la Magie)* is dedicated to the all-time great magician and Blois native, Jean-Eugene Robert-Houdin, originally a clock-maker by trade. Robert-Houdin (whose last name was a hyphenated combination of his own last name, Robert, and his wife's last name, Houdin) was much admired by the escapist, Houdini, who adopted a variation of his idol's name.

Before Robert-Houdin, magic had a dubious reputation. The *Inquisition* repressed the practice of magic, considering its practitioners to be charla-tans and quacks. Robert-Houdin changed all that. In 1845, he created his own theater in Paris and devised "Soirées Fantastiques" where he, fol-lowed by his successors, delighted and astonished generations of Parisians for the next 75 years. He later took his show to England, and was equally popular there as "the French conjurer."

As you approach the house, pause to look up at the windows, where the 6-headed dragon, "guardian of the magic temple," appears every hour, on the hour. When the mechanical clock is set in motion, the windows slide open, and the dragon's six golden heads emerge, jaws snapping. Two clawed hands crush the balcony railing, and a serpentine tail waves from the attic window.

The *Maison de la Magie* museum offers five floors of interactive exhibits featuring Robert-Houdin's fascinating life and inventions—clocks, robots, optical games, and grand illusions. Take time to walk through the *hallucino-scope*, designed by Gérard Majax, where special glasses create the illusion that you are crossing a disintegrating bridge, hopping between stepping stones, and wandering through a vividly-colored maze. Other exhibits show the history of magic, and the life and work of Robert-Houdin.

Attend a magic show in the *Magician's Theatre*, if possible, to experience grand illusions and magic tricks. Also, check out the gift shop to take some magic home with you.

Traverse the Architectural Timeline of Blois Castle

 TIME TARGET: Aim to enter Blois Castle before 5:00 pm to allow yourself at least an hour for your visit before it closes a6 6:00 pm.

Blois Castle

http://www.chateaudeblois.fr/

Open from 9 am to 6 pm (7 pm in July and August)

A Little History of Blois Castle

Blois Castle is another of François I's major renovation projects, in this case at the request of his wife, Queen Claude. But the history of the castle goes back to the 10th century and *Thibault the Cheat*, first Count of Blois. Thibault was a descendent of one of the 350 counts that Charlemagne appointed in the 9th century to administer the 350 counties of his empire. Perched on its promontory overlooking the Loire, the castle held an excellent defensive position.

Blois Castle was home to seven French kings and ten queens, and a place where Joan of Arc stayed. It has 75 staircases and 564 rooms (100 are bedrooms), each with a fireplace.

There are four distinct sections of the castle, spanning from the 13th to the 17th centuries, that include:

- *Medieval* (13th century),

119

- *Flamboyant Gothic.* Look for Louis XII's porcupine insignia,

- *Early Renaissance.* Look for François I's salamander insignia, and

- *Classical* (17th century).

Stand in the Courtyard to Orient Yourself!

You will already have your ticket, so you can skip the line. But do pick up the English audio guide (€4 adult, €3 child), with a 1-hour dramatized tour that features guides who assume roles of people who lived in the castle—knight, architect, master of ceremonies, servant—each with stories to tell and secrets to reveal.

The castle is square, with a large central courtyard at the entrance. From the courtyard you will be able to spot the variety of architectural styles that transformed the ancient fortress into a stunning castle. Take some time to stand in the courtyard and get oriented. As you study the architecture, you will have a visual introduction to the timeline of the castle's royal occupants.

First, locate the modest section of the castle, built of native red and blue brick, and decorated with *Louis XII's* porcupine insignia. *Louis XII* built this section, replacing the walls, ramparts and keeps of the former fortress with a modest manor house. The simplicity of this section demonstrates the carefulness of *Louis'* expenditures. Unlike the kings who followed him, Louis actually reduced taxes during his reign.

Next locate the wing that *François* built, easily recognized by its elegant and extravagant Italian Renaissance style, with carved stone, an open circular stairway, and salamander insignias.

Grandeur of this magnitude is what you likely have come to expect from this free-spending king. *François* also created here one of the period's most important libraries. *François'* library was moved to *Château de Fontainebleau* after his wife's death, and is now the core of the *Bibliothèque Nationale de France.*

The Medieval part of Blois Castle dates back to the 13th century, and houses the famous *Hall of the General States,* used by the Counts of Blois as a courtroom. The classical wing was added during the 17th century, integrating three orders of arches and an eclectic mix of Doric, Ionic and Corinthian style columns. So what appears to be the oldest section of the castle is actually the most recent.

Find the "Scenes of the Crimes"

Blois castle is noted not only for its architecture, but for stories of murder and intrigue, particularly during the Medici days. Your audio guides will recount juicy stories of the wedding-cake staircase, where on December 23, 1588, the "Day of the Daggers," *Henri III* (son of *Henri II* and *Catherine de Medici*) summoned the *Duke of Guise* (Scarface) to his bed chambers, then had him ambushed and hacked to death. The next day, the Duke's brother, the *Cardinal of Lorraine,* was murdered in prison.

The popular Guise brothers, members of the powerful *House of Guise* family, were leaders of the radical *Catholic League*, proponents of aristocratic over royal power, and responsible for the massive execution of Huguenots at Amboise. The brothers' deaths were avenged a year later when a monk assassinated King Henri himself, using the pretense of whispering a secret message in his ear to get close enough to plunge a knife into his abdomen.

Paintings that depict the murders of the Guise brothers hang from the walls of the castle, along with a painting of their mother, *Madame de Guise*, who lost two sons in two days. Henri III's mother and manipulator, Catherine de' Medici, died at Blois Castle in 1589, a few days after the Guise brothers were murdered. Her "Queen's Cabinet," dating from 1530, is noted for its 180 sculpted oak panels, with four secret cabinets to conceal jewels... or poison.

In the 17th century, *Louis XIII* banished his own interfering Medici mother, *Marie de' Medici*, here to *Blois Castle*. But the plump matron escaped using a coat to slide down a mound of dirt, left by the builders, into the moat.

Take the Train Back to Amboise

 TIME TARGET: Aim for the 6:44 pm train back to Amboise.

Your train back to Amboise leaves at 6:44 pm, arriving at 7:08 pm.

Depending on when you leave Blois Château, you may have some time to wander the cafés and shops below the Château in *Place Louis XII,* looking for treasures, or picking up a snack for your train ride home. There is a comfortable café in the train station should you end up with waiting time before your train. Just find a seat, order a glass of wine or a beer, and write postcards or post pictures to Facebook while you wait.

If you miss your 6:44 pm train, or if you decide to pause awhile in Blois before heading home, there is a later train at 7:03 pm (arriving Amboise at 7:18 pm). The last train back to Amboise leaves at 10:19 pm.

Eat Dinner Outdoors or Picnic While Watching the Sunset

This will be your final evening in Amboise. Spend it as you like. If you've made reservations for dinner at *Chez Bruno, l'Epicerie* or *Le Lion d'Or,* then bon appétit. As an alternative, picnic while watching the sunset from your room or in a park beside the river.

During dinner, have some fun playing "International Châteaux Hunters." Which of the five châteaux you have visited would you most want to live in: *Amboise Castle, Clos Lucé, Chenonceau Castle, Chambord Castle* or *Blois Castle?* In your château of choice, where would you be most likely to hang out? What bedroom would you sleep in?

As night falls, drink a final toast to your time here in the *Valley of the Kings.* Tomorrow will be a long travel day, and it will begin early, as you head for Mont Saint-Michel. But what lies ahead at the end of your journey will be one of the most remarkable places you will ever experience in your life.

CHAPTER 6:
To the Incomparable Mont St Michel

Moving from Renaissance castles to medieval abbeys, you will now traverse Brittany, from the Loire Valley to the Atlantic Coast of France, at the border of Brittany and Normandy, to visit the phenomenal *Mont Saint-Michel.*

Because the Mont is so entirely unique, it is heavily visited during the day. And so you will actually be staying for two nights in a hotel on the Mont itself-- an experience that will be unforgettable. After the crowds of visitors have left the Mont, you will dine at a terrace restaurant, looking out over the bay as the tide moves 8 miles in, then 8 miles out, at the "speed of a galloping horse"—12 miles per hour—360 yards per minute—18 feet per second.

The narrow, ancient streets will be beautiful and serene once they empty of crowds each evening and you have the place to yourself. And you will experience many lovely views out across the water.

Staying on the Mont will have its challenges, as would be expected, given its geography and surroundings—a craggy rock, topped by an Abby, and surrounded by water when the tide comes in. Remember that the word "Mont" means "mountain"!

You will spend your first night near the train station in Pontorson, a small town close to the Mont. This will put you within a short bus ride to the Mont tomorrow for your two-night stay in the medieval city itself, a once-in-a-lifetime experience.

Day 5 (Wednesday): Overnight Stop in Pontorson

Before You Set Off for the Day: Call your next hotel: *Hotel Ariane* in Pontorson (1-866-599-6674) to confirm your arrival. Ask that they make dinner reservations for you for 7:00 pm at the *Relais Hotel,* with a table overlooking Mont Saint-Michel (0)2-33-60-14-25.

Today you will travel by train from *Amboise* to *Tours* to *Caen* to *Pontorson...* a distance of around 125 miles, but a train journey of over 7½ hours. *Pontorson* is the small town closest to your next destination, the entirely unique and breathtaking *Mont Saint-Michel.*

TIME TARGET (confirm these times):

8:38 am train from Amboise to Tours, arriving at 8:50 am.

9:22 am train from Tours to Caen, arriving at 12:13 pm.

2:13 pm train from Caen to Pontorson, arriving at 4:13 pm.

There are very few train options for the final leg of your journey today. So plan to take the earliest train available. Leave Amboise on the *8:38 am* train at the latest. This will allow you 32 minutes to find your next train in the vast *Tours* train station, and also to pick up a breakfast sandwich or snack for the 4-hour train ride from *Tours* to *Caen*, departing *Tours* at *9:22 am* and arriving in Caen at *12:13 pm.*

Eat lunch at a Brasserie on *Place de la Gare*, across the square from the Caen train station. Three options with outdoor tables are: *La Consigne*, *L'Escapade* and *La Gitane.* Or stop in the Fast Market for sandwiches, drinks and fruit to eat on the train.

Then catch the 2:13 pm train to Pontorson, arriving at 4:13 pm. Check the timetables to confirm the schedule has not changed for the day you are traveling.

Stay Overnight at Hotel Ariane in Pontorson

Hotel Ariane

50 Boulevard Clémenceau

1-866-599-6674

You will be spending the night at the *Hotel Ariane*, a charming hotel in a quiet neighborhood, within a two-minute walk of tiny Pontorson train station. Turn left as you leave the station, and walk to the intersection. Look across the intersection toward Boulevard Clemenceau, where you will see the stone building and gardens of your hotel straight ahead on your left.

Hotel Ariane has an outdoor terrace, free Wi-Fi access and a year-round indoor pool. Some rooms have small balconies. A full buffet breakfast is provided every morning.

Use your stay at *Hotel Ariane* as an opportunity to do any necessary web checking and to make your phone calls home. Phone reception and Internet access on the Mont can be quirky at best.

Another option for staying near, but not too near, the train station in Pontorson is *Hotel le XIV* (14 rue du Docteur Tizon).

Drinks & Dinner on the Terrace, Overlooking the Mont

Relais Hotel Restaurant

Address: Route du Mont Saint-Michel

Phone: (0)2-33-60-14-25. *reservation@le-relais-du-roy.com*

Plan to check in quickly and set off for Mont-Saint-Michel for a drink on the terrace of the *Relais*, enjoying the music and the stunning views as evening falls over the Mont. You will have already made reservations to stay for dinner.

For the 15-minute ride to the *Relais*, you will have two options—the bus or a taxi. The bus is more economical, costing around €6 for two, each way. A taxi costs upwards of €26 each way (€32 after 7:00 pm). To update these taxi fares, use the estimation tool at *http://www.taxiproxi.fr*.

TIME TARGET (confirm these times):

5:20 or 6:00 pm bus to the Relais (across from the Mont).

Check times for the return bus from the Mont to Pontorson, or take a taxi.

To catch the bus to the Mont, walk back to the bus stop in front of the train station. Get off the bus at the *Route du Mont* stop. To confirm current bus schedules, visit the official welcome site for the Mont: *http://www.bienvenueaumontsaintmichel.com*.

Plan your return to Pontorson while you are on the bus heading toward the Mont. Make note of when the last bus back to Pontorson leaves from the *Route du Mont* stop. If you miss the final bus back to Pontorson, plan to ask the *Relais Hotel* desk staff to call you a taxi. And remember to confirm the cost before you get in. Evening taxi fares from the Mont to Pontorson will be higher, averaging around €32 after 7:00 pm.

The bus will take you through the *Visitors' Entrance Gate*, stopping in *La Caserne*, the hotel and shopping hamlet on the mainland, immediately across from Mont-Saint-Michel. The bus then crosses the causeway to the entrance gates of the Mont. This evening, get off the bus at the *Route du Mont* stop in *La Caserne*. Tomorrow, you will ride the bus all the way to the Mont.

Take note when you pass through the *Visitors" Entrance Gate*. Entry through this gate is limited to visitors who are staying at a hotel in La Caserne or on the Mont. If you miss the last bus to Pontorson later this evening, and call a taxi to take you home, you will need to meet your taxi driver outside this gate.

The *Relais Hotel* will be on your right, near the dam and immediately facing the Mont. Look at the shops as you walk past, and possibly stop in a few, if they are open, to pick up supplies to take with you to the Mont tomorrow.

For more time flexibility, take a taxi both to and from the Mont, arranging a time and a meeting spot to reconnect with your driver outside the *Visitors' Entrance Gate*. If you need help making your taxi arrangements, ask the staff at the *Hotel Ariane* desk.

Taxi from Pontorson

Phone: 02 33 60 33 23 or 02 33 60 82 70

Dinner at the *Relais* will be an unforgettable experience. Request a window table or a table on the terrace overlooking the Mont. As evening falls, and the lights on the Mont come on, soak in the ethereal vision of the dramatically-lit Mont rising from sea. The 3-course "Pilgrim's Menu" at the Relais starts at €19.50. The 4-course menus range from €28.50 for the "Relais Menu" to €39.00 for the "Discovery Menu."

This may seem like a lot of trouble and expense to go to at the end of a long travel day. But seeing the Mont lit up at night is an experience of a lifetime. Your efforts will be well rewarded.

If, instead, you opt to eat dinner in Pontorson, after having drinks at *Le Relais*, take an earlier bus back to the train station and dine at one of the many restaurants within a short walk of your hotel. Some options include:

- *La Squadra.* 102 rue Couesnon. (0)2-33-68-31-17. Outstanding pizzas. Good prices. Friendly staff. Plenty to share if you order one pizza and one salad.

- *Le Grillon.* 37 rue Couesnon. (0)2-33-60-17-80. Superb value Menu (three courses for under €17), with delicious options. Very popular, so book early.

- *La Casa de Quentin.* 102 rue Saint-Michel. (0)2-33-48-61-95. Excellent *Cassoulet Fruits De Mer* ("fruits of the sea") and varied dishes of mussels, including bacon & cream mussels.

- *Au Jardin Saint-Michel.* 37 rue de la Libération. (0)2-33-60-11-35. Set Menus start at 17€, with specialties such as baked scallops, grilled steak with camembert sauce, pasta and pizzas, followed by rice pudding, chocolate fondant or berries crumble.

Important Note about Tomorrow...

Be prepared for tomorrow's task of hefting your luggage on and off the bus, then through the gates of the Mont, and up the steep cobblestone streets and stone stairways to reach your hotel. Once inside your hotel, you likely will be carrying your bags up more steep stairways to get to your room.

The Mont is a magical place. And the experience that lies ahead of you will definitely make your efforts well worth it. But managing your luggage here is decidedly a challenge. Since you will know in advance what to expect, you will be well prepared to manage your load gracefully, deposit it as quickly as possible, then walk out your door to take in this most remarkable of places.

Where Will You Be Staying for the Next Two Nights?

There are only around 150 hotel rooms total on the entire Mont, and they book up quickly. You will need to make your reservations very, very early, preferably as soon as you know the dates for your trip. If your travel schedule is somewhat flexible, it may even work best to find dates when you are able to book lodgings on the Mont, then plan the rest of your trip around these dates.

Enter your dates in booking.com, and use the aerial view to zoom in to see what options are available on the Mont itself. If you find there are few options on this site, consider calling each hotel in turn, or visiting their individual websites, to find what may be available.

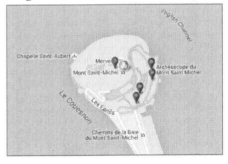

Given how quickly rooms fill up on the Mont, and depending on how far in advance you book, you may or may not be able to reserve a room within its walls. If nothing is available on the Mont, check the locations along the water's edge, across from the Mont. Then, if necessary, continue working your way back through the village until you find a vacancy.

As a first choice, stay within the walls. As a second choice, book a room with a view of the Mont. If all these rooms are taken, work your way back through the village. And if the entire village is already full, just remain in Pontorson at the *Hotel Ariane* and use the bus from the train station to go back and forth to the Mont.

Some "Full Experience" Places to Stay on the Mont

One good choice is *Le Mouton Blanc* (19 rooms). In its historic 14th century location below the abbey, *Le Mouton Blanc* offers rooms with views of the bay, the Abbey, or the *Grande Rue*. Rooms in the main building are more comfortable, if you have a choice.

Le Mouton Blanc
Phone: (0)2-33-60-14-08. *www.lemoutonblanc.fr*

Alternative places to stay on the Mont, starting near the gate and moving up, include:

- *Mere Poulard* (27 rooms). *Grande Rue.* (0)2-33-89-68-68. With rooms that overlook the Bay, Abbey, or medieval city. Piano bar with views of the Bay. Home of the famous fire-cooked omelets. *http://en.merepoulard.com/*.

- *Terrasses Poulard* (29 rooms). *Grande Rue.* (0)2-33-89-02-02. In a historical building overlooking the sea, with a garden for guests, and a restaurant with panoramic views over the bay. *http://en.terrasses-poulard.fr/*

- *Auberge Saint-Pierre* (23 rooms). *Grande Rue.* (0)2-33-60-14-03. In a 15th-century wood-framed house. Some rooms have exposed beams, leaded-glass windows and sea views. *http://www.auberge-saint-pierre.fr/uk/index.php*.

- *La Croix Blanche* (31 rooms). *Grande Rue.* (0)2-33-60-14-04. With bay-view rooms, a terrace, and a bar. Half-board packages include breakfast and dinner (excluding drinks). *http://www.hotel-la-croix-blanche.com/uk/index.php.*

- *Logis St. Sebastion* (3 rooms). *Grande Rue.* (0)2-33-60-14-08. In a picturesque 14th century home, with simple rooms, charm and character. *http://en.logis-saint-sebastien.com.*

- *Hotel Du Guesclin* (10 rooms). *Grande Rue.* (0)2-33-60-14-10. Rooms face the Bay or village. *http://www.hotelduguesclin.com.*

- *La Vieille Auberge* (11 rooms). *Grande Rue.* (0)2-33-60-14-34. With a restaurant, bar, and terrace overlooking the Bay. *www.lavieilleauberge-montsaintmichel.com.*

- *Hotel Le Saint-Michel* (6 rooms). (0)2-33-60-02-16. A small family hotel at the foot of the parish church, with rooms that overlook the island of Tomberlaine or the ramparts. Half-board option includes breakfast and dinner (excluding drinks) at *Les Terrasses Poulard. www.hotel-saintmichel.com.*

Day 6 (Thursday): Mount the Mont

Enjoy breakfast at your hotel, then strike out for the Mont to get there ahead of the crowds. Wear comfortable shoes, and carry an umbrella and a daypack for hands-free convenience while climbing stairs, walking the ramparts, and navigating cobblestone streets. Plan to drop off your luggage first.

Take the Bus from the Pontorson Station to the Mont

 TIME TARGET (confirm these times):

8:20 am or 9:35 am bus to the Mont.

Catch the earliest direct bus you can manage, leaving from the train station. Your goal is to arrive at the Mont before 10 am, so you will be slightly ahead of the crowds. From 11 am until 4 pm, the Mont is packed with throngs of modern-day pilgrims and tourists, nearly 3½ million per year.

As you approach the tiered wedding cake of the Mont, look up at it. Once you are *on* the Mont, you will have other views. But this will be your best chance to see it as a whole and get your bearings.

The lower tier of the Mont is made up of medieval fortifications. The top tier is a fortified Benedictine Abbey that has been a popular destination for pilgrims for over 1200 years, topped by a statue of Saint Michael, weigher of souls. Between the fortifications below and the soaring abbey on top, is a compact and steeply-sloped medieval town, with a single main street, *Grande Rue*.

As you cross the causeway, observe the current state of the tides. The influx and outgo of tides is a remarkable feature of the Mont, with changes in water depth of as much as 49 feet from low to high tide. The Mont goes from land to island and back again daily.

This tidal island, only 656 yards from land, has always been accessible at low tide, and thus could be reached by pilgrims. Yet it could be defended from assailants, who were drowned or stranded by the rapidly incoming tides, or sucked down into the surrounding pools of quicksand. By capitalizing on these natural defenses, the Mont remained unconquered during the Hundred Years' War, with only a small garrison needed to successfully defend it against British attacks.

The tides are caused by the action of heavenly bodies, principally the sun and moon. When sun and moon are in line with the earth, the attraction is multiplied, causing the highest tides—spring tides. And when sun and moon form a right angle, the attraction is reduced, causing a period with lowest tidal movement—neap tides. Since the recent building of the dam to protect the bay, there are times when the water does not reach the Mont, and the differences in low and high tides are not as dramatic.

As you cross the Causeway, you may see people walking across the sand, or even riding on horseback. Be aware that although these can be interesting activities, they should only be undertaken in the company of a professional and very experienced guide.

It is possible to journey across the sand at low tide, but many have perished over the course of the centuries through miscalculations while making these crossings. Never assume that because the water is only ankle-deep when you start out, you will have plenty of time to make the crossing. Treat the sea with great respect.

Other hazards of these innocuous-looking sand flats are pockets of quicksand. Tomorrow, when you visit the *Museum of History*, you will see a Capellani sculpture (1909) that dramatically depicts a man as he is being overcome by quicksand.

Enter Through the Gates

As you enter through the formidable gates to Mont Saint-Michel, imagine yourself as a pilgrim arriving here 1200 years ago, passing through these same three gates… *Porte de l'Avancée, Porte du Boulevard,* and *Porte du Roi.* Pause to look up and around, and snap some photos.

Stop to Pick Up Schedules & Maps

As you enter through the first gate, stop by the *Tourist Information Center* (TI) in the small Burgher's Guardroom to the left and up a few steps to pick up a larger map, as well as other information you will need, including: 1) bus schedule, 2) English tour times for the Abbey, and 3) tides table (*Horaires des Marées*).

If the *Tourist Information Center* (TI) is crowded, come back later today or early tomorrow. The TI is open from 9 am to 6 pm March through June and September through October (9 am to 7 pm in July and August). It closes daily for lunch from 12:30 pm to 2 pm.

Take a moment to study the map and orient yourself. Start by finding the gates where you are standing. Then study two main ways to get to the top of the Mont from here. The primary route is along *Grande Rue* ("Grand Street") to the *Grande Degré* ("Grand Staircase"). A longer route is by way of the medieval ramparts that once protected the Mont. As you walk the ramparts, you will pass seven towers: *Tour du Roi, Tour de l'Arcade, Tour de la Liberté, Tour Basse, Tour Cholet, Tour Boucle* and *Tour du Nord*. You will be making use of both of these routes during your stay here.

Locate the smaller church, Saint-Pierre, with its lovely open area in front, a perfect spot to pause for a break. And find the Archéoscope Museum, the first of the museums you will be visiting tomorrow. You now know enough to make your way.

Walk the Grande Rue

Follow the *Grande Rue*, curving counterclockwise steeply up and up, paralleling the outer edge of the Mont. Although "grande" implies large, this street is, in fact, very narrow. Because it is the main access to the Abbey, and also lined with restaurants and shops where people pause, it becomes very congested during the peak hours for visitors.

Grande Rue was similarly crowded 1200 years ago during the Middle Ages, when Mont Saint-Michel was one of Europe's major pilgrimage destinations. Then, as now, visitors walked up this steep winding street through the village on their way to the Abbey, passing eateries and shops like those you see today, and pausing for refreshments and souvenirs of their journey.

The Abbey became a renowned center of learning, attracting some of the greatest minds in Europe. There was no causeway then, so crossing the sand flats to reach the Mont was treacherous. It is said that the journey to the Mont was considered to be so dangerous, pilgrims were advised to make out their wills before they set out since they were unlikely to return.

As you walk along *Grand Rue*, watch for the stairs to your right. You will use these tomorrow, or later this evening, to reach the ramparts. The *Grande Rue* eventually arrives at the *Grande Degré* ("Grand Staircase"), leading to the Abbey.

Locate Your Hotel and Drop Off Your Bags

Most hotels on the Mont are accessible from the *Grand Rue*. Have the location of your hotel firmly in mind before you enter the maze. And keep a watch out for *small* signs. Otherwise you may walk right by your hotel and climb higher than necessary, then need to double back. And that would be regrettable!

Begin to orient yourself as you walk up and past the restaurants and shops. You will be returning here later.

Arrive, Unload, Catch Your Breath & Set Off to Explore

Check in and leave your bags, then set off to explore. Your quest while you are here on the Mont is to *"Go where the crowds are not."* You should be slightly ahead of the deluge at this point, so head immediately up to the Abbey to get there ahead of the throngs. As a temporary "resident" of the Mont, you will have the luxury of coming back later to any areas that are clogged with tourists.

Pause to Book a Window Seat for Dinner

Stop in briefly at *Les Terrasses Poulard Restaurant* along your way and make your dinner reservations for around 8 pm, after the crowds have left. This is an excellent restaurant, with a splendid view of the Bay. Request a window table, if possible, explaining that you wish to watch the tides. Or call (0)2-33-89-02-02.

As always, speak at least some French when you make your wants and needs known to the hectically busy wait staff. Say hello. Make you request clearly known. Say thank you and goodbye.

"Bonjour madame. Nous voulons une table à côté de la fenêtre a vingt heure (20:00 = 8 pm), s'il vous plait. Merci, madame. Au revoir"

Visit the Abbey First

Benedictine Abbey
Open: 9 am to 7 pm, May to August; last admission 6 pm. 9:30 am to 6 pm, September to April; last admission 5 pm.
Rates: €9 for 25 and over; €5.50 for 18-25 year-olds; no charge for under-18 year-olds visiting with their families.

If all goes according to plan, you will reach the eighth-century Norman Abbey before the mobs arrive. If this doesn't work out, plan to make your visit later in the day, when the crowds begin to dwindle after 4 pm. As you climb up the *Grande Degré*, be careful on the steep stairs. When you complete your visit, plan to walk back down by way of the ramparts or past Saint-Pierre and along the gardens, avoiding the *Grand Rue*.

Rent an individual or a couples headset (for €6) for the audio tour to learn the history of the Abbey, and the stories that surround it. If you are willing to relinquish your freedom to see the Abbey at your own speed, you may be able to catch a tour in English.

There is no entrance fee to attend daily Mass at the Abbey, celebrated by the resident order (*Fraternités Monastiques de Jérusalem*). Mass is celebrated weekdays at 7:00 am (8:00 am on Saturday and Sunday), and every day except Monday at 12:15 pm (11:30 am on Sunday). Vespers are held at 6:30 pm every day except Sunday. Arrive at the entrance of the Abbey 15 minutes ahead of the service to be escorted into the chapel by a Sister or Brother before the service begins.

Confirm these times on the Mont website when you know the exact dates of your visit at *http://www.ot-montsaintmichel.com/en/agenda/mont-saint-michel.htm*. Also, check for any concerts or other special events.

Spot these Highlights of the Abbey

As you follow the one-way route through the Abbey, passing through the looming Gothic rooms, look for these highlights:

- *The Abbey church*: Replaced in the 15th century after the original chancel (choir) collapsed.

- *The Cloisters*: A tranquil garden area high above the sea. Look down through the glass to the precipitous drop below.

- *The Saut Gautier Terrace*, with stunning views of the bay and reclaimed farm-land below. Named for the prisoner who jumped from here to his death.

- *The Wheel*: Once used to lift two-ton loads of stones and supplies up to the Abbey, powered by six workers walking the wheel like hamsters.

- *The refectory*, where the monks ate in austere silence.

Late Lunch Higher Up or Out By the Ramparts

Plan to eat a light lunch since you will be dining royally later this evening. Chose a restaurant located toward the top of the Mont, on a back street, or out along the ramparts, to avoid the crowds filling the restaurants lower down on *Grande Rue*. Watch your timing for lunch, since some restaurants close from 5 to 7 pm to give the staff a break between lunch and dinner.

One good option is *Le Tripot*—(0)2 33 68 24 07—a sandwich shop on your right as you walk down the *Grande Rue*, with continuous service, offering sandwiches as well as other dishes such as mussels and chips or lamb pré-salé (pre-salted lamb, from sheep that graze the salt flats surrounding the Mont).

Another option is *Creperie du Chapeau Rouge* ("Red Hat")—(0)2-33-60-14-29—part way up *Grande Rue*, serving a selection of *"galettes"*—buckwheat pancakes, with various fillings, including ham, cheese, smoked salmon, potatoes, mushrooms, "fruits de mer" ("fruits of the sea"). A very tasty choice here is the *Galette Terroir*, made with potatoes ("pomme de terre"),

137

camembert cheese, and bacon (lardon). There is a reasonably-priced "Menu" here as well. *Chapeau Rouge* is also open for breakfast, so consider returning here tomorrow morning.

A third choice is *Du Guesclin Brasserie*—(0)2-33-60-14-10—located between the *Grande Rue* and the ramparts. The Brasserie is open for lunch, and the panoramic restaurant for dinner (where you may want to return tomorrow). For a light lunch, consider ordering one of the huge and fluffy omelets, perhaps an *Omelette du Mont-Saint-Michel* (soufflé) or an *Omelette Jambon/Fromage* (ham and cheese), accompanied by frites and a salad. Or order one "Menu" (Lunch Menu: 14.90€) and one omelet, then share.

When eating on the Mont, adjust your expectations to the realities and challenges inherent in the location. Anticipate that restaurants on the Mont will be small, with very busy kitchens and wait staff. So relax, have a glass of wine, converse, and forgo being in a hurry. If you adapt to the surroundings, you will enjoy yourself tremendously.

Also, as you approach the restaurant of your choice, remember to use your French language and manners. Offer a greeting, say please and thank you, and speak French to the degree you are able. Request recommendations from your waiter to aid you in making your selections, and politely request the check when you are finished. Review these essential phrases to be prepared:

- Quelle est votre recommandation? What do you recommend?

- Du vin rouge (or "blanc" or "rosé"), s'il vous plait." Red wine (or white or Rosé), please.

- L'addition s'il vous plait. The check please.

- Merci monsieur/madame. Thank you sir/ma'am.

Free Time After the Crowds Leave to Explore Until Dinner

By now you should be able to check into your hotel room. Settle in, and take a break until after 4 pm, when the crowds begin to thin out. Then head back out to search through the shops for treasures or to walk the ramparts until dinner. The gauntlet of shops along *Grande Rue* date back 1000 years, when they sold mementos to the pilgrims visiting the Mont. They may, at first glance, seem to be just another set of shops selling tee-shirts and trinkets. But slow down and walk inside. There are treasures to be found in these shops, and fun to be had exploring them.

By now the tour groups will have thinned out, so you will have these tiny shops essentially to yourself. The shopkeepers will have time to spend with you now that they are free of the maddening hoards, clamoring to pay for postcards.

I found a wonderful shop on the Mont, with a lovely and helpful shopkeeper, and many treasures. I came away with a happy assortment of gifts and personal finds: tapestry bags, knight figurines, garden elves, an intriguing map showing the layout of Europe during Roman times, and a sword-in-a-sheath letter opener. The shop owner helped me herself, and offered me a discount unasked since I was making my multiple purchases. She asked which items were going to be gifts ("cadeaux"), and wrapped them up beautifully, and with enthusiasm…a memorable cultural connection.

Dine at Les Terrasses Poulard with a View of the Bay

As you dine at *Les Terrasses Poulard*, on Grande Rue near the *Boucle Tower*, glance out the window at the tides. Hopefully you will have a chance to watch the phenomenon of the tides racing in, flooding across the 8 miles of sand at the amazing rate of 12 miles—over 63,000 feet—per hour, until the Mont is surrounded by water. If the tides are going out, the water drains off, leaving the Mont surrounded by sand once again.

One story from history about these tides and sands… William the Conqueror, during a battle with Conan II (Duke of Brittany), almost lost some of his knights on horseback to the quicksand surrounding the Mont. Harold, Earl of Wessex—who later usurped the throne of England and became Harold II—rescued William's knights. This dramatic event is memorialized in the 70-meter-long 11th century *Bayeux Tapestry*, in a scene that shows a horse stumbling and throwing his rider into the quicksand. You will visit the *Bayeux Tapestry* in Bayeux, the next stop on your trip.

Walk Out to the Causeway to See the Mont Illuminated

After dark, the Mont is aglow and reflecting. Walk back out through the gates and part way across the causeway to look back at the Mont, spectacularly illuminated nightly from dusk to midnight.

Take along your cell phone if you wish to make calls. Phone reception is better from the causeway than on the Mont where you are surrounded by rocks.

Kick Back at the Piano Bar at Mere Poulard

Return to the warm and cozy piano bar at *Mere Poulard*, with stunning views out across the Bay.

Make this your evening spot, and plan to come here one or both evenings during your stay on the Mont to enjoy music as you watch the tides rise and fall on the marsh.

Day 7 (Friday): Experience Life on the Mont

Early in the Day: Make dinner reservations at *Restaurant du Gueslin*— (0)2-33-60-14-10—located between the *Grande Rue* and the ramparts.

This morning you will awaken in your deserted island fortress. The Mont faces southwest, so the morning light can be amazing. If you arise early, you will still have the place pretty much to yourself until the crowds begin to build up by around 11 am. By now you are very familiar with how to come and go around the Mont. And you fully understand the benefits of going where the crowds are not.

Start your day at *Creperie du Chapeau Rouge*—(0)2-33-60-14-29—part way up *Grande Rue*, opening at 8 am. Order from their main menu a *"Complète,"* with ham, egg and cheese, or a *"Super Complète,"* with ham, egg, cheese, tomatoes and mushrooms. Also available are the standard French breakfast of coffee, tea or hot chocolate, with bread and juice. Or, if you prefer, visit *Mere Poulard,* near the base of *Grande Rue,* for one of their famous, if pricey, omelets.

Following breakfast, take advantage of your chance for some pre-crowd shopping to gather supplies for the day, and possibly to track down more treasures. Then take a rampart walk along the outside edges of the Mont, surveying both land and sea, like the soldiers who defended the fortress from the British in the 1400s.

After lunch high on the Mont where the crowds thin out, or a picnic in a spot off the beaten track, you will visit four intriguing small museums. Then, as the masses depart for the day, and the Mont becomes yours once again, you will dine at another Bay-front restaurant, *Restaurant du Gueslin,* where you will have made reservations for a table with a view.

Pre-crowd Shopping for Picnic Sandwiches and Treasures

It may seem odd to be thinking about lunch already, after your breakfast of omelets or crêpes, but now is a good time to be planning out the rest of your meals for the day. Now is also a good time to visit several more gift and specialty shops, so as to avoid them later when the *Grande Rue* has been transformed into a flood of humanity.

Since you ate a restaurant lunch yesterday, today may be a good day for a picnic in one of the grassy areas, along the ramparts, or even back in your room. Gather supplies or sandwiches for your picnic while the coast is clear, and before the *Grande Rue* fills with people. One good option is the sandwich shop, *Le Tripot*—(0)2 33 68 24 07—on your left as you walk up the *Grande Rue.*

If you prefer to lunch at a restaurant, go back to one of yesterday's list of options, or consider other places you have spotted yourself. Some additional options (lower to higher) are:

- *La Croix Blanche* (near Liberty Tower), with fine window tables and bay views.
- *La Vielle Auberge* (near Boucle Tower), with window tables and bay views.
- *Les Terrasses Poulard* (near Boucle Tower), where you ate last night.

Again, select a restaurant that is either higher up, or off the beaten path, to avoid the crowds. Make your lunch choice now so that you can reserve a table, either by stopping by or calling.

Walk the Ramparts Up and Up, then Down and Down

Every time you walk the ramparts will be a new and different experience. Look out. Look back. Look up. Look down. Learn your seven towers as you walk counter-clockwise, from lower to higher. Imagine the face of a clock, with these towers spanning from 6 o'clock to 1 o'clock.

1. *Tour du Roi* (King's Tower)—6 o'clock.

2. *Tour de L'Arcade* (Arcade Tower)—between 6 and 5 o'clock.

3. *Tour do la Liberté* (Liberty Tower)—5 o'clock.

4. *Tour Basse* (Lower Tower)—4 o'clock.

5. *Tour Cholet* (Cholet Tower)—3 o'clock.

6. *Tour Boucle* (Boucle Tower)—between 3 and 2 o'clock.

7. *Tour du Nord* (North Tower)—1 o'clock.

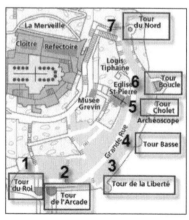

Explore Two of the Four Little Museums

There are four mini-museums on the Mont. Plan to visit two museums now, and the other two after lunch.

These are small, but earnest and informative, and well worth the modest price of €18 for the *4-Museum Pass* (€9 for ages 18-25. Under 18 free).

1. *Archeoscope Museum*

2. *Maritime & Ecology Museum*

3. *Museum of History*

4. *Logis Tiphaine* (Tiphaine's house)

Adjust your expectations, and visit these to learn more about the Mont, its history, the tides, and a remarkable couple who resided here on the Mont in the 14th century.

Archeoscope Museum

> *Archeoscope Museum*
>
> *Grand Rue*. Phone: (0)2-33-89-01-85

First, visit the Archeoscope Museum, to explore the myths and legends of the Mont through a sound and light show that takes you on a multimedia journey through time and history, with the Archangel Michael as your guide. Go back to the time when the Mont was under construction, then follow through its sacred and military history. The show is all in French, but you will be able to get the gist of what is happening.

Maritime & Ecology Museum

> *Maritime & Ecology Museum*
>
> *Grande Rue*. Phone: (0)2–33–60–85–12

This small museum explores the science of the phenomenon of the tides surrounding the Mont, and the dangers of this "beautiful and wild nature."

143

Here you will come to understand the siltation conditions that threatened to leave the Mont permanently land bound and bring an end to the unique phenomenon of its daily becoming an island surrounded by the sea. This threat led to the "Grand Project"—one of the "largest ecological projects in the world"—to reverse the extensive accumulations of sand and silt deposits, and preserve the Mont's remarkable relationship with the sea.

The museum also displays a magnificent collection of 250 model ships—ranging from ancient ships of war to vessels for trade, fishing and recreational activities—illustrating maritime modes of transport in and around the bay that surrounds Mont-Saint-Michel, from the Middle Ages through the present.

Lunch Away from the Crowds

Take a break for your lunch picnic in one of the lovely garden areas (shown in green on the maps of the village). Or lunch higher up where you made your reservations earlier. Watch the people walking by from your vantage point as a temporary resident of the Mont who knows where to go and how to get the most enjoyment out of your time here on the Mont.

Now More Little Museums…

After lunch, and possibly a siesta break back in your hotel room, visit the other two museums in the order, and at the speed, of your choice.

Museum of History

Museum of History
Grand Rue. Phone: (0)2–33–60–07–01

The *Museum of History* illustrates 1300 years of history, starting with the monks who built the Abbey, and presents old weapons, paintings, sculptures, watches, and a famous 19th century periscope. You will:

- Learn about the monks who built the Abbey.

- Visit the prisons and dungeons of the Mont, with wax models of some of its famous prisoners.

- View collections of ancient weapons, watches and medieval instruments of torture, including Louis XI's iron cage.

- See the Paul Capellani sculpture of a man succumbing to quicksand on the sand flats surrounding the Mont.

- Look through a famous periscope to see the bay from here.

The Logis Tiphaine

Logis Tiphaine
Grand Rue. Phone: (0)2–33–60–23–34

The *Logis Tiphaine* is the home that *General Bertrand du Guesclin* built in 1365 for his wife, *Tiphaine de Raguenel.* *Bertrand* was a well-known and heroic knight of 14th century France, and a fierce ally of the cause of French independence. He was courageous and fierce, but so ugly his mother rejected him at birth. *Tiphaine,* his wife, was a renowned beauty, and a famous astrologer. This profession was associated with sorcery at that time, and thus was a highly dangerous pursuit. So Guesclin installed his vulnerable wife on the Mont, one of the most secure and protected locations in the kingdom during those dangerous times.

The legend of their union is an example of "courtly love" between a ferocious man and a lovely woman. Tiphaine was as cultivated and faithful as her husband was homely, illiterate and absent. As *Bertrand* rode off to battle, *Tiphaine* read the stars to foretell who would be the victor.

Appointed constable (chief military leader) of France by King Charles V, *Bertrand* reconquered much of France from the English during the Hundred Years' War. He was nicknamed very early "The Black Dog of Brittany" due to his ugliness and bravery.

Special exhibits at the home of *Bertrand* and *Tiphaine* include:

- Period furniture, tapestries and paintings displaying their 14th century lifestyle,

- The bridal chamber,

- A medieval chastity belt,

- Bertrand's armor, and

- Tiphaine's astrologer's study.

Dine Royally with a View of the Bay

You have made dinner reservations for a window table at the lovely bay-view restaurant, *Restaurant du Guesclin*—(0)2-33-60-14-10—50170 *Grande Rue,* serving traditional French cuisine, with an emphasis on seafood. The 3-course Menus start at €19.50. Even if you are seated away from the window, you will be able to see out through the wall of windows. Have another slow and memorable meal while watching the tides "perform" in the bay. Make a mental picture to mark this moment and this spot to remember always.

More Silence & Lights

By now the streets have grown quiet again, and the Mont is yours for the evening. You know your way now, so pick your own favorite spot from which to view the spectacle of the illumination of the Mont. From the ramparts. From outside the gates. From part way across the causeway. From the terrace of the *Relais* hotel. Your choice.

What you are seeing this last evening, most people only see in photographs. And, as you now know, photographs cannot possibly do justice to the "real thing." Whatever challenges you may have encountered while you were here on the Mont will soon be forgotten. But your experience of the Mont will be etched in your memory for life.

Tomorrow... Bayeux

Rest well tonight in your island fortress. Tomorrow you will leave the Mont by bus and return to Pontorson to catch the train to Bayeux, where new stories and experiences await you.

CHAPTER 7:
Normandy Conquerors & Liberators

Bayeux will be your home base for the next four nights. From here you will immerse yourself in heroic stories that changed the course of history—from Norman conquerors in the 11th century to American, British, and Canadian liberators in the 20th.

The 11th century saga involves *William of Normandy* (also known as *William the Bastard*, and later *William the Conqueror*), who, in 1066, launched his army of 16,000 Norman troops from Bayeux to cross the English Channel from France to England. His quest was to take back the English crown that the childless and dying King Edward II had bestowed on him.

In Bayeux you will view the remarkable *Bayeux Tapestries*, a detailed visual account of William's tale, from his early alliances and battles, to his preparations to transport his troops and horses across the English Channel, to his valiant march through the south of England, to his decisive victory in the Battle of Hastings, where the usurping King Harold was killed by an arrow in his eye. After Harold's defeat, William successfully took back the throne and ruled as king of England for the next 21 years.

Moving ahead in time nine centuries to the 20th century story, the purpose of the epic battles fought—the dramatic *D-Day Landing ("Jour J,"* in French)—was to liberate, not to conquer. Bayeux was, once again, among the focal points. The 75-mile coast of Normandy, 110 miles from England across the English Channel, was Hitler's "Atlantic Wall," northernmost defensive barrier of his "fortress Europe." This coastline, located 6 miles from Bayeux, was the scene of the *D-Day Landing*, codenamed *Operation Overlord*.

From Bayeux, you will venture out on three daytrips. Your first daytrip will be by train to nearby Caen for more about *William the Conqueror*—visiting his castle and the abbeys he built as atonement for marrying his cousin. This will be followed by lunch, shopping, and wandering the streets of the medieval Vageaux district.

For your second daytrip venture, you will travel by taxi to *Arromanches*, epicenter of the D-Day landings. Here you will see the artificial harbor, *Port Winston*, constructed as a port-of-entry to offload Allied troops, vehicles and supplies. After viewing fascinating models and displays of the fabricated harbor, and the seemingly impenetrable beaches that surrounded it, you will visit Omaha Beach, where you will imagine the scene that played out there during this critical turning point in history, and comprehend how tenuous the success of this venture was at the time.

Your third daytrip will take you back to Caen, this time to see the remarkable *Memorial Museum*. Descending a spiraled walkway that takes you through the chain of cause and effect that followed in the wake of the First World War, you will descend ever deeper into the abyss, witnessing the gradual unhinging of a world unable to retain its grasp on its newly established and fragile peace.

A Little History of Conquerors & Liberators

Back at Mont Saint-Michel, you were introduced to part of the 11th century story, where the English Harold rescued William's men from the quicksand around Mont Saint-Michel.

Having no heir, King Edward of England chose as the next king of England his French cousin, William, over his British brother-in-law, Harold. But when Edward died, Harold turned rogue, betrayed his allegiance to William, and scurried back to England to crown *himself* king. Big mistake! William set out from Bayeux to reclaim his throne, leading an army of 16,000 troops, drawn to the quest through promises of sharing the spoils of the conquest. A fleet of 700 ships was built to transport the army across the Channel, along with 2,500 horses and all necessary supplies (including kegs of wine, of course).

William arrived in England, speaking only French, marched to Hastings, built a castle as a military base, and waited for Harold and his Saxon armies to return from the north. Harold was killed at the *Battle of Hastings*. And so William retrieved the crown, demolished all opposition, and became King of England.

Bayeux and the D-Day Landings

While William crossed to conquer, the D-Day troops crossed to liberate. On June 6th, 1944, a force ten times the size of William's, totaling 160,000 American, British and Canadian troops, crossed the English Channel, this time in the opposite direction, from England to France, to liberate France and Western Europe from Nazi control.

Bayeux had a key role in both the 11th and 20th century stories. Bayeux is where William and his troops constructed the fleet to transport French troops to England. And Bayeux was the first city to be reclaimed by the Allies on the day after D-Day, June 7, 1944. Unlike the other towns and cities near the Normandy coast, Bayeux was recaptured without being subjected to bombing, and thus emerged from the war virtually undamaged.

Day 8 (Saturday): To Bayeux

> **Before You Set Off for the Day:** Call your next hotel to confirm your arrival. Ask that they make 12:30 lunch reservations for you at *La Fringale, (43 rue St. Jean;* (0)2-31-21-34-40), at an outdoor table. Also request that they make your dinner reservations for 7:30 or 8:00 pm at *La Reine Mathilde Brasserie,* on the terrace, with a view of *Bayeux Cathedral (23 rue Laracher;* (0)2 31 92 08 13**).**

Leaving the Mont

TIME TARGET (confirm these times):

7:30 am hotel check-out and walk to bus stop.

8:45 am bus to the train station.

9:16 am train to Bayeux.

Today you will need to be up and away right on schedule, and with great focus on achieving your goal of catching the morning train to get yourself to Bayeux in time for lunch. You have a *9:16 am* train to catch from the little station in Pontorson (be sure that you have confirmed this time after making your own reservations).

It is essential that you check the current train schedule for updated train time from Pontorson to Bayeux. Train schedules change frequently. And YOU DO NOT WANT TO MISS THIS TRAIN.

But first, in order to get to your train, you will need to run the gauntlet that brought you onto the Mont two days ago, this time in reverse.

FRI 20 MAY	SAT 21 MAY	SUN 22 MAY		
	09:16 PONTORSON MONT ST **11:03** BAYEUX	1h 47m Direct		TER
	17:37 PONTORSON MONT ST **19:31** BAYEUX	1h 54m Direct		TER

It is crucial that you make your train with time to spare. This is why you will be starting early to allow plenty of time. Since you will be traveling between two small stations, Pontorson and Bayeux, there will be very few trains. If you miss the morning train, you will have many hours to wait before the afternoon train at 5:37 pm.

These are the five tasks ahead of you as you leave the Mont:

1. Check out of your hotel at around **7:30 am.**.

2. As you wind your way back down the *Grand Rue*, pick up breakfast sandwiches and drinks to eat on the train.

3. Walk out through the gates to the bus drop-off point. You will be traveling against the crowd, so allow time accordingly.

4. Aim to be near the front of the line for the *first* bus, leaving the Mont at **8:45 am,** and arriving at the Pontorson train station at *9:03 am,* just in time for the *9:16 am* train.

5. Catch the **9:16 am train** (confirm your own train time).

Catch the Morning Train to Bayeux

Once you are aboard your train, and stow your luggage, you will have around 1¾ hours to relax and eat the breakfast snacks you brought along.

Since you will arrive in Bayeux at around 11 am, set 10:50 am as your time target to begin your preparations to get off the train. Again, if you begin to doze off during the train ride, set an alarm to be sure you wake up in time to gather yourself and your belongings and move toward the door at least five minutes before your scheduled arrival time.

Arrival in Bayeux: Look Around You

When you arrive at the small Bayeux station, walk out to the street and call a taxi to take you to your hotel.

02 31 92 92 40
CONTACTEZ NOUS !

Another option, depending on the location of your hotel, is to walk. The town is small. Walking from the station to the vicinity of the *Tapestries* takes only about 8 minutes. Wind your way around to your right from the station, then around the traffic circle, and walk into town along *rue de Crémel*.

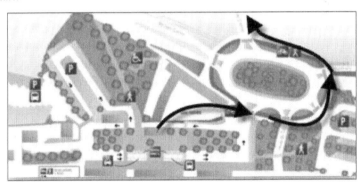

Locate Your Hotel and Check In

Your reservations hopefully will be in a small hotel or a bed & breakfast close to either the *Tapestries Museum*, the 11th-century *Notre Dame Cathedral*, or along *rue Saint-Jean*. When you arrive, it will likely be too early to check into your room. Ask your hotel to allow you to deposit your bags until check-in time. Request a map from the hotel desk, and have the attendant point you in the direction of the pedestrian Street, *rue St. Jean*.

Some "Full Experience" Places to Stay in Bayeux

A word to the wise… Bayeux is tiny, and a popular home base for travelers who are visiting the D-Day beaches. All the little hotels book up very early. By October, many options are already sold out for the following May. So book your rooms as soon as you know your travel dates. If you use _booking.com_ and select a room that offers "Free cancellation," you will be able to make changes and cancellations later if need be.

Again, to find a full-experience hotel with local charm, enter your dates on _booking.com_ and use "Map View" to zoom in on the area where you want to stay. In this case, plan to stay in the _Old Town_, close to either the _Tapestry Museum_ or _Notre Dame Cathedral_, or along the quiet pedestrian street, _rue Saint-Jean_.

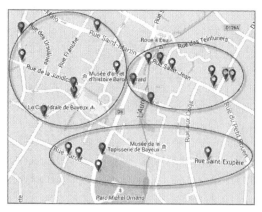

Some options are:

- _Villa Lara_ (28 rooms). _6 Place du Québec_. In the historic center, facing the _cathedral_, a 2 minute walk from the _Bayeux Tapestry_.

- _Le Lion D'or_ (29 rooms): _71 rue Saint Jean_. Located in a former 18th-century post office, ¼ mile from the _Tapestry Museum_.

- _Churchill Hotel_ (32 rooms). _14 rue St. Jean_. In the heart of the historic center, 430 yards from the _Bayeux Tapestry Museum_. Departure for the D-Day beach tour is just behind the hotel.

- _Hotel Reine Mathilde_ (22 rooms). _23 rue Larcher_. In the medieval district, 330 yards from the _Bayeux Tapestry Museum_ and within view of the _Notre Dame Cathedral_.

- *Chambres d'Hotes Villa Aggarthi* (5 rooms). *13 rue Saint-Exupère.* Located 230 yards from *Bayeux Tapestry Museum,* in an 18th-century building with enclosed gardens. Continental breakfast and access to communal kitchen included.

- *Logis de Saint Jean* (4 rooms). *77 rue Saint-Jean.* 380 yards from the *Tapestries* and a 5-minute walk from the cathedral. Offers a courtyard with outdoor seating. Breakfast includes pastries, bread, homemade cake, fresh fruit, juice and homemade jam.

- *Le Castel Guesthouse* (5 rooms). *1 Boulevard Sadi Carnot.* A 1937 Art Deco villa near the *Tapestries* and cathedral. Breakfast provided. Some rooms have terraces and cathedral views.

- *La Plus Petite Maison De France. 1 Passage De L'Islet.* Small but charming apartment on the river, steps from *rue Saint-Jean.* Bike rental is available at the property; popular area for biking.

- *Hotel d'Argouges. 21 rue Saint Patrice.* A centrally-located 18th century townhouse. Rooms have beautiful views over the garden or central courtyard. Breakfast ($15) is served in the living room or the gardens. Book a larger room.

Time to Learn Your Way Around: Orienteering

If all goes smoothly, you will have dropped off your luggage at your hotel by noon, with time to walk around a bit before lunch, and afterwards visit the *Saturday Market* on *Place Saint-Patrice* before it closes at 2:30 pm. Ask to be pointed toward the pedestrian street, *rue St. Jean,* then set off to learn your new hometown.

You will be lunching at *La Fringale (43 rue St. Jean.* 02 31 21 34 40), where you have already made reservations for 12:30 pm, hopefully at an outdoor table. This will be your starting point to get fully oriented in Bayeux.

After a relaxing lunch, and a brief visit to the *Saturday Market,* you will take a walkabout of Bayeux, locate the river, and learn an initial set of four rues. From this point on, you will be able to locate the pedestrian street, the *Tapestry Museum* and Bayeux's *Notre Dame Cathedral* on your own.

Lunch Outdoors at La Fringale

La Fringale is one of the nicest of the many pavement restaurants along the pedestrian *rue Saint-Jean,* offering good-value lunch menus from €9.

Consider ordering an inexpensive, but good, jug of the house wine. Then sit back, enjoy your meal, watch the people, and congratulate yourself. Once again, *you have arrived!* *La Fringale* may become the first of your

favorite restaurants in Bayeux... a place you will want to return to later for meals or for a snack or a glass of wine after shopping or exploring. Decide if you want to make this your "go to" meeting spot to get back together if and when you split off in different directions.

Attend the Saturday Market

After lunch, walk 10 minutes down *rue Saint-Jean*, crossing the bridge over the *River Aure*, and continuing on until you reach *la Place Saint Patrice*, a square that serves as a parking lot during the rest of the week, but is transformed into a bustling weekly market every Saturday, rain or shine. The market closes at 2:30 pm, so this activity will depend on your timing.

This will be the first leg of your orientation walk. Later you will follow a box-like pattern that will take you to the *Bayeux Cathedral*, then to the *Tapestry Museum*, as shown, then described, below:

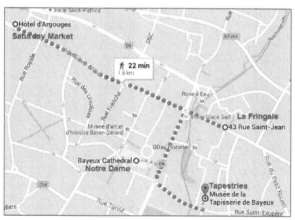

> ➤ Continue straight along *rue Saint-Jean*
>
> ➤ The street will change to *rue Saint-Martin*, then *rue Saint-Malo*, and then *rue Saint-Patrice*.

> ➢ The Saturday Market is on your right in *Place Saint-Patrice*, in the large parking lot across from *Hotel d'Argouges*.

As you cross the bridge, look down to spot the colorful umbrellas of cafés along the river on *passage de l'Islet*. Locate the stairs to walk down to river level, and plan to return here later. Take a few minutes for some great photo ops.

Stop by the *Tourist Information Office* on your right as you cross the bridge to pick up a good map of Bayeux and a calendar of events.

As you walk along *rue St. Jean* on your way to the Saturday Market, watch for ATMs, interesting shops, and places you may want to visit later for supplies for picnics or to take back to your room.

At a minimum, notice these essential shops:

- *"Pharmacie,"* in case you need some Band-Aids later, after all this walking.

- *"Tabac,"* in case you need to purchase more minutes for your French phone.

- *"Patissier & Chocolatier,"* for pastries and chocolates to take on your day trips to Caen and the D-Day beaches.

- *"Marché Plus,"* where you will come for groceries.

- *"Charcuttier"* (deli), to pick up entrées to go.

- *"Cave"* (wine shop), where you may request a "degustation" (wine tasting), and select a few nice bottles of local wine.

Soon after the bridge and the TI, watch for *rue Larcher* on your left. This is the intersection you will return to after your visit to the Saturday Market. At the Saturday Market, the entire perimeter of the square at *Place Saint-Patrice* is devoted to food. Cheese ("fromage"), both local and from all over France... Wine, Calvados, and Normandy cider producers, offering samples of their wares... Breads, sausages, cut flowers... Local fruits and vegetables... Seafood trucks selling an array of Normandy seafood, including local mussels... Vendors offering pizza, paella, sweet and savory crepes...

In the center of the square you will find new and used books for sale, as well as an array of clothing, shoes, jewelry, scarves, handbags pottery and market baskets.

Visit Notre Dame of Bayeux

Bayeux Notre Dame Cathedral

Open daily: 10 am to noon and 2 pm to 5:30 pm.

Evening hours: Tuesday, Thursday & Saturday, 8:30 pm to 10:30 pm.

Frequent choral and organ performances offered. Check *http://www.notredamedubessin.org.*

After visiting the market, continue your orientation walk-about.

> ➤ Retrace your steps toward *rue Larcher,* walking back along *rue Saint-Patrice* until it becomes *rue Saint-Malo,* then *rue Saint-Martin.*

> ➤ Turn right on *rue Larcher* before you reach the bridge, to reach the *Bayeux Notre Dame Cathedral.*

The narrow street will open up as you continue along. Look right to spot the Merry-Go-Round, and left to locate *Brasserie Reine Mathilde*, across from the *Notre Dame Cathedral*. This is the restaurant where you will be dining later this evening.

Pause to visit *Notre Dame Cathedral*, a soaring masterpiece of Norman architecture, consecrated on July 14th, 1077 by Bishop Odo, in the presence of his illustrious half-brother, *William the Conqueror*. Magnificent both inside and out, the cathedral is as large or larger than *Notre Dame* in Paris, and equally impressive. Later, when you visit the Paris *Notre Dame*, you can be the one to decide which Notre Dame is more splendid.

The inside of the cathedral is serene, light and airy, with many gothic details, and some of the most striking stained glass in the world, miraculously unharmed during World War II.

On the day the cathedral was consecrated, the 230-foot *Bayeux Tapestry* was displayed along the walls of its massive sanctuary, communicating to a primarily illiterate populace the details of William's heroic saga. After taking in the exterior architecture, go inside and take a seat.

Take a Break at Le Normandises or in a Park

Before or after your visit to the cathedral, claim an outdoor table at *Le Normandises* across the street, and take a break, with a view of the cathedral. Order your choice of wine, beer or ice cream, and rest up for your visit to the *Bayeux Tapestries*. Or find a bench in a park near the cathedral and enjoy some of the treats you found at the Saturday Market. But plan to arrive at the *Tapestry Museum* by 4:30 pm, 5 pm at the latest.

Walk to the Tapestry Museum by 4:30–5:00 PM

After you visit the cathedral, continue your walk-about:

157

> ➤ Continue along *rue Larcher.*
>
> ➤ Turn left on *rue de Nesmond* (toward the *Tapestry Museum*).
>
> ➤ Turn left at the sign for the *Tapestry Museum* on *Allée des Augustines.*

When you turn along *Allée des Augustines,* in the direction of the *Tapestry Museum,* you are on a path that would take you back to the now familiar *rue St. Jean* (with a jog to the right on *Place de Quebec,* then to the left on *Allée de L'Orangerie).*

You will be stopping at the *Tapestry Museum* now. But lock this basic box-shaped route into your mind so you will know enough to make your way around town from now on. To *rue Saint-Jean* for shops and restaurants… Across the *Aure River* and down the stairs to the walkway along the river… Along *rue Larcher* to the cathedral… Down *rue de Nesmond* to *Allée des Augustines* for the *Tapestry Museum*…

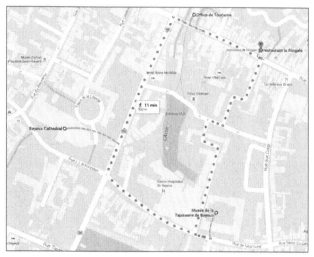

Visit the Tapestry Museum by 4:30–5:00 PM

TIME TARGET (confirm these times):

Visit Tapestry Museum by ***4:30 pm***

Tapestry Museum

Open daily: 9 am – 6:30 pm (7 pm from May to August); last admission 45 minutes before closing (5:45 pm).

Cost: *9€* for *Tapestries Museum* alone. *12€* for two museum combination ticket; *15€* for all three museums.

Additional museums: *Museum of Art & History (37 rue du Bienvenu)* and/or the *Memorial Museum of the Battle of Normandy (Boulevard Fabian Ware)*.

Note about other museums on the Combo Ticket

Museum of Art & History: housed in the *Bishop's Palace* beside the cathedral. Exhibits include fabulous Bayeux lace samples, pottery, china, and paintings.

Memorial Museum of the Battle of Normandy: a unique museum that immerses you in the battle of Normandy from the allied point of view, as well as the German perspective, spanning from preparations for D-Day (June 6, 1944) to the aftermath.

You will have time to fit in one or both of these additional museums, one each at the end of the days you travel to Caen.

If you will only be visiting one museum in Bayeux, the *Tapestry Museum* is the "must do." This remarkable museum is now housed in an impressive eighteenth-century seminary. Enter the courtyard on your right. The *Bayeux Tapestries* illustrate, comic-strip style, the complex and dramatic 11th century saga of *William the Conqueror*. This is an amazing piece of work, comprising 230 feet of vividly intricate embroidered scenes—58 scenes in all.

French legend claims that the tapestry was created by William the Conqueror's wife, *Queen Matilda*, and her ladies-in-waiting. You will learn more about the dauntless Mathilde tomorrow, when you visit the royal couple's castle and abbeys in Caen. Most scholars, however, believe that the tapestry was stitched by nuns at the behest of William's half-brother,

159

Bishop Odo of Bayeux, probably at the same time he was overseeing the construction of the cathedral. Whatever its genesis, the tapestry is a veritable marvel. And the fact that it has survived from the 11th to the 21st century is nothing short of miraculous.

If a visit to a museum of tapestries sounds low key to you, consider why the tapestry was created at the time. Imagine yourself alive during William's conquest—this seemingly impossible, and insanely heroic, venture across the English Channel to wrest back the throne of England from the usurper, Harold. How would you have learned the story, in all of its glory?

The graphic version of the tale displayed in the tapestry would have been your primary means to discover what had happened, given that, in that day and age, you most certainly would not have had access to radio, TV or the Internet. All of these means of communication were far in the future. Most probably, you would not even have been able to read. And if you were, you would have had very limited access to written accounts.

So, to learn the story, you would have gone to the Cathedral, along with all of your neighbors, to view the saga in the "living technicolor" of the day. *William's tale of bravery and sacrifice, loyalty and love, was passed on, and then preserved for the next 1000+ years, through this very tapestry you are about to see.* This Norman work of art, a key resource for the history of earlier civilizations, was added to the UNESCO "Memory of the World" Register in 2007.

Don't Miss the Model of William's Ships

Start in the courtyard, where you will view a model of the ships William and his army built in Bayeux to traverse the English Channel and retake the English crown.

As you view the tapestry, look for the portrayal of William's horses aboard these boats.

First Time Seeing the Tapestry

Once you are inside the museum, there are three main areas to view, all highly interesting. On the ground floor is the 11th century *Bayeux Tapestry*, very old and extremely fragile, yet retaining much of the vivid color of the original. You will be able to examine the tapestry up close, displayed behind glass for protection. Use the audio guide commentary to hear the saga as you move past each of the 58 scenes along the tapestry's length.

The original tapestry ends with the death of King Harold at the Battle of Hastings, and before William is crowned. This is not the end of the story! The full tale is cut short because part of the tapestry has been lost. These missing scenes now have been tirelessly and meticulously redesigned and recreated by stitchers on *Alderney* in the *Channel Islands* in England, in a style that exactly matches the original. The recreated panels carry the tale through to its historic conclusion... the coronation of *William the Conqueror* on Christmas Day, 1066.

Second Walk Through of the Tapestry

The audio-guide moves along very quickly. So when it ends, you will have the sense that you have missed a lot of the story on your first walk-through. But you are allowed to remain inside the gallery for as long as you like. So plan to take a second walk-through to "read" more of the tapestry. This will give you time to look more closely at each of the scenes and to decipher the story as it unfolds.

One interesting point in the chronology shows William's ships setting sail to England. Hundreds of vessels spread out across the Channel, carrying soldiers, weapons, horses and wine, with the horses peering calmly out over the high sides of the ships.

See What Life & War Were Like Back Then

After viewing the tapestry, take the grand staircase to first floor exhibition room, and immerse yourself in the world of William and his armies. Here you will find fascinating displays of knights in armor (including William), the history of the Normans in Britain, and some beautifully-built scale model dioramas of Norman buildings. These exhibits will answer many of your questions about life in Normandy and England in William's time.

Catch the Movie in English

Plan to catch the final English showing of the 16-minute movie at 5:15 pm. The Cinema is on the second floor. Shows alternate between French and English.

> English: 9:55am- 10:35am- 11:15am- 11:55am- 12:35pm- 1:15pm-
> 1:55pm- 2:35pm- 3:15pm- 3:55pm- 4:35pm- 5:15pm (+5:55pm 1 May
> to 31 August)

Free Time Until Dinner

Enjoy some free time on *rue St. Jean* before heading back toward *Notre Dame* for dinner at *Brasserie Reine Mathilde* (named in honor of William's wife, Queen Mathilde), across the street from the cathedral. You know your way around now. Go where you wish. Window shop or pause at a café or meander along the river.

Dinner at Brasserie Reine Mathilde

You will have made reservations for 7:30 pm or 8:00 pm at *Brasserie Reine Mathilde* (23 rue Larcher), on the terrace, with a view of the cathedral. This place is considered by some to be "a find."

Sample Reviews

"Cozy atmosphere inside, or dine under the awning. Great food at reasonable prices. Helpful and friendly service."

"Great outside seating and view of cathedral. We liked it so much we ate two breakfasts, one lunch, and two dinners here."

So now relax. You have arrived in Bayeux. Breathe the fresh air. Watch the lights of the cathedral come on. You know your way around well enough to take a leisurely stroll "home" after dinner.

Day 9 (Sunday): William the Conqueror's Caen

> **Before You Set Off for the Day:** Make reservations for lunch at *Le Bouchon du Vaugueux* (*12 rue Graindorge*; 02-31-44-26-26) in Caen for 12:30 pm.
>
> Also make dinner reservations in Bayeux for 7:30 or 8:00 pm at *Le Moulin de la Galette* along the river (*38 rue de Nesmond*; 02-31-22-47-75).
>
> Note: Take along a backpack and/or marketing bag to carry around your finds from today's shopping.

Today you will take a short train ride to Caen (pronounced "cong," that rhymes with "honk," but without the "k"). Caen is known as the town of a hundred spires. On today's visit to Caen, you will focus on the medieval city of William the Conqueror.

Features of the day will include visiting the Saturday Market and lunching at an outdoor table in the charming *Vaugueux* area, the valley located between the ducal castle and the high ground on which the collegiate church of *Saint-Sepulcre* is built. After lunch you will ride the *"Petit Train"* from one end of William's town to the other, passing William's 11th century castle, as well as the *Men's Abbey*, where William is buried, and the *Ladies' Abbey*, where his wife is buried. William built these impressive abbeys as peace offerings to the church to atone for the "sin" of marrying his distant cousin, Matilda of Flanders.

Later you will have ample opportunity to wander at will inside and atop William's castle walls, and to visit the remarkable *Normandy Museum*. This will be followed by free time to shop along *rue St. Pierre* or to stroll through the *Botanic Gardens* or the *Art Museum*.

Take the Train to Caen, then the Tram to St. Pierre

Caen is less than 20 minutes by train from Bayeux, with efficient tramways running back and forth from in front of the Caen train station to the center of the city. Since there is much for you to see and do today, it will be best for you to catch an early train and arrive in Caen by around 9 or 10 am.

8:37AM Bayeux	**8:53AM** Caen	0hr 16min	SNCF Intercités 3302
9:20AM Bayeux	**9:38AM** Caen	0hr 18min	SNCF TER 52614

Taxi or Tram to the Old Town

Although the taxi may seem easier, it may be more fun to use the convenient *Twisto Tram & Bus* system for your ride into town. And it certainly will be much more economical. You will quickly get the hang of this convenient and efficient option, and should have no problems, since both the tram and the bus run regularly and use the same ticket.

If you opt for the Tram, walk out of the station to the first shelter—do not cross the tram tracks. Take either Tram A or B, leaving every 4 minutes. Purchase your *Twisto* tickets from the machine before boarding the tram. Remember to validate your ticket when you board the tram.

To save yourself money and effort, opt for the best pass for your situation. For two or more traveling together, purchase a 24-hour family ticket for €5.95. Then you'll be set for the day. Do the same when you return to Caen in two days. For an individual, the 3-day pass saves money at €7.50 for three days of unlimited journeys.

1 JOURNEY	Magnetic ticket valid for 1 hour after being stamped/punched.	1.40€
24 HOURS	Magnetic ticket valid for 24 hours counting from the moment it is first stamped/punched for an unlimited number of journeys	3.90€
3 DAYS PASS	Magnetic ticket valid for 3 days for an unlimited number of journeys.	7.50€
FAMILY	Magnetic ticket valid for 24 hours for a family of 2 to 5 persons travelling together including at least one accompanying adult.	5.95€

If you elect to save time and effort, taxis are usually waiting outside the station. Just walk out the front door and spot a driver.

Making Sense of the Caen Tram/Bus System

As you have come to expect in France, the key to understanding the tram system is to learn the *end points* for the journeys you plan to make. Make sure that the tram you board is heading in the direction you want to go.

You will be using one of two tram lines, *Line A* (Orange) and *Line B* (Red). The directions *Line A* travels are: *"Direction Campus 2"* or *"Direction Jean Vilar."* Directions for *Line B* are: *"Direction Saint-Clair"* or *"Direction Grâce de Dieu."*

To head into town, you will need to take:

- *"Direction Campus 2"* for *Line A* or

- *"Direction St. Clair"* for *Line B.*

When you head back to the station at the end of the day, take:

- *"Direction Jean Vilar"* for *Line A*, or

- *"Direction Grâce de Dieu"* for *Line B.*

Get off at the 3rd tram stop—*Bernières* to head over to the *Sunday Market* at *Place Courtonne*, bordering the marina. If you are planning to skip the market and make your way straight to the castle, wait until the 5th stop and get off at *Quatrans*.

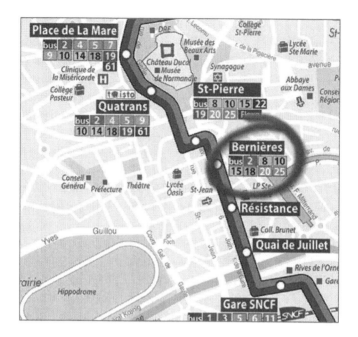

Visit the Sunday Market at Place Courtonne

Open 8:00 am to 1:00 pm

Around the *Port de Plaisance*. (*quai Vendeuvre, place Courtonne*). *Sunday Market* is the main Caen market of the week.

Like most markets in France, Caen market is lively, colorful, and noisy, with a large number and variety of products. Sunday is the main market day, with regional crafts, cider, cheeses, apple products, jams, jellies, and preserves. This is said to be the 5th largest market in France, with 400 traders offering their wares from all around the region.

The setting for this market is interesting in itself, as it borders the marina located in the center of the city. This a great place to wander and buy local produce.

166

Walk to Lunch, then the Office de Tourisme

TIME TARGET

Lunch at **12:30 pm**. *Petit Train* at **2:00 pm**

From the market at Place Courtonne, walk first to lunch at *Le Bouchon* in the Vaugueux area (old town), and from there to the *Tourist Information Center*. Your walking path is shown on this map.

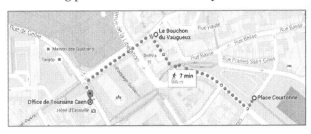

Lunch at Le Bouchon du Vaugueux

> ### *Le Bouchon du Vaugueux*
>
> *12 rue Graindorge*
>
> (0)2-31-44-26-26

Pause for lunch at 12:30 pm at *Le Bouchon du Vaugueux*. This restaurant comes highly recommended by online reviewers, who cite "a fantastic menu, great food and wine" and "small, cozy and busy... friendly and welcoming... good food, reasonably priced."

Catch the "Petit Train Touristique" at the Tourist Information Center

---

Tourist Information Center & the Petit Train

12 Place Saint-Pierre (0)2 31 27 14 14

Train departs every hour on the hour, 10 am to 7 pm (minimum of 4 riders) Thursday to Sunday (April and May), then daily (June through September).

Cost: €6 for adults, €4 for children (3–12), free under 3.

Board at *Church of Saint-Pierre*, opposite the Tourist Office.

Take a moment to step inside the Tourist Information Center (TI) to pick up a good map and any other brochures of interest. Confirm the schedule for the *Petit Train* and purchase your tickets for the 2 pm departure.

Ride a Full Circuit

Outside the TI, step on board the Petit Train for a 45-minute tour, with audio commentary in French and English, that will give you an overview of the city and its rich heritage. You will see:

- Church of Saint-Pierre,
- *William the Conqueror's* Ducal Castle,
- The port,
- The *Ladies' Abbey*,
- The *Men's Abbey*.

A Little History

William the Conqueror was born October 14, 1024 in Falaise, Normandy, France, the illegitimate son of *Robert II "The Magnificent,"* 6th Duke of Normandy, and his mistress, *Arletta of Falaise,* a tanner's daughter. Thus William's initial nickname, "William the Bastard." William grew up to be a handsome and athletic man, robust and burly in appearance, with a guttural voice, and tall stature for the time—approximately 5'10". He was a formidable warrior.

When he was 25 and still a Duke, William married his distant cousin, Mathilde. He built *Caen Castle* while he was 36, and set out to conquer England and become its king when he was 42. His reign as King lasted 21 years (1066–1087). He enjoyed excellent health and stamina into "old age," and died from a fatal fall from a horse at the age of 63, four years after his beloved wife, Mathilde.

The Conquest

As you saw in the *Bayeux Tapestries,* William was named next king of England by the dying King Edward. But Harold usurped the throne, declaring himself king instead. William gathered together an army, built a fleet of ships, crossed the English channel, and advanced on Harold and his troops. Harold was killed in the Battle of Hastings in 1066, and William reclaimed the crown. Pope Alexander II himself sanctioned William's invasion and kingship.

When gathering together the forces he needed to invade England, William promised to grant them the lands he confiscated from defeated Saxon nobles in exchange for their pledges of service and loyalty. This arrangement set the new precedent of a Continental system of feudalism, where loyalty to the king overrode fealty to an immediate lord.

William as Ruler

King William was reputed to be an efficient but harsh ruler, fierce in protecting his domain. Although he was known as a conqueror, he also imposed the "Truce of God" to restrict warfare and violence to a maximum of 80 days total per year, and never on holy days or feast days. He prescribed "permanent peace" for churches and their grounds, women and pilgrims, merchants and their servants, cattle and horses, and men at work in the fields.

In 1085 William started the *Domesday Book*, sending men all over England and Wales to record landowner holdings in land and livestock, and determine their total worth. This assessment covered a total of 13,418 domains throughout the shire, and was used to ascertain what lands had been owned by the prior King Edward and what taxes had been paid to him. This comprehensive inventory was used to establish what land was now owned by King William, and what taxes were due him as the new king. The *Domesday Book* was the last such accounting of land ownership until a census was taken almost *eight centuries later* in 1873. These ancient volumes from 1085 have been preserved and protected throughout the ages, and are now housed in the British National Archives.

The Love Story

In 1053, when he was 25, William married his 22-year-old cousin, *Matilda of Flanders*. Matilda was the daughter of the *Count of Flanders*, one of the wealthiest and most powerful realms in Europe at that time. On her mother's side, Matilde was the granddaughter of the King of France.

Extremely well-educated, lovely and very petite (only four-foot-two), Matilda attracted the adamant attention of her cousin William, as well as many other suitors. As a much sought after potential bride, she considered herself to be too high born to consider marrying a "bastard," although by this time William had succeeded his father as *Duke of Normandy*.

William adamantly pursued Matilda, declaring that he had fallen in love with her the first time he saw her at the French court. He was so passionately enamored of her that he declared he would do anything necessary to claim her, even if it required using force.

When Matilda refused William's offer of marriage, and publicly denounced him as a bastard, William accosted her on her way home from church and dragged her from her carriage by her hair. This outraged Matilda's father, the Count of Flanders, who began making preparations to attack William's dominions. But then, to the astonishment of all, Matilda intervened on William's behalf, announcing that she would marry no other than him. "He must be a man of great courage and high daring who would venture to come and beat me in my own father's palace."

This marriage between cousins displeased the Pope, who excommunicated them both. William appealed, and the Pope relented on the condition that the couple build two abbeys, one for monks and one for nuns. You saw these abbeys today during your ride on the Petit Train.

Despite the discord and drama of their so-called courtship, William and Matilda went on to enjoy a successful and happy marriage. The pair were devoted to each other, faithful and affectionate, and went on to have 10 children, four sons and six daughters, including two future kings, William II and Henri I. William was proud of his wife, taking her with him on royal tours to show her off to his subjects. And, unprecedented for the period, William remained staunchly faithful to her.

Matilda's Role in the Kingdom

Matilda was passionate, steadfast and wise, yet utterly ruthless and tenacious in the pursuit of her goals. She supported and sympathized with all of William's projects, social and political, and was the only person capable of taming her formidable husband. She confounded the traditional views of women in medieval society by seizing the reins of power when she had the chance, directing her husband's policy, and, at times, flagrantly disobeying his orders. She was known to have a talent for architecture that she inherited from her father.

Before William set off to conquer England, he sought help in his preparations from Matilda, who assisted him by convincing the barons to follow William "beyond the Sea." Since she controlled her own property, wealth and income, she was able to use her own funds to build and equip a secret ship, called the *Mora*, that she presented to her husband as a gift to

171

support his venture across the Channel. William took the *Mora* as his flagship.

The king of France, *King Philip I*, considered William's plan to annex England to be absurd, asking who would be left in charge of Normandy while William was off running another country. To this William confidently replied that Matilda was fully capable of ruling Normandy in his absence. Before he left for England, William appointed Matilda as Regent of his dominion, with their 13-year-old eldest son, Robert, as her assistant.

After William was crowned king of England in Westminster Abbey, he arranged for Matilda to join him to be crowned Queen. She was crowned in *Winchester Cathedral* in 1068.

Matilda died in 1083, at age 51. William was bereft, and plunged into a deep depression. He died four years later, at age 63, after a fall from his horse.

Enter the Walls of Caen Castle to Wander the Ruins

Caen Castle, one of the largest medieval fortresses of Western Europe, was built by William the Conqueror in around 1060. The walls of the castle are beautifully preserved, with fantastic views of the city from atop the walls.

The ruins of the castle's keep, a large square section with round towers at each corner, all surrounded by a moat, have been undergoing excavation. Over 6,000 cubic meters of earth have been removed, revealing elements of the early structure that include:

- the base of the keep,
- a better view of the 12th-century north-west wall,
- the cellar of a 15th-century private home,
- a powder magazine,
- a 14th-century forge, and
- the traces of the stables.

The grounds of the 11th century castle also house the *Musée des Beaux-Arts,* with one of the world's finest collections of European Art, as well as the *Musée de Normandie.*

Enter through the castle walls to wander the ruins of the château and explore the ramparts, at will. The castle has two fortified gateways: *porte sur la ville* ("door to the town") and *porte des champs* ("door to the fields"). For a fuller view of this remarkable medieval site, climb to the top of the recently restored northern rampart.

Visit the Musée Normandie

> *Musée Normandie*
>
> *Open:* 9:30 am–6:00 pm, Wednesday to Monday. *Closed Tuesdays until May 3.* Open daily beginning June 1st.
>
> *Cost:* €5.20 (€7.20 to include the special exhibits). Free to anyone under age 26, and for everyone on the first Sunday of each month.
>
> *Combo tickets:* Purchase a *Pass Murailles* for entry to both the *Normandy Museum* and the *Musée des Beaux-Arts.* 15 € for one person; 25 € for two.

The *Normandy Museum* is now housed in the 14th-century building that was once the residence of the captain of the château, and later the Governor of Caen. It provides an excellent and interesting introduction to the history of Caen and its wider region.

The museum goes back in history, presenting an overview of regional people's lives throughout Normandy, from prehistoric times to the great migrations in the Middle Ages and to modern times. Permanent exhibitions cover each historic period, from the earliest traces of human activity to the present age, illustrating the life of Normandy through the centuries.

Free Time Options

After visiting the castle and the *Normandy Museum*, you will have your choice of three excellent options to pursue:

1. Browse the shopping streets in city center,

2. Stroll the *Botanical Gardens*,

3. Visit the *Musée des Beaux-Arts,* inside the walls of the Castle.

You may opt for one or more of these, as you choose, in whatever order, allocating your time according to your interests. Since you and your travel companion may have differing priorities during this free time, this may be a good time to part ways for an hour or so, and meet up later.

Browse the Shopping Street, rue St. Pierre

Rue Saint-Pierre is a popular shopping street in Caen's city center. As you walk these pedestrian streets, pause to wander in and out. Flowers, chocolates, jewelry, clothing, lingerie, treasures of Normandy…

Even if you are not a shopper by nature, take a stroll along this pedestrian street, pausing to look at the window displays. Check out *Le Chocolaterie Hotot (13 rue Saint-Pierre)*, offering a cornucopia of chocolate products. Stop by *Nature & Decourvertes (88-90 rue Saint-Pierre)*, for decorations, gifts, garden accessories and books on the theme of nature. Then wander through one or two other shops that look interesting. If shops are closed, make note of the ones you would like to visit when you return to Caen in two days.

Agree on a meeting spot where the non-shoppers can perch while the seasoned shoppers enjoy themselves browsing through the boutiques. If the non-shoppers are feeling energetic, they may venture over to the *Botanical Gardens* or the *Musée des Beaux-Arts* until time to meet up with the shopping enthusiasts in their midst.

Visit the Botanical Garden

The *Botanical Gardens (Jardin des Plantes)* are a 15-minute walk from the Vaugueux area. Walk along *Geole Street*, with the castle wall on your right. Turn left on *Bosnieres* to reach *Place Blot* and the entrance to the gardens. The *Jardin des Plantes* has been a beautiful botanical haven in Caen for over three centuries—a living museum of the flora of the Normandy region. Admission is free.

Stroll Through the Musée des Beaux-Arts

Located within the walls of William's castle, in a contemporary building, the *Museum of Fine Arts* offers a rich collection of 16th and 17th century European painting—Italian, French, Flemish and Dutch. A sculpture park was added in 2007.

The history of the museum goes back to 1801, when the French Minister of Interior of the time selected Caen as one of 15 cities in France to serve as depots to display the large number of paintings that had been confiscated during the French Revolution and the Napoleonic Wars.

The collections housed in Caen went largely unharmed throughout Nazi occupation. But the Allied bombings of 1944 destroyed much of the artwork, a total of 540 paintings and 400 drawings. After the final Allied air raid on July 7, most of the museum had been flattened. The surviving artwork—567 paintings and miniatures, ceramics and porcelains—was hastily stored in the unsound ruins of the *Hotêl Escoville* and the *Langlois Museum*.

In 1963, almost 20 years later, it became possible to rebuild the art museum. The stored collections were inventoried, in addition to what remained of a considerable collection donated in 1872 by Caen bookseller, Bernard Mancel. Mancel had purchased many of his holdings from the collections that had belonged to Napoleon I's uncle, Cardinal Fesch.

Through intense effort, this historic art museum was reestablished as a major museum, and promoted to the rank of "*musée classé*," in recognition of the importance of its collections.

Take Tram Line A or Line B back to the Train Station

When you are ready to return to the train station, walk to the *St. Pierre* or the *Quatrans* tram stop and board the tram using:

- *Line A "Direction Jean Vilar"* or

- *Line B "Direction Grace de Dieu."*

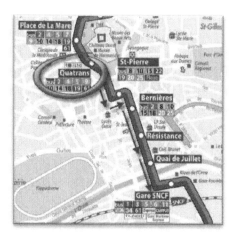

Take the Train "Home" for Dinner in Bayeux

Then take the train back to Bayeux. Aim to arrive back in Bayeux by around 6:00 pm so you will have some down-time before dinner.

Dinner in Bayeux at Moulin de la Galette

> **Le Moulin de la Galette**
>
> *38 rue de Nesmond*
>
> (0)2-31-22-47-75

You will have made dinner reservations for 7:30 or 8:00 pm at *Moulin de la Galette*. Relax and enjoy your time here, dining along the Aure River.

Day 10 (Monday): D-Day Beaches

> **Before You Set Off for the Day:** Make *12:30 pm* lunch reservations (or ask your hotel to make your reservations) at *La Marine (1, quai du Canada;* (0)2-31-22-34-19).
>
> Make *7:30 or 8:00* pm dinner reservations at:
>
> - La Rapiere (*53 rue Saint Jean*; (0)2-31-21-05-45) OR
> - Au Petit Bistrot (*31 Ter rue Larcher*; (0)2-31-92-30-08).

Today you will make your way by taxi. This will preserve your independence so you will be free to take as much time as you want at each stop, include a lunch break overlooking the former harbor at Arromanches, and pause for drinks at Omaha beach.

Beginning in Bayeux, you will travel northeast to Arromanches, the location of Port Winston, the temporary harbor built and used for the

177

landings on the Normandy coast. The second leg of your drive will take you west along the coast to *Saint Laurant sur Mer*, scene of the *Omaha Beach* landing. The final leg of today's circuit will bring you back home to Bayeux.

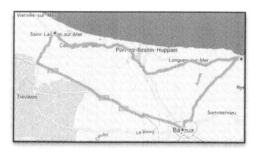

This first leg of taxi rides will take 15 minutes, a distance of just over 6 miles, and will cost around €25 (about $28). The second leg, from Arromanches to the *American*

Cemetery & Memorial overlooking *Omaha Beach*, will take around 45 minutes, a distance of 14 miles, and will cost about €35 ($39). Your third and final leg, from *Omaha Beach* back to Bayeux, will take about 30 minutes, a distance of just over 12 miles, and will cost around €40 ($45). Planning ahead for your day's transportation, figure on a total cost of around €100 ($112) to complete the full loop. Be sure to carry enough cash with you to pay your drivers.

BAYEUX TAXIS - ARROMANCHES
TAXI
BAYEUX
Tél. 06 70 40 07 96
www.taxisbayeux.com

GIE TAXIS DU BESSIN
BAYEUX CEDEX
Tél. 02 31 92 92 40
www.bayeux-taxis.com

TAXI SERVICES +
BAYEUX
Tél. 06 74 49 77 67
www.taxi-lecornu-bayeux.fr

If €100 seems steep for a single day trip, consider that a full-day group tour to the *D-Day Beaches* from Bayeux, would cost around €100 ($112) per person. So by sharing a series of taxis, your total cost for two will be cut in half, and you will save €100 (or more).

Also, if you book a group tour, you will need to lock in your reservations well in advance of your trip, and make full payment at the time of booking. This can become even more of a problem if you later need to make changes. Generally you will not be entitled to a refund for cancellations made within one week of the tour.

Programmed group tours to the beaches generally include visits to several landing locations. This means that the time allotted to each stop is extremely limited. And most tours do not include a visit to *Arromanches*, one of the essential sights of your day. Also, if you opt for a programmed tour, you will be bound by a prescribed schedule, and will not have the latitude to lunch overlooking the sea, or walk along the beach looking back up at the cliffs. You will spend your day with scant time to take in each stop before you head back to the bus or van to meet your group.

If, despite these sacrifices to your full experience, you still would prefer to exchange your freedom for a full-day guided group tour, one option is *Bayeux Shuttle* (*http://www.bayeuxshuttle.com*).

Otherwise, call a taxi and set off, first to *Arromanche*.

A Little History of Arromanches

Arromanches lies along the stretch of coastline, designated *Gold Beach,* that was liberated by British troops. Within 12 days after D-Day on June 6, 1944, Arromanches was transformed into a *Mulberry Harbor* (temporary and portable), one of two such harbors built along the Normandy coast to offload troops and supplies to support the Allied troops.

The second *Mulberry Harbor,* was located at *Omaha Beach* to support the American landing troops. It was destroyed by a large storm only days after it began to operate.

These temporary harbors at *Gold Beach* and *Omaha Beach* were built in great secrecy, while the Allies were still under fire from German troops. To form *"Port Winston,"* the synthetic harbor at *Gold Beach*, a protective breakfront was floated over from England under cover of night, made up of 17 derelict ships, sunk end-to-end 1½ miles offshore, supplemented by 115 cement blocks ("block ships"), each the size of a football field.

Together these shielded the landing vessels against turbulent seas, opening an entry point into the Nazi's "fortress Europe" through which soldiers, vehicles and provisions were supplied for the march across France, then on to Germany, to liberate Europe from the Nazis and bring World War II to a close.

Within the area protected by the breakfront, 10 miles of floating pontoon roads were constructed to offload vehicles, troops and supplies. Although *Port Winston* was designed to last only 3 months, it was heavily used for 10 months, offloading a total of 2.5 million troops, 500,000 vehicles, and 4 million tons of needed supplies.

Sections of Arromanches *Mulberry Harbor* still remain today, with huge concrete blocks sitting in the sand and farther out at sea.

View the Beach from Above & Visit Arromanches 360

Arromanches 360 Circular Cinema and Memorial

Open daily: 9:30 am to 7 pm; last show at 6:40 pm

Cost: €5 per person. Children, teachers, soldiers, students, disabled, and people over 60 receive a discount.
Combo tickets: *Twin Ticket* for €20.50 (includes entry to the *Caen Memorial Museum* you will visit tomorrow).

Note: The *Twin Ticket* saves €3.50 each (about $4), and also allows you to skip the ticket line at the *Memorial Museum*.

Have your taxi drop you off on the cliff above Arromanches for a panoramic view down to the beach. Contemplate what the landing forces faced.

Then visit the *Arromanches 360 Circular Cinema and Memorial* to watch the film that relives this episode in history, showing archived footage of actual battles. Learn the incredible story of how this artificial harbor was built.

Visit the Disembarkment Museum

Walk 5 minutes down the hill and along the sea front to visit the small but fascinating *Musée du Débarquement*.

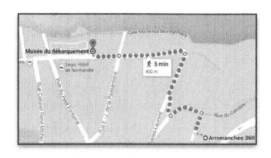

Musée du Débarquement

Place du 6 Juin

Open daily: 9:00 am to 7:00 pm, May through August.

Cost: €7.90 per person.

This museum offers an engrossing collection of working models and dioramas, as well as archival film footage that brings to life the complex jigsaw puzzle of this dramatic harbor construction operation. Immerse yourself in learning about this strategic undertaking that was so key to the Allies' success. The self-guided tour takes about 1 ¼ hours.

Walk Down to the Water & Look Back Up

Walk down to the beach to see the concrete blocks that remain from the breakfront out in the water. This is what now remains of Port Winston, the temporary harbor.

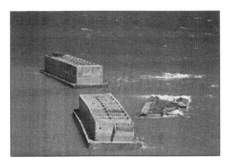

Then turn around and look back up the cliff wall to understand what the liberating troops faced as their landing boats dropped them into the surf against enemy fire.

Lunch at La Marine on the Water

La Marine
1 quai du Canada
(0)2-31-22-34-19

You have made 12:30 pm lunch reservations at *La Marine*, with a view of the beach. The restaurant is a 2-minute walk from the museum, and offers splendid views out to sea, overlooking what is left of the artificial harbor. Try the huge bowl of mussels or a plate of fresh seafood.

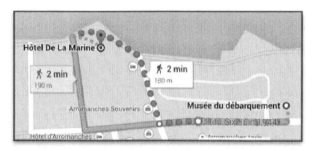

Take a Taxi to the American Cemetery at "Omaha Beach"

Call a taxi for the 14 miles drive along D514 toward *Saint Laurant sur Mer*, to the *American Cemetery & Memorial*, overlooking *Omaha Beach*, one of the landing points that was taken by the American troops on D-Day.

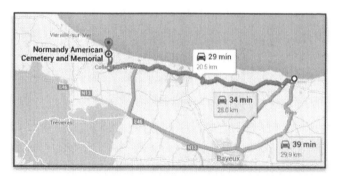

The Memorial is open to the public daily from 9 am to 6 pm (April to September), with reduced hours in off-season. Set aside at least an hour for your visit.

About the Omaha Beach Landing

"Omaha Beach" is the code name for one of the five sectors of the Allied invasion of German-occupied France. As you will see for yourself, this 5-mile strip of coastline to the West of Arromanches is composed of steep chalk cliffs that rise precipitously one hundred feet or more above the sea.

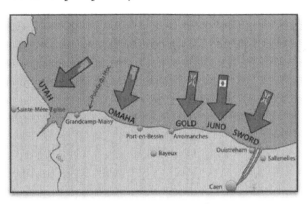

Landing at *Omaha Beach* was necessary in order to link the British *Gold Beach* landing to the east, with the American *Utah Beach* landing to the west. When combined with Juno and Sword beaches, this provided a continuous 5-beach lodgment along the Normandy coast—Utah, Omaha, Gold, Juno and Sword.

Taking Omaha Beach fell to the American troops, who suffered heavy losses, earning this beach the name "Bloody Omaha." If the Normandy landings were to have failed anywhere, it would certainly have been at *Omaha Beach*. Of the five landing zones, *Omaha Beach* was the most heavily defended, with the well-organized and resolute German 352nd Infantry Division defending the high bluffs with machine guns, mortars, and artillery, and formidable anti-invasion obstacles placed on the beaches, including heavy obstructions made of angled iron.

General Eisenhower sent a message to these troops prior to the invasion, saying: *"You are about to embark upon the great crusade toward which we have striven these many months. The eyes of the world are upon you, I have full confidence in your courage, devotion to duty and skill in battle."*

The first American assault offloaded waves of engineers, tanks, and infantry. These troops took heavy casualties, and succeeded in blowing only a few gaps through the beach obstacles. Of the 16 tanks that initially landed, only two survived. This resulted in grave delays for successive landings.

The heavily defended vehicular routes off the beach were impassable at first. This backed up traffic, and resulted in the beach being closed to all but infantry landings.

At one point, the Allied commanders considered abandoning the beachhead. But small contingents of infantry pushed their way forward, often in ad-hoc groups supported by surviving tanks and whatever other equipment they could muster. Eventually these groups infiltrated through the coastal defenses and scaled the bluffs between the strongpoints. Subsequent waves of infantry exploited these initial penetrations.

By the end of D-Day at Omaha Beach, American troops had fought their way across 300 yards of open beach, scaled the heights overlooking the channel, and occupied the plateau where the *American Cemetery* is now located. They suffered more than 3,000 casualties during the attack, the highest for any Allied landing zone.

On D-Day, a combined total of around 156,000 Allied soldiers, including 73,000 Americans, landed on the five beaches. Over the following days, the Allies expanded these tenuous beachheads, and within a week, with the aid of constant naval and air support, the five separate landing sectors were linked.

Visit the American Cemetery

The vast 170-acre *American Cemetery and Memorial*, with its panoramic view of *Omaha Beach*, is a fitting spot for a cemetery dedicated to the Americans who lost their lives during the liberation of France. This breathtakingly beautiful, peaceful and solemn cemetery is lovingly cared for by the people of Normandy. A winding trail leads down to the beaches.

Here lie the graves of 9,386 American soldiers known to have died at Normandy. Names of another 1,557, whose bodies were never recovered, are inscribed on a memorial wall in the *Garden of the Missing*. Also buried in this cemetery are two of President Theodore Roosevelt sons, Teddy Roosevelt, Jr., recipient of the *Medal of Honor*, and his brother, Quentin, who lost his life in World War I.

The Visitor's Center houses an informative museum, with exhibits that illustrate the personal side of war, highlighting stories of individuals who fought here. A moving film features men who wrote to their families during the war, many of whom died in France.

As you walk from row to row of perfect marble markers, with the sounds of the sea crashing on the beach below, and a cool breeze blowing off the water, you will come to grasp the magnitude of this turning point in human history.

Walk to the D-Day Monument on Omaha Beach

Walk down the winding path to the beach, then west (left). Look back up at the cliffs to better appreciate the bravery and commitment of the soldiers who fought here, and to contemplate the daunting task they faced.

Continue along the beach, or the road that parallels the beach (*rue de la 2ème Division US*), for about 15 minutes, until you reach the remarkable *D-Day Monument* at the ocean's edge.

Pause for Drinks and a Snack at Restaurant l'Omaha

Restaurant l'Omaha
Rue du 116eme Regiment USA, Saint-Laurent-sur-Mer, (0)2-31-22-41-46

From the *D-Day Monument* it will be a short walk to *l'Omaha Restaurant* for a drink and snack at an outdoor table before you call a taxi to take you "home" to Bayeux. Walk away from the beach for 2 minutes, turning right on *rue du 116eme Regiment USA*.

Pause here for a well-needed break to enjoy the wonderful view from the terrace, and to process all you have seen and experienced today. The local cider served here is made right up the road, and is very good.

Taxi Back to Peaceful Bayeux

Call a taxi to pick you up at *Restaurant l'Omaha* for the 12-mile drive back to peaceful Bayeux. Make an effort to engage your driver in conversation on the way. He may have an interesting viewpoint, or even family memories and stories, to add to your day.

After such an intense day, make it a point to treat yourself to some lounging time, and maybe a walk along the river, during your free time before dinner.

Dinner at La Rapiere in Old Town

You have reservations for a relaxing dinner at *La Rapiere* on the pedestrian street (53 *rue St. Jean* (0)2-31-21-05-45), or at the less expensive *Au Petit Bistrot* (*31 Ter Rue Larcher* (0)2-31-92-30-08).

La Rapiere is an atmospheric restaurant that is housed in a late-1400s mansion, with stone walls and large wooden beams. It specializes in Norman cuisine such as terrines, duck, and veal with Camembert. There are three fixed-price menus (€29–€52), as well as a la carte options. The food is excellent, and worth the splurge.

At the lower cost option, *Au Petit Bistrot* the Menus start at €23.

Day 11 (Tuesday): Caen Memorial Museum

Before You Set Off for the Day:

Make lunch reservations for 12:30 pm at *La Terrasse Restaurant* at the *Memorial Museum*. (0)2-31-06-06-00.

Make dinner reservations for 7:30 or 8:00 pm in Bayeux at: *Le*

> *Conquerant (38–40 rue de Nesmond;* (0)2-31-10-36-02) OR *Le Volet qui Penche,* along the river *(3 Passage de L'islet;* (0)2-31-21-98-54).

Today will be another intense day, starting with the brief train ride to Caen. Much of the day will be devoted to the thoughtfully arranged *Caen Normandy Memorial Center for History and Peace,* built on top of the underground headquarters of General Richter, commander of the 716th German infantry division. Here you will "enter" history, and come to understand it in a whole new light.

After 3–4 intense hours in the *Memorial Museum,* "experiencing" the devastation and suffering of invasion, occupation, and eventual liberation, with a pause midway for lunch and a walk in the Memory Gardens, you will take the bus back to the 11th century, to spend more time in the Vaugueux district you visited two days ago.

Or you may opt to take an earlier train "home" to Bayeux to visit the *Museum of the Battle of Normandy,* the *Museum of Art & History,* or the *Lace Museum,* or to stop by a shop that has caught your eye during your time in Bayeux.

Train to Caen, then Tram & Bus to the Memorial Museum

This morning, you will head back to the now-familiar *Bayeux Gare* (train station) to take the short train ride to Caen.

8:37AM	8:53AM	0hr	SNCF
Bayeux	Caen	16min	Intercités 3302

9:20AM	9:38AM	0hr	SNCF
Bayeux	Caen	18min	TER 52614

187

Walk out to the first shelter and take either Tram A or B in the direction of the old town (*Direction Campus 2* for *Line A. Direction St. Clair* for *Line B*), leaving every 4 minutes. Get off at the 5th tram stop—*Quatrans.*

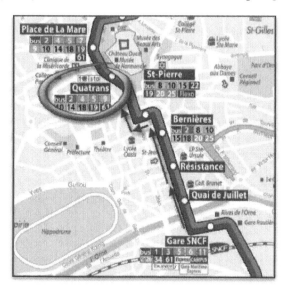

Spot the bus stop and take *Bus #2* in *Direction La Maladrerie.* If you have any confusion or misgivings as the bus pulls up, politely ask your fellow riders or the driver if this is the bus to the *"Mémorial de Caen."* Remember to validate your ticket when you board the tram and *again* on the bus when you transfer.

A second option to get to the *Memorial Museum* is to take a taxi, a ride of 2.3 miles, and arrange to be picked up again at around 3:00 pm.

A Little History of Caen During World War II

The German command center for Normandy was located in an underground bunker in Caen. So it is not surprising that the city was completely destroyed during the hundred days of battle following the Normandy landings. During this massive assault on "Fortress Europe," that ultimately involved a total of 3 million men, the local residents of Caen paid a heavy price, along with the liberating forces. All across Normandy, civilians were trapped by these war efforts and crushed by the bombs. More than 20,000 inhabitants of Normandy were killed during the liberation, and towns were razed to the ground in the massive bombing attacks.

To quote from the website for the *Mémorial de Caen:* "The war years taught people to live in a daily atmosphere of blind violence, inhuman treatment, racial hatred, aggression, rule bending and lawless behavior that had lost all power to surprise. The trivialization of all that is worst in us is part of the second world war's tragic heritage."

Have the Full Experience of the Caen Mémorial Museum

Caen Mémorial Museum

Esplanade Général Eisenhower. (0)2-31-06-06-44

Closed on Mondays.

Open: 9:30 am to 6:00 pm.

Cost: €19 (€16.50 reduced rate). *Audio guide*: €4/person. Reduced rates for: seniors (60+), students, children (10+), teachers, and soldiers. Free for veterans, children under 10, unemployed, disabled, journalists, and tourism staff.

If you purchased a *Twin Ticket* when you were at the *Arromanches 360 Museum* yesterday, you will be able to walk right in and skip the line. You may want to add the audio guide, which is excellent and will bring your visit to life. Watch the ticket line to purchase the audio guide when the line is relatively short.

Today's visit is best broken into segments, with a break at the museum restaurant. One possible schedule for your visit is to:

- 10:00 am showing of the *Jour J* ("*D-Day*") movie. Arrive at least 10 minutes before the show starts.

- Follow the sign marked "*Begin Visit Here*" ("*Debut de la Visite*"), and enter the downward "spiral" that takes you from the end of World War I into the devastation of World War II.

- Meet up for an early lunch break before noon, followed by a walk through the *Memorial Gardens*.

- Then reenter the exhibits where you left off for another hour or so of immersion. Plan to meet around 2:00 pm in the gift shop or beneath the airplane suspended in the lobby.

- OPTIONAL: Visit the "Hall of Peace," with exhibits where many different cultures define their concept of peace.

- OPTIONAL: Visit General Richter's underground command post bunker at the foot of the Memorial.

The Movies

Jour J ("*D-Day*") movie

Show times: 10:00 am to 5:30 pm, starting every 30 minutes (arrive at least 10 minutes before the show).

Jour J ("*D-Day*") is a powerful 15-minute film dramatizing the build up to the landings. By using dual images, the movie shows both the German and the Allied forces on the eve of the invasion.

The Descent into Chaos

Note the "*Debut de la Visite*" ("*Start of Visit*") signs to your left as you enter the museum. This downward spiral draws you "helplessly downward into the abyss." Beginning with the tentative peace at the end of World War I, your descent will take you through the stirrings and sequence of events that led to World War

II. A series of media displays—magazine covers, newspaper clippings, video footage—demonstrates the "gradual unhinging of a world that had just found peace."

The peace that was negotiated after World War I in the *Treaty of Versailles*, and guaranteed by the *League of Nations*, was swiftly challenged and threatened by the rise of totalitarian governments. As you descend the curving ramp, you will witness a Germany trapped in an increasing spiral of debt and economic misery. These hardships spread to the rest of Europe, with severe impact on Wall Street in 1929. This set in motion a chain of cause and effect that precipitated the "disintegration of the ideal of peace," the rise of Hitler, and the Second World War.

You will see amazing footage that chronicles the Nuremberg rallies in the 1920s and 30s, the rise of fascism, the Japanese invasion of Manchuria, the financial crash of Germany, and Hitler's being named *Chancellor of the Third Reich* in 1933.

At the bottom of the spiral, you will view exhibits, documents and photographs that display the rise of Nazism—a force that "seemed completely unstoppable at the time." You will enter a "dark sphere, resonating with the distorted voice of Hitler, accompanied by the sound of marching boots."

You will pass through exhibits that depict the "Phony War," where a weary France gathered what remained of its forces behind the *Maginot Line*, and engaged in a "strategy of waiting." This was followed by a brief but violent month of actual fighting that culminated in French defeat in June 1940. German forces arrived in an undefended Paris on June 14, 1940.

In a circular room, you will stand surrounded by woods, listening to actual recordings of voices from the train car where France signed its terms of surrender. Under the terms of this armistice, Germany would occupy the north and west of France, Italy would control a small Italian occupation zone in the south-east, and the remaining unoccupied zone, the *zone libre*, would be governed by the French Vichy government, led by the French Marshal Pétain.

As you proceed through "France in the Dark Years"— the four years of the Nazi occupation—you will be faced with the range of options available to the occupied citizens of France... Disobey? Resist? Wait? Collaborate? You will experience the French feeling of helplessness "as onlookers of the barbarity."

Film Clips to See

Pause to watch the films throughout the exhibition area, including:

- Kristallnacht ("night of broken glass"), 1938.

- Hitler's speech of January 30, 1939.

- Pogrom in Lvov, Poland, 1941.

- Inauguration of *The Jew and France Exhibition* in Paris, 1941.

- Siege of Leningrad, 1941–1944.

- German propaganda film of the Warsaw ghetto, 1942.

- Goebbels's speech on total war, 1943.

- Dutch Jews departing for the death camps.

- Battle of Britain.

- Interviews with Holocaust survivors.

Stop for lunch before you begin looking through the *D-Day Landings* and *Battle of Normandy* sections of the museum. Your reservations are for 12:30 pm. By now you will need to take a break!

Lunch Break & Memorial Gardens

Enjoy your lunch at *La Terrasse*, sitting outdoors, if the weather cooperates. *Les Menus* start at €15.50. Then take a walk in the Memorial Gardens as part of your break before you return to see the rest of the Memorial.

D-Day Landings & the Battle of Normandy

Here you will see displayed every detail of the *Invasion of Normandy*, starting on the night of June 5th when airborne troops parachuted down, supported by bombers who pounded the German coastal artillery batteries. Meanwhile, an armada of 5000 ships, including a thousand battleships, crossed the English Channel to take their positions along the beaches.

These strategic maneuvers went undetected by the Germans who had lost several strategic radar stations over the past few weeks, and were being battered by a still-raging storm. And so the surprise was total when, at 5:45

am, the battleships opened fire on the Atlantic Wall defenses, and landing craft transported the first wave of assault troops toward the beaches.

The *Battle of Normandy* was expected to last only a few weeks, but went on for 100 days, finally ending on September 12th. By the end of this 100 days, 20,000 inhabitants of Normandy had been killed—a third of all the French civilians killed during the entire war. The city of Caen endured a month-long siege before it was finally liberated on July 9th, when Canadian and British troops entered the city after a frontal attack and heavy aerial bombing.

American troops broke through enemy lines to the west of Saint-Lô, opening up a passageway. Armored divisions swept through the breach and overran the German armies, forcing their retreat across the Seine, then back across the German border.

General Richter's Command Center Bunker

Under the *Caen Memorial Museum* lies a former quarry that was once used as a firing range by the French Army. This rock-bound citadel was converted

to a German command headquarters in 1943 under General Wilhelm Richter, commander of the 716th German infantry division.

A tunnel was dug into the limestone rock, measuring 3 meters tall and 70 meters long (think of a 10-foot high tube reaching underground for ¾ the length of a football field). A power generator, water cistern, and ventilation system were installed, as well as transmission technology. The three entrances to this command post were defended by a small garrison of troops, and blocked by armored doors that were embedded with automated machine guns that stood ever at the ready.

Within the thick limestone shell of the bunker, officers, secretaries, telephonists, and cartographers worked constantly. During the *Battle of Normandy*, the Germans also used the bunker as a shelter for troops and later a makeshift hospital.

The Allies learned about this structure from information provided by the French Resistance. On June 23ʳᵈ, the Germans abandoned the bunker, and on July 9ᵗʰ Canadian soldiers took possession of the premises.

Take Bus #2 Back to the Historic Center of Caen

When you are ready to return to town, catch *Bus #2* across the street from the Museum. Remember to revalidate your pass as you board the bus. Get off the bus at the *Quatrans* stop.

As you get off the bus, look at the half-timbered *Maison des Quatrans* in front of you. Built by Jean Quatrans in the late 14th century, this is the oldest timber-framed house remaining in Caen today. Confiscated by the British in 1417 and given to an English knight, the *Quatrans House* was rebuilt in the late 15th century. Today it houses the *Association for "Music in Normandy"* and the *International Institute for Human Civil Rights and Peace*.

Head for the Vaugueux

Walk along the castle wall to the Vaugueux area, a dry valley below the rocky outcrop on which *William the Conqueror* established his castle. Pause a minute to get your bearings. You are on *rue de Geôle*. Keeping the castle on your left, walk to the corner and follow the castle wall, turning left on *rue Montoir Poissonnerie*, then left on *Avenue de la Liberation*.

194

Cross the street on the pedestrian crosswalk, then walk left, then right, then left, circling around to *rue du Vaugueux,* a short, quiet, but very pretty street in the historic center, with buildings dating back to the *Middle Ages.* This popular area is worth visiting, both for its history and because it has retained its mediaeval charm.

Take a Café Break in the Vaugueux Quarter

Find yourself an outdoor table at *O Chato* (28 rue du Vaugueux. (0)2-31-94-35-70). This will be your chance to relax, decompress and absorb all that you have seen today. Or select another café or restaurant with outdoor tables, and find a seat outside.

Head Back to the Shopping Street, Rue St. Pierre

If some of the Caen shops you wanted to visit were closed when you walked along *rue St. Pierre* two days ago, or if you just ran out of time, take an hour or so now for more shopping before you head back to the train station.

If you would prefer, head back to Bayeux early to visit the *Museum of the Battle of Normandy,* the *Museum of Art & History,* or the *Lace Museum,* or to stop by one or two final shops in Bayeux. This will be your final evening in Bayeux, so you will know by now what you most want to do.

Catch the Tram, then the Train Back to Bayeux

Then take the Tram back to the station in time for your 15–20 minute train ride to Bayeux. You will be many train schedule options between 5:00pm and 6:00pm, including these:

5:00PM Caen	**5:16PM** Bayeux	0hr 16min	SNCF Intercités 3311
5:29PM Caen	**5:45PM** Bayeux	0hr 16min	SNCF TER 52817
5:35PM Caen	**5:55PM** Bayeux	0hr 20min	SNCF TER 52733
5:55PM Caen	**6:11PM** Bayeux	0hr 16min	SNCF TER 52131

Last Evening in Bayeux

Tonight will be your final evening in the sweet little town of Bayeux, your home for the past four days. You will have made reservations in advance at the restaurant of your choice, at: *Le Conquerant* (*38–40 rue de Nesmond*; (0)2-31-10-36-02) OR *Le Volet qui Penche*, along the river.

Enjoy yourself. Relax. Reflect on the many experiences you have had, as well as your responses to them. These few days have been intense and compelling, not soon to be forgotten.

Tomorrow you will leave for Paris.

CHAPTER 8:
Now Off to Paris, City of Lights

And now you are off to Paris, a city that is beautiful and romantic, as well as fascinating. You will quickly discover why Paris is the city most visited in all the world.

By the end of the day today, you will have gained an overview of Paris, and will know your way around your own neighborhood. You will have cruised the Seine, from Notre Dame to the Eiffel Tower and back, noting key sights along the river, many of which you will return to later.

As the lights on the bridges come on this evening, you already will have begun to love this incomparable city and to make it your own, with hopes, or even plans, to return to it again and again.

Day 12 (Wednesday): To the Isles, Birthplace of Paris

> **Before You Set Off for the Day:**
>
> Make reservations for a 12:30 pm lunch at an outdoor table at *Brasserie Esmeralda* (*15 rue Lamartine*; (0)1-42-81-58-08), across from the buttresses of *Notre Dame*.
>
> Make 7:00 pm dinner reservations at *Le Flore en L'Ile* (*42 Quai Orleans*; (0)1-43-29-88-27) on the smaller island, Ile Saint-Louis.

As you board the train to *Paris St. Lazare*, you will say farewell to small medieval French towns, and prepare yourself for the dazzle and sensory abundance of Paris, your home for the next four nights. Immediately after you arrive and check into your accommodations, you will set out to learn your way around "your neighborhood," then head off to lunch on *Ile de la Cité*, with a view of the buttresses of *Notre Dame*.

The rest of the day you will spend on the two small islands in the Seine, *Ile de la Cité* and *Ile St.-Louis*. The larger of these, *Ile de la Cité*, is where Paris had its beginnings as a small fishing village, settled by Celtic tribes known as the *Parisii* during the third century BC.

In 55 BC the Romans destroyed and sacked this settlement, then rebuilt the town to their own design, with forum, theater, baths, and arena (used for circuses, theatrical shows and gladiator fights) on the *Left Bank*, and a temple on the island (where Notre Dame now stands).

Take the Train to Paris

Plan to catch an early train from Bayeux. If you leave at 8:37 am, you will arrive in Paris *Gare St. Lazare* before 11 am. During your 2-hour ride between Bayeux and Paris, read ahead in your trip day pages and prepare to hit the ground running when you arrive.

Upon arrival, you will have three immediate goals: 1) find your hotel on the *Left Bank*, 2) start to learn your neighborhood, and 3) locate the *River Seine*. Then you will be off to lunch on *Ile de la Cité*, with a close-up view of *Notre Dame Cathedral*.

Arrive in "Your Neighborhood"

Your home base will be either in the *Latin Quarter* on the *Left Bank* of the Seine, within close walking distance to the river, or on the smaller island in the Seine, *Ile St.-Louis*. By staying near the river, or on the smaller island, you will quickly become oriented and learn to find your way around.

You will be using the river as your primary means of transportation, each day venturing further from your familiar home base as you experience an ever-widening swath of Paris.

Paris is large. But it is made up of smaller neighborhoods, each distinct, located on the *Left Bank* or the *Right Bank* of the Seine. Today you will learn your way around the two Iles in the river. Tomorrow you will add Saint-Germain and the Latin Quarter on the Left Bank.

Friday you will cross the river to the Right Bank, and experience the incomparable Tuileries and Champs-Elysees districts. Saturday will take you to bohemian Montmartre and the lively Marais neighborhood.

Your cruising will begin tonight, as you travel up and down the river admiring Paris at night, aglow with lights, and passing under many of the 37 bridges across the Seine, some of them quite beautiful. Tomorrow you will start using the Batobus ("boat bus") as your main mode of transportation, hopping on and off at will, and beginning to derive a clear sense of where you are, what is where, and in which direction you need to go to get there.

Where You Will be Staying on the Left Bank

When you selected your accommodations in Paris, you were advised that Paris is an excellent place to splurge a bit. So you will be staying in a superb location on the *Left Bank*, near Notre Dame, or on *Ile St.-Louis*. The additional expense will be well worth it.

By staying within a 3-5 minute walk of the river, you will be well located to come and go by foot or by boat as you visit the famous sights of Paris— Notre Dame, St. Chapelle, d'Orsay, the Louvre, the Arc de Triomphe, the Eiffel Tower. And by using the river as your main transportation route, the getting there will be as rich an experience as the arriving.

You will be able to walk out your door and stroll along the Seine, pausing at the book stalls. The delightful open air market at *place Maubert* on *Boulevard Saint-Germain* will be minutes away, where you can purchase cheese and fruit, and perhaps a brightly colored scarf or tie, or one of those quintessentially French striped pullovers. In the evenings, you will venture back out to stand on a bridge watching the river boats and the lights, or to stop in for a drink on a boat bar along the river.

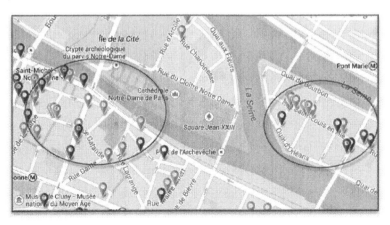

To ensure that you will have the best choice of places to "call home" during your stay in Paris, you will need to book your room or apartment well in advance, hopefully as much as 6-8 months before your trip. Use the *Map View* feature on www.booking.com to explore your options by hovering over the markers in the best locations, then clicking to follow the links to the details about hotels or apartments that look interesting.

Apartments can be even better options than hotels, giving you your own kitchen, sitting and dining areas, and opening up the possibility of shopping the markets and eating at "home" when you wish to. Using www.booking.com, you will be able to manage all of your bookings, including apartments. And if you select lodgings that offer free cancellation, you will be able to make adjustments as needed.

Some Full Experience Places to Stay

One example of an interesting hotel in a superb location on the Left Bank is *Hôtel Les Rives de Notre-Dame* (15 Quai Saint-Michel. (0)1-43-54-81-16), across the river from *Sainte-Chapelle* and 4 minutes from *Notre Dame*. The hotel has only 10 rooms total, each charmingly decorated in traditional Parisian style. Room sizes are typical for hotel rooms in central Paris— small! (161 square feet for a standard room; 226 square feet for superior).

Another excellent choice of "home-base" in Paris is *Hôtel de Lutece* (*65 rue Saint Louis en l'Ile*. (0)1-43-26-23-52), on the smaller island, *Ile Saint-Louis*, within a 4-minute walk to *Notre Dame*. Housed in a beautiful 17th-century building, with a lovely lobby and stone fireplace, *Hôtel de Lutece* offers 23 charming soundproofed and air-conditioned rooms (145 square feet for a standard room; 161 square feet for superior).

A studio apartment option on *Ile Saint-Louis* is *Appartement des Deux Ponts* (*9 rue des Deux Ponts*), with a view of the Seine, and 700 meters from Notre-Dame. The apartment features exposed beams and a fully equipped kitchenette, with dishwasher and microwave.

Additional Options

Hôtel des Deux-Iles (*59 rue Saint-Louis En L'ile*. (0)1-43-26-13-35). Located on *Ile Saint-Louis* in a 17th century building, with *Notre Dame* only 5 minutes away. This hotel has slightly larger standard rooms (194 square feet) for the money, and is in a superb location.

Hôtel le Notre Dame Saint Michel (1 Quai Saint Michel). On the banks of the Seine, near *Petit Pont.* A charming boutique hotel, with stunning views of *Notre Dame.*

Hôtel le Clos de Notre Dame (22 rue de l'Hirondelle). Rooms feature exposed beams and stone walls. 5 minutes from *Notre-Dame.*

Relais Hotel du Vieux Paris (9, rue Git-le-Coeur). A boutique hotel near the *Seine, Place Saint-Michel* and *Notre Dame Cathedral.* Rooms have unique decorations, featuring exposed wooden beams.

Hotel Saint-Louis en L'Ile (75 rue Saint-Louis en L'ile). Located 800 feet from *Notre Dame,* with visible stone walls, old terra cotta and oak beams, and an elevator.

Take Your Orienteering Walk-About

After checking in, begin your walk-about to find the river and locate your nearest shops for wine, cheese, bread and deli.

As you walk around, learn your immediate surroundings—your own street, the connecting streets at each corner of your street, and the direction of the river. In the process, pick a nearby café to be your designated meeting spot when you go off in separate directions.

Next begin to learn your bridges (ponts). Start by finding the bridge nearest your hotel that crosses over to the larger of the Iles, *Ile de la Cité.* Later you will expand your range of bridges, locating the bridge that connects *Ile de la Cité* to *Ile St.-Louis,* then the bridges that cross from each of the two Iles to the *Right Bank.* While walking across the bridges, you will identify the docks where the cruise boats and the Batobus stop.

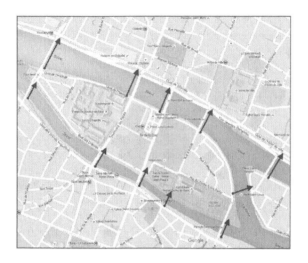

A Word to the Wise to Avoid Pickpockets

Paris is a safe city, but pickpocketing remains a problem, particularly in crowded areas such as the metro and around popular tourist attractions such as the *Eiffel Tower* and the *Sacre Coeur Basilica*. Pickpockets are known to operate in areas frequented by tourists, and use fairly predictable strategies that target the unaware. By learning what these strategies are, taking a few key precautions, and remaining vigilant at all times, you will be protected from pickpockets. For more about traveling safely, read the *"How to Stay Safe While Traveling"* section in Chapter 10.

Walk Past Notre Dame for Lunch at Brasserie Esmeralda

> *Brasserie Esmeralda*
>
> *5 rue Lamartine*; (0)1-42-81-58-08

Make your way to the river, and cross the bridge to *Notre Dame Cathedral* on the larger of the two islands, *Ile de la Cite*.

Stop part way across the bridge to watch the boats along the river. Look back at the Left Bank to locate the landing where you will be boarding the *Bateaux Parisiens* cruise later this evening. Also locate the other landing where the Batobus will drop you off each day when you return from your day's explorations. And look for the boat bar so that you can come back later.

Pause in front of *Notre Dame,* looking up at its façade and towers. This

202

massive structure was begun back in the 11th century, and took two centuries to complete. The thin walls and lovely stained glass windows of this Gothic-style cathedral made it vulnerable to collapse from the weight of the roof pushing the walls outward. Flying buttress (arched exterior supports) were added to brace the walls, making it one of the first buildings in the world to use external buttresses.

You will be back later to spend more time at the cathedral, and to venture inside. But you have 12:30 pm lunch reservations at *Brasserie Esmeralda* (*15 rue Lamartine*), and you are probably ready for sustenance and fine wine at this point! So head for your outdoor lunch behind the cathedral, with an up-close view of the buttresses and the bridge that crosses to *Ile Saint-Louis*. Celebrate your arrival in Paris.

To reach *Brasserie Esmeralda,* walk past Notre Dame and turn right, keeping the cathedral on your immediate right. This street is called *rue du Cloitre Notre Dame* ("street of the *Notre Dame* cloister"), a busy little street with an assortment of shops and cafés. As you walk along, notice cafés or shops you may want to return to later. You will walk the full length of *Notre Dame*, passing the buttresses at the back and the lovely park behind the cathedral. Your destination is on your left, almost at the end of the island. If you are coming from *Ile Saint-Louis, Brasserie Esmeralda* is immediately on your right after you cross the bridge.

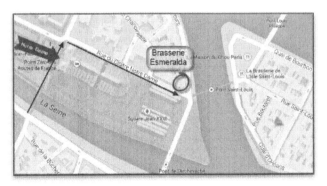

Order escargot with a salad, or the excellent onion soup with a "Crepe Esmeralda" (ham, cheese and tomato). Save room for sorbet, or plan to come back for desert later.

While you sip wine and wait for your food to arrive, look around you and reconcile your position with your map of the city. Note how the *River Seine* bisects Paris, with two islands in the river, and bridges that connect the islands to each shore—the *Left Bank* and the *Right Bank*—and also to each other. By fully understanding this geography of the islands and the river, you will begin to feel "at home" in Paris, and Paris will be yours, in all its glory.

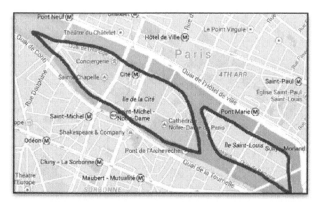

From where you sit, look across the bridge—*Pont Saint-Louis*—to the smaller island. You will be crossing this bridge this evening to enjoy dinner at *Le Flore en L'Ile* (*42 Quai Orleans*; (0)1-43-29-88-27). If you have not already booked your table for this evening, call the *Le Flore en L'Ile* to book an outdoor table for 7 pm (19:00). Or take a few minutes after lunch to cross the bridge and make your reservations in person. Make note of how to come back here tonight.

As you enjoy your lunch, consider whether you may want to return here to *Brasserie Esmeralda* tomorrow morning, when not many people are out and about, for a typical French breakfast of coffee and a fresh croissant. Also, since you and your travel companion(s) now know how to find your way here, consider using this as one of your meeting spots when you set out independently for shopping or other individual activities.

Walk Quai aux Fleurs to the Marche aux Fleurs

After lunch, walk left toward the *Right Bank*, rounding the tip of the island to the *Quai aux Fleurs*. As you walk along this side of the island, pause to watch the boats cruise by, and to look across to the *Right Bank*. *Quai aux Fleurs* becomes *Quai de la Corse* after you pass *Pont d'Arcole*.

When you see *Pont Notre Dame* ahead on your right, look to your left for the green metal pavilions of the *Marché aux Fleurs*—flower market—open daily from 8:00 am to 7:30 pm.

Dating back to 1808, the picturesque *Marché aux Fleurs* is an absolute and total delight, offering spectacu-
lar displays of beautiful plants
of each season. On Sundays the
*Bird Market (le Marché aux
Oiseaux)* is added, showcasing
vibrant and rare species of all
types, with all the accessories to
go with them. Stroll through the
delightful selections of exquisite
orchids, exotic cacti, and vivid
hibiscuses. Check out the shops
for accessories. Find the garden
elves. Photograph the flowers.

Continue Walking Along the River to the Island's End

As you leave the *Marché aux Fleurs*, continue your walk along the river. The imposing building you pass on your left is the *Conciergerie*, where Marie Antoinette and many others spent their final days before losing their heads. *Place Dauphine* on your left, opening to *Square du Vert-Galant*, brings you to the other tip of the island.

Pause to admire the statue of Henri IV. From the end of the island, look down the river to spot the *Louvre* on the *Right Bank* and *d'Orsay* on the *Left Bank*. You will see these again this evening during your river cruise. And you will visit them both, *d'Orsay* tomorrow and the *Louvre* the day after.

View the Stained Glass Windows of Sainte-Chapelle

 TIME TARGET (confirm these times):

Visit Sainte-Chapelle by ***4:00 pm***

Sainte-Chapelle
8 Boulevard du Palais; (0)1-53-40-60-80
Open weekdays: 9:30 am – 1:00 pm, 2:15 pm – 6:00 pm. Last admission 30 minutes before closing.
Open weekends: 9:30 am – 6:00 pm.
Cost: 10€ or Paris Museum Pass. Free for under 18.

Walk around the tip of the island, and along *Quai des Orfèvres* on the *Left Bank* side of the island, back toward *Notre Dame*. Turn left on *boulevard du Palais* heading for the small royal chapel of *Sainte-Chapelle*.

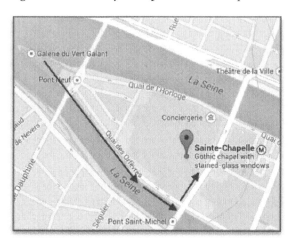

Sainte-Chapelle is an ethereal treasure of Gothic architecture hailed as "one of the greatest architectural masterpieces of the Western world." Worshippers in the Middle Ages considered this chapel to be a "gateway to Heaven." Here you will see stained glass that virtually surrounds you in color and light, preserved since the 13th century, some of loveliest in all the world. This is truly an experience you will carry in your mind's eye for life.

Louis IX built this splendid chapel as a shrine to house the *Crown of Thorns* he acquired from the Emperor of Constantinople in 1239. The king later added to the shrine a fragment of Christ's cross that he purchased in 1241. Reputedly Louis paid nearly three times as much for these relics as he did to construct the chapel.

Purchase and Use Your 4-Day Paris Museum Pass Here

Before you visit *Sainte-Chapelle*, cross the street from the entrance to purchase your *4-day Museum Pass* in the small tourist shop, *Souvenirs et Services*, at *5 Boulevard du Palais*, next to the café, *Les Deux Palais* (open Monday through Friday from 7:30 am to 7 pm; Saturday and Sunday from 10 am to 7 pm). The best plan will be to divide and conquer, with one person in your party walking over to *Souvenirs et Services* to buy your passes, and the other claiming a place in the entrance line for *Sainte-Chapelle*.

The *4-day Museum Pass* will be extremely valuable to you throughout your stay in Paris because it will: 1) save you money, 2) allow you to move to the head of the line at most museums and sights, and 3) make it easy to decide whether or not to enter a museum or other sight, since your entry already will be paid for.

Although your *Paris Museum Pass* will allow you to skip the line at the ticket office at *Saint-Chapelle*, you still will need to join the line on *boulevard du Palais* in order to pass through the security check-point. Be aware that access to *Sainte-Chapelle* is controlled by the gendarmerie, and it is strictly forbidden to be in possession of any pointed or sharp metal instruments such as knives or scissors. So don't forget to leave your cheese knife back in your room!

Consider Returning for a Concert

The *Souvenirs et Services* shop also sells concert tickets for *Sainte-Chapelle*, if you plan to return. The chapel is the venue for over 100 classical music performances each year. If you have the option of attending a concert at *Sainte-Chapelle*, make this a priority. If there's anything more stunning than viewing the purple and blue glow of all this stained glass, it is sitting for an hour surrounded by all this beauty while listening to lovely music. Concerts begin at 7 pm and 8:30 pm. Most famous of the classical concerts in *Sainte-Chapelle* is Vivaldi's *Four Seasons*.

If you decide to return for a concert, today's visit to *Sainte-Chapelle* could be just a walk by, since you will have ample time during the concert to enjoy the beauty of this chapel at your leisure while listening to classical music performed by excellent soloists and ensembles. When you attend a concert here, plan to arrive at least 45 minutes before concert time to be close to the front of the line and get good seats. To plan in advance, and to be certain you will be able to purchase tickets for the concert of your choice, check the concert schedule at *http://www.classictic.com*, and buy tickets before you leave on your trip.

Look Through the Gates at Palais de Justice

After visiting *Sainte-Chapelle*, continue walking along *Boulevard du Palais*. Peer through the massive golden gates at the impressive courtyard of the *Palais de Justice*. This site has been occupied since Roman times. *Palais de Justice* served as the seat of royal power until Charles V moved his royal court to the Marais area during the 14th century.

Pause at Brasserie Les Deux Palais

If you are ready for a break before you continue on to *Notre Dame*, cross the street to *Brasserie Les Deux Palais* and find an outdoor table to enjoy a snack or a glass of wine here.

View the Exterior of Notre Dame

Continue down the pedestrian street, *rue de Lutèce*, toward *Notre Dame*. Turn right along *rue de la Cité*, and left past the *Crypte Archeologique* (open 10 am to 6 pm, admission: €4 or free with the *Museum Pass*), where you may wish to return later to see the ruins, dating back to the Romans and before, that were discovered under the square.

In the square in front of the cathedral, find a place to sit for a few minutes to take in its full grandeur. *Notre Dame* represents a thousand years of history, but it is still a living place of worship. Look up at the row of statues of the *Kings of Judea*, lined up across the façade of the cathedral, under the circular stained-glass window. The heads of these statues are replacements. During the Revolution, a Paris mob, thinking that these were statues of French monarchs, loped off their heads and tossed them on the debris piles from their rampages.

208

These piles of broken stone were sold to a wealthy lawyer as building materials for the foundation for his new home. Being a devout Catholic, the lawyer obeyed church law dictating that religious objects removed from a church must be burned or buried. He had the heads buried, all facing in the same direction. Here they remained, missing and forgotten, for the next 184 years until 1977, when workmen who were enlarging a bank basement accidentally discovered them buried in a wall of plaster. You will see the real heads, and learn more of their fascinating story, when you visit the *Cluny Museum* tomorrow.

Enter Notre Dame, Sit Down and Look Up

> ### *Notre Dame*
>
> ***Open daily:*** 8:00 am – 6:45 pm (7:15 pm Saturdays & Sundays).
>
> ***Cost: Free.*** English audio guides (also French, German, Spanish, Italian, Portuguese, Japanese and Chinese) available at reception.
>
> **Mass Monday to Saturday noon:** *8:00 am, 9:00 am, 12:00 noon, 5:45 pm vespers, 6:15 pm.* Sundays: *8:30 am, 9:30 am, 10:00 am, 11:30 am, 12:45 noon, 5:45 pm vespers, 6:30 pm.*
>
> **Concerts:** Check the *Calendar of Music* at *http://www.musique-sacree-notredamedeparis.fr/*

Make your way to the entrance of *Notre Dame*. Of the two lines in front, the one you want is the line on the right facing the entrance. This line will move quickly as people flow through the massive doors into the vast space inside the vast sanctuary. Check to be certain that you are in the correct line. The slow line is waiting and waiting to climb up the towers, with only a few people allowed entry at a time.

As you move toward the entrance, look up to study the carvings above the door. These carved images were used to communicate to the illiterate masses of the time the stories and warnings in the Bible. "Read" your way through them as best you can.

Once you are inside the cathedral, take a seat. Look around you, including up. Take your time inside the cathedral, moving from one seat to another to experience the full effect of the stunning rose windows, glowing blue and purple, many of them still with their original medieval glass.

If you happen to arrive in time for a late afternoon service (5:45 pm Vespers; 6:15 pm Mass on Monday–Saturday, 6:30 pm Mass on Sunday), stay to hear the mighty organ. This is an organ you will *feel* as well as hear. Check the music schedule, and consider returning later for a concert if at all possible.

Free Time Until Dinner at 7:00 PM

Ooh la la!!! What a day this has been. Now take any time that remains before your 7:00 pm dinner to do whatever you choose. By this point, you likely will have some good ideas about what you would enjoy.

You may just want to head back to your accommodations and relax, possibly purchasing a bottle of wine on your way "home." Maybe you would enjoy wandering the streets of the smaller island, *Ile Saint-Louis*, spotting interesting shops to return to another day.

This also might be an optimum time to lose yourself browsing the stalls (green metal boxes) of the *Bouquinistes*—second-hand booksellers—along the river, in search of something that appeals to you. Or to visit the rose garden behind *Notre Dame*... Or to stop in the middle of a bridge to watch the boats drift by... Or to find a good spot for people watching...

If you have found the *Boat Bar* anchored across from *Notre Dame*, capture a front row seat to watch the parade of activity along the river.

Already you know your way around Paris enough to set yourself loose for a while, and move about at will. Just be certain that you carry with you a copy of your Paris address, as well as your French cell phone, so you can rescue yourself should you wander too far from what is familiar. And always keep in mind which direction to walk to get yourself back to the river (generally downhill).

This is Paris, after all. And *you are here* in this iconic city. Anything you chose to do is likely to be wonderful.

Dinner on the Little Isle

Now take yourself back to the little island, *Ile Saint-Louis*, for your 7:00 pm dinner at *Le Flore en L'Ile* (*42 Quai Orleans*; (0)1-43-29-88-27). Sit at your table watching the sun set over the *Seine* and *Notre Dame*, and possibly the street performers on the bridge. Order the delicious burgers, onion soup, foie gras and/or salad, accompanied by what reviewers term "the best fries ever" and, of course, good wine. This restaurant is also a favorite for breakfast. You may decide to return in the morning.

Plan to finish up dinner by around 9 pm at the latest to allow yourself time to catch the 10 pm cruise (10:45 pm on Friday and Saturday) along the Seine, from *Notre Dame* to the *Eiffel Tower* and back.

Night Cruise on the Seine

 TIME TARGET (confirm these times):

Catch the ***10:00 pm*** cruise (confirm the correct time)

Bateaux Parisiens Seine Cruise
Open daily: 11 am – 10:00 pm, April through June; 11 am – 10:45 pm, July & August).
Cost: 14€ for adults; 6€ for age 3 to 11; children under 3 free.

Tonight you will take a one-hour cruise, with commentary, on *Bateaux Parisiens* (*http://www.bateauxparisiens.com/english.html*), from *Quai de Montebello* (across from *Notre Dame*) to the *Eiffel Tower*, and back. Plan to catch the 10:00 pm boat. But confirm the time your boat is scheduled to depart during the planning phase of your travels, and possibly purchase your tickets in advance of your trip. You also can book your cruise by calling (0)1-76-64-14-45. Sailing times change, so it is essential that you know the your correct departure time.

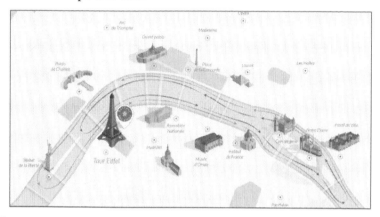

If you purchased and printed your cruise vouchers online in advance of your trip through *http://www.bateauxparisiens.com*, redeem these vouchers at the ticket desk at *Pontoon #3* on *Quai de Montebello* (on the *Left Bank*, across from *Notre Dame*) before boarding. Present your confirmation e-mail to exchange it for your tickets. If you have not already purchased vouchers, buy your tickets directly at the ticket desk before your cruise.

Arrive well in advance of departure time to get an open air seat at the front and have the best views. Try for a seat on the left side of the boat, if possible, to have a clear view of the *Eiffel Tower*. If the evening is a bit chilly, there are also seats in the covered area. Restrooms are available on the boats.

Whether you sit inside and watch the sights from behind the glass, or secure a seat on the upper deck to breathe in the fresh air, you will have panoramic views of the many major sights of Paris that border the river—*Notre Dame*, *d'Orsay*, the *Louvre*, the *Grand Palace* (*le Grande Palais*), and the *Eiffel tower*. And you will gain a good sense of the Seine riverscape, lined with old quays, and crossed by 37 beautiful bridges, including the city's oldest bridge, called the *Pont Neuf* ("New Bridge"), as well as the pedestrian bridge covered in lovers' locks, *Pont des Arts*, and the ornately gilded *Pont Alexandre III*.

Paris is stunningly beautiful at night. You will never forget this experience of seeing Paris illuminated as you drift along the river.

Tomorrow... Art & Markets, Gardens & Palaces

Tomorrow, your second day in Paris, you will awaken with all this remarkable city has to offer at your doorstep, and much to explore and experience. Your focus will be on the *Left Bank—Maubert Market, d'Orsay*, Sainte-Germain and *Latin Quarter* antique shopping, the *Cluny Museum of the Middle Ages*, the *Pantheon* and *Luxemburg Gardens*.

The next day your focus will shift to the *Right Bank*, from the *Louvre* through *Tuileries Gardens* and *l'Orangerie*, down the *Champs-Élysées* to the *Arc de Triomphe*, then back past the *Petit Palais* and on to the *Eiffel Tower*.

On your fourth and final day in Paris, you will head up the hill to *Montmartre* to the artist's square and the *Sacré-Coeur Basilica*, then back down to the *Marais* area, with stops at vintage clothing and other eclectic shops, as you walk to the fountains beside the *Pompidou Center*.

If you are traveling on the recommended 15-day schedule, tomorrow will be Thursday, and you will have no problems. However, if you have altered the schedule, and if any of your remaining three days in Paris fall on a Monday or Tuesday, you may need to shift the order of these days to adjust for museum closings. Of the museums you will be visiting, the Monday or Tuesday closings are:

Monday Closings	Tuesday Closings
D'Orsay	Louvre
Carnavalet	Cluny

Day 13 (Thursday): d'Orsay & the Left Bank

> **Before You Set Off for the Day:**
>
> Make lunch reservations at the *Restaurant of the Musée d'Orsay* (0)1-45-49-47-03) OR *La Frégate (1 rue du Bac.* (0)1-42-61-23-77), beside the Seine.
>
> Make dinner reservations at *Le Jardin du Roy* in the Latin Quarter (*28, rue de la Huchette.* (0)1-40-79-56-01).

A Snapshot of the Day

Today you will visit the open air market at *Place Maubert* in search of treasures and delectables. Then you will board the *Batobus* to travel down the river to *d'Orsay*—the former train station, built for the *1900 World's Fair* at the location along the Seine where *d'Orsay Palace* once stood. Queen Margot, first wife of Henri IV, built *d'Orsay Palace* directly across the river from her former residence, *Louvre Palace,* after the king divorced her and married *Marie Medici.*

D'Orsay is now one of the world's most remarkable art museums, where you will wander through a stunning collection of Impressionism, from Renoir to Monet to van Gogh to Cezanne.

After lunch in the magnificent restaurant of the former *Grand Hotel* of the train station, or at *La Frégate* along the river, you will make your way back to the *Saint-Germain* area for some antique shopping, and a walk through the *Buci Market.* Your walk through *Saint-Germain* will take you to the *Cluny Museum,* housed in what was once a Roman bath. Here you will see the *Lady and the Unicorn* tapestries, as well as the "real" heads from the statues of the *Kings of Judea* above the entrance to *Notre Dame.*

Next you will walk, or possibly bike, deeper into the *Left Bank* to *Luxemburg Palace and Gardens.* This palace was built by the "other wife" of Henri IV, *Queen Marie Medici,* after her husband died. As a Medici, Queen Marie's goal in building *Luxemburg Palace* was to create a palace and gardens for herself that was reminiscent of her beloved Florence.

So this morning you will see the riverside location of Henry's first wife's home, and this afternoon the domain of his second wife, Queen Marie. Decide for yourself which wife had the better location for her palace.

After *Luxemburg Palace*, you will walk or bike to the *Pantheon*, final resting place for a long list of famous figures from history—Voltaire, Rousseau, Victor Hugo, Marie Curie. Then back to the *Latin Quarter* to turn in your bikes before making a quick stop at the famous *Shakespeare & Company* bookshop, followed by a stroll along the river, browsing the stalls for books and memorabilia.

After dining at *Le Jardin du Roy*, in the *Latin Quarter*, you will meander the *Latin Quarter* in search of a *Piano Bar* for some jazz.

Explore the Open Air Market at Place Maubert

If you are following the prescribed schedule, today is Thursday, and you are in luck. Thursday (also Tuesdays and Saturdays) is market day at *Place Maubert* on *Boulevard Saint-Germain* at *rue des Carmes*—next to the *Maubert-Mutualité Métro Station*.

To fully experience life as a Parisian, take every opportunity you have to frequent the open-air markets. There are over 70 outdoor markets in Paris—each its own "monument" of sorts, and worthy of a visit. Parisians have visited these markets since the 1500's, thereby making something of a party out of what otherwise would be routine shopping to purchase food, clothing, household items, and, of course, flowers.

Many of the stall owners at Parisian markets drive hundreds of miles to market their food and wares, some from as far away as Italy. Farmers, bakers, fishermen and other merchants from throughout France sell their products at these markets, and become well known for their specialties.

At these markets you will be able to purchase the finest fresh ingredients, buy a range of delicious food gifts for the gourmets back home, or select fully prepared dishes, from pâtés to roasted chickens. You will enjoy creations by local artisans who are proud of their wares, and love to talk about them… And there will be profusions of flowers… And people-watching.

At *Maubert Market* you'll find great buys on beautiful pashmina or silk scarves and shawls, leather goods, Provençal napkins and tablecloths, herbal-scented soaps and candles, shoes, and clothing (including vintage and Italian).

Behind the market stands are wonderful permanent shops: *Fromagerie* (cheese), *Charcuterie* (cold cooked meats), *Vin* (wine), *Patisserie* (pastry), *Boulangerie* (bakery).

Some important pointers about shopping in Parisian markets:

- Take along a good supply of cash, since most vendors do not accept credit cards. And carry an expandable marketing bag.

- Walk the full length of the market first to pinpoint the best-quality items at the best prices.

- Unless you see a sign that says "service libre" ("free service"), you are not meant to handle the food yourself. Point to what you want to purchase; the vendor will gather your selections together for you.

- In crowded markets, keep your wallet in a safe place, and do not flash money around— pickpocketing is not uncommon.

Take the Batobus to d'Orsay

 TIME TARGET: Aim to catch the Batobus **before 10 am** (check the schedule). Bring along your *Paris Museum Pass.*

Boats run: Every 20 minutes, *10 am–9:30 pm* April to September. Every 25 minutes, 10 am–7 pm September to April. Confirm schedule at *http://www.batobus.com/english/index.htm.*

Cost: 1-day pass €16; €8 for children over age 3; free under 3.

2-day pass €18; €9 for children over age 3; free under 3.

Today you will head toward the river to the *Notre-Dame* stop of the *Batobus* ("*Boat Bus*"), at *Quai de Montebello* on the *Left Bank*, near where you boarded the *Bateaux Parisiens* yesterday evening. On this second ride along the river, you will make nearly the full circuit, this time enjoying the views in daylight, before hopping off at *d'Orsay*. The *Batobus* circuit travels in a counterclockwise loop, making eight stops, three on the *Right Bank* and five on the *Left Bank*.

Along the Right Bank
Hôtel de Ville, close to *Pont d'Arcole*
Louvre, between *Pont du Carrousel* and *Pont Royal*
Champs-Élysées, close to *Pont Alexandre III*
Along the Left Bank
Eiffel Tower, at *Port de la Bourdonnais*
Musée d'Orsay, at *Quai de Solférino*
Saint-Germain-Des-Pres, at *Quai Malaquais*
Notre Dame, at *Quai de Montebello*
Jardin des Plantes, close to *Pont d'Austerlitz*

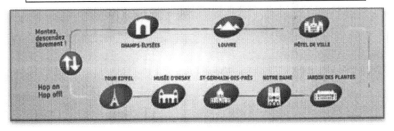

Purchase a 2-day pass. You will be using the Batobus again tomorrow when you visit the Louvre and the Eiffel Tower.

You will have a beautiful ride, with excellent views through the glass roof of the boat, or standing on an outside deck. This will be your opportunity to orient yourself to the layout of Paris in regards to the river, and to learn what is where. After today's ride you will know which way to go on the river to get to where you're going.

Start to Learn Your Bridges

As your boat travels up and down the river, it will pass under a sequence of bridges. Today you will learn to identify five of these.

From where you board at the *Notre Dame* stop, the *Batobus* will travel up river, passing the small island, *Ile Saint-Louis,* on your left and cruising as far as the *Jardin des Plantes* on the *Left Bank,* before turning around to head back down river along the *Right Bank.* Your first stop along the *Right Bank* will be at the *Hôtel de Ville* dock. Pay attention as you stop here, noting the bridges before and after where your boat docks. Tomorrow you will start your day's travel by boarding at this Batobus stop.

Pont d'Arcole

The bridge before the *Hôtel de Ville* stop is *Pont d'Arcole.* Built in 1856, this was the first wrought iron bridge in Paris. The bridge forms a single arch, 80 meters long, connecting the *Ile de la Cité* with the *Right Bank* at *Hôtel de Ville* (Town Hall).

Pont Notre Dame

The bridge after the Batobus stop is *Pont Notre Dame,* also linking *Ile de la Cité* with the *Right Bank.* This bridge is located where the first bridge in Paris was built. But it has been replaced many times.

The 1400s version of the bridge, with 60 houses atop it, 30 on each side, collapsed in 1499 due to structural weaknesses caused by lack of repairs. A stone version of the bridge, built in 1853, was nicknamed *pont du Diable* (Devil's Bridge) because it caused more than 35 water traffic accidents. This hazardous stone bridge was  replaced in 1919 by the metal bridge you see now.

Like *Pont d'Arcole, Pont Notre Dame* is made from metal. To tell these two bridges apart, note that *Pont d'Arcole* is constructed as a single metal arch, while *Pont Notre Dame* has a metal arch in the middle, with a stone arch on each end, like bookends.

Pont Neuf

As you cruise downriver, the next bridge for you to learn is *Pont Neuf.* Although the name "*Pont Neuf,*" means "*New Bridge,*" this is actually the oldest bridge in Paris that is still *in its original form. Pont Neuf* crosses the downstream tip of *Ile de la Cité*, connecting the island to both the *Left Bank* and the *Right Bank.*

Pont Neuf is to recognize, with its lovely stone structure and semicircular bastions (rounded projections) supported by "cutwaters" that project out into the river. These bastions provide wonderful spots to pause along the bridge and look out over the river.

Even easier to remember are all the little heads of bearded men at the bases of the decorative corbels. As you pass under the bridge, look up for a close-up view of these heads.

So far you have learned three bridges:

1. Wrought iron, single arch—*Pont d'Arcole*

2. Iron center arch, with a stone arch on each end—*Pont Notre Dame*

3. Bastions and little heads—*Pont Neuf*

Recognize Your Left and Right Bank Palaces

After your boat passes the western tip of the *Ile de la Cité*, your next stop on the Batobus will be at the *Louvre*. While the boat pauses at the *Louvre* for passengers to disembark and board, look ahead to the *Pont Royal* that crosses between the *Louvre* on the *Right Bank* and *d'Orsay* on the *Left Bank*. These two gargantuan edifices make for quite a story.

Henri IV, known as "Good King Henry," gained the throne through his wife's lineage, not his own. His wife, *Queen Margot*, was the daughter of *Henri II* and *Catherine de Medici*, and the sister of *King Henri III*, who died childless, and passed the throne to Margot's husband, *Henri IV*. As well as gaining her husband the throne, *Margot* also saved Henri's life during the St. Bartholomew's Day massacre.

Apparently this was not enough to sustain the marriage. Margot and Henri (shown below on the left) both kept other lovers, and quarreled frequently. Henri had Margot locked up, then divorced her in 1606, with plans to marry his mistress, *Gabrielle d'Estrées*, mother of his three children.

Since marrying Gabrielle clearly was not a possibility, Henri instead married *Marie de' Medici* of Florence (shown below on the right), entering yet another unhappy marriage. Gabrielle died giving birth to Henri's fourth child, a stillborn son. But Henri continued to keep an "official mistress" even after Gabrielle died.

As second wife, Queen Marie became a sympathetic friend and supporter of first wife, Queen Margot. It was through Marie's urgings that Henri allowed Queen Margot back into his realm. Such were the comings and goings of royal marriages during that period.

The rejected Queen Margot crossed the river from her ex-husband's palace in the Louvre to build a mansion on the opposite bank. This structure was later expanded into a palace—Palais d'Orsay.

With one wife on each side of the river, Henri may have considered it to be something of an advantage that the only way across the river at the time was by ferry. The *Pont Royal* bridge was built some 26 years later in 1632.

Palais d'Orsay was destroyed in 1871 by a fire set by the Communards during their uprising—the same fire that consumed *Tuileries Palace* across the river. Margot's palace sat in ruins for the next 30 years, a highly visible eyesore along the banks of the Seine.

With the World's Fair looming in 1900, the French government was understandably anxious to remove the destroyed palace and replace it with something suitably magnificent. This coincided with the need for a new train terminal in central Paris to serve World's Fair attendees. So the ruins of *Palais d'Orsay* were demolished, and the impressive *Gare d'Orsay*, with an attached 370-room grand hotel, was built in its place.

The new train station combined the vaulted halls of Roman baths with the grandeur of a Basilica—architectural designs that were fashionable at the time. To complete this impressive building in time for the 1900 World's Fair, work continued around the clock, employing 300 workers during the day and 80 at night.

The station's exterior was covered in white limestone to match the prestigious neighborhood and the nearby *Louvre Palace*. Sculptures along the river-front façade represent the principal cities served by the *Compagnie des Chemins de Fer d'Orléans Train Line* that once ran 200 trains a day through this station.

Some 66 years later, in 1966, permission was granted to demolish the now-abandoned train station. This intent was met by such a public outcry that all plans to tear down the derelict building were canceled, and the structure was listed in the Historical Register. Some 20 years later, the now almost

90-year-old former train station was converted to *d'Orsay Museum*, opening in 1986.

While your boat pauses at the Louvre stop, look to your right at the *Louvre*, where you will be returning tomorrow. Then look across the river for your best view of *d'Orsay*, the almost palatial former train station where you are going today. With its two large clocks, it's seven glass arcades, and its allegorical sculptures along the roof, does this look like a train station to you?

Two More Bridges

Pont Royal

The bridge ahead of you is the *Pont Royal*. Note its distinctive design so you will recognize it from now on.

Pont Royal was built in 1632 to replace the Tuileries ferry—the only way to cross the river back when *Henri IV* had a wife on the Right Bank and an ex-wife on the Left.

The original version of this bridge, composed of fifteen arches, was made of wood and very fragile. By 1649, when it was 17-years-old, major repair work was required. Five years later, in 1654, the bridge burned down and was replaced. Two years later, in 1656, it was damaged by flooding, then completely rebuilt in 1660, propped up in 1673, and finally carried away by flood waters in 1684.

The current bridge, completed in 1689, and this time constructed out of stone, was financed by *Louis XIV*, who gave it the name *Pont Royal*.

Pont Alexander III

As you continue your cruise, the next stop will be *Champs-Élysées*. You will be boarding the *Batobus* here tomorrow after your visit to the *Arc de*

Triomphe and *Champs-Élysées*. Note how to get down to the boat dock in preparation for tomorrow.

While the Batobus is stopped, look up at the opulent bridge ahead of you. This is the *Pont Alexander III,* built in time for the 1900 World's Fair, and named after Czar Alexander III to symbolize Russian-French friendship. Atop the bridge are golden statues astride winged horses. These are the mythological "Fames," Art, Science, Commerce and Industry. They are joined by an exuberant collection of cherubs and nymphs.

This bridge is considered to be a marvel of 19th century engineering, with its 20-foot single-span steel arch. It also is thought to be the most extravagantly decorated bridge in Paris.

The Little Statue of Liberty

As your boat crosses the river, then turns back to cruise along the *Left Bank,* look toward the tiny island, *Île des Cygnes* ("Island of Swans") to spot the ¹/₃-scale version of the *Statue of Liberty,* standing 37 feet, 9 inches tall (the NY City statue is 151 feet tall).

An even smaller version of the *Statue of Liberty* now stands inside the entrance to *d'Orsay.* This is Bartholdi's bronze model, created in preparation for building the full-sized statue that stands in New York Harbor—a gift from France to the newly liberated United States of America.

Bartholdi donated his small working model of the statue to the city of Paris in time for the *1900 Exposition Universelle*. It stood in the *Jardin du Luxembourg* until 2012, when the original working model was moved to the entrance of *d'Orsay*, and a replica left in its place in *Jardin du Luxembourg*. Since you will visit both *d'Orsay* and *Jardin du Luxembourg* today, you will have a chance to view all three versions of the statue now standing in Paris.

Hop Off at Musée d'Orsay

As your boat pulls up to the dock at the *Musée D'Orsay* and you hop off, look up at the two huge clocks that decorate the façade. Later when you take a break in the *Café Campana* on the fifth floor of the museum, you will be looking out through the glass of the clock on the right.

Revel in Impressionism at d'Orsay

> ### *Closed Mondays*
>
> Open Tuesday to Sunday: 9:30 am to 6 pm
>
> Open until 9:45 pm Thursdays

Your *Paris Museum Pass* covers entry to *d'Orsay Museum*. This will allow you to use *Entrance C* and skip the ticket line at *Entrance A*. You will pass through a security check on your way in. Coat check is immediately inside the entrance. You will be asked to check long umbrellas or large backpacks. Drop off everything you can do without to lighten your load while you visit the museum.

Descend to Where the Train Tracks Used to Be

As you enter the museum and descend the stairs into the grand hall, look out into the massive glass-roofed space and imagine how it would have appeared to the excited crowds arriving in central Paris by train to attend the *1900 World's Fair*. Pause to look back up at the huge clock that was once a prominent part of the train station.

When you reach the base of the stairs, you will be at the level of the tracks, surrounded by balconies where travelers once stood, observing the comings and goings as they waited for their trains. A conveyor belt once followed a trajectory from tracks to entryway. This was used to carry luggage up from the trains.

The balconies of the former train station are now *Sculpture Terraces*. The grand restaurant, once part of the impressive train hotel attached to the station, has been restored. This is where you will be having lunch in a few hours.

Pause to observe the layout of the Museum, and to form a quick idea of how to organize your visit and where to meet up should you get separated. The museum is arranged on three levels:

- **Ground floor (Floor 0)**—with sculptures where the tracks used to be, and painting galleries opening out on either side of the central area.

- **Second floor**—with sculptures displayed on the terraces, and paintings in the adjoining exhibition galleries. The magnificent *Museum Restaurant* is also located on this floor.

- **Fifth floor**—galleries high above the entrance lobby and along the river. This is where you will find *Café Campana*, with its view out to the river through the glass of the huge clock.

Immerse Yourself in Impressionism on the 5th Floor

Start by taking the escalator up to the large gallery on the 5th floor—*Galerie des Impressionnistes*—devoted to the stunning works of the Impressionists who stirred up the Paris art world in the late 19th century with their vivid colors and non-traditional themes. Here you will find paintings by Monet, Renoir, Manet, Morisot, Degas, Cezanne, Toulouse-Lautrec and others.

Impressionist Paintings	
Monet	29 works exhibited
Renoir	28 works exhibited
Manet	29 works exhibited
Bertha Morisot	4 works exhibited
Degas	31 works exhibited
Toulouse-Lautrec	9 works exhibited
Cézanne	3 works exhibited
Pissarro	9 works exhibited
Mary Cassatt	1 work exhibited
Sisley	4 works exhibited

Time will go quickly as you wander room to room, surrounded by one of the most bountiful displays of well-loved and time-proven artwork in the world. If you decide to separate from your travel companion as you walk among these paintings, set a time to meet again later in the *Café Campana* next to Salle 37 (Room 37) on the 5th Floor.

Being surrounded by this much incredible art can be almost overwhelming. As you let your eye lead you around the rooms, take the time you need to get a full look at each painting that speaks to you. Walk up to these paintings, and give yourself a full minute to take them in before you allow others to step in front of you and block your view.

The museum website, *http://www.musee-orsay.fr/en/visit/welcome.html*, provides the option of planning and printing out in advance your personalized "Trail" through *d'Orsay*. This feature allows you to search the museum's collections by artist and determine which of their paintings are currently on display, and where they are located in the museum. To select the paintings you particularly want to see, click the icon that looks like a folder, and they will be added to your "personal album." Click on the icon that looks like a map to print out your personalized *Trail Plan*, with your choices listed in order by floor and by room.

Van Gogh, Vincent
Portrait de l'artiste
Ⅺ Salle 71

Van Gogh, Vincent
L'église d'Auvers-sur-Oise, vue du chevet
Ⅺ Salle 71

Armed with this map of your visit, you will be sure not to miss seeing any of your top picks, although artwork locations are updated daily before the Museum opens, and some of the specific paintings you are looking for may have moved.

Meet Up in the Café Campana for a Break

Your designated meeting spot will be at the café with the clock, *Café Campana*, on the 5th floor, outside the *Impressionists Gallery*. Set a time to meet at this interesting café, with its outstanding views through the glass of the clock, out across Paris and up to *Sacre Coeur Basilica* in *Montmartre*. This is the clock you noted from the river as your boat docked alongside the museum.

Plan that the first to arrive will get a table and place a prearranged order for everyone. Hot chocolate? Ice cream sundae? Cappuccino? A foot-long chocolate éclair?

When you finish your treat, walk out to the roof-top patio next to the café to enjoy more city views across the river before you return to the museum exhibits with renewed vigor.

Down to the Second & Ground Levels for Sculpture & More Paintings

Now head off in search of the 15 displayed Van Gogh—paintings one of the greatest treasures in the museum. Also seek out the 38 masterpieces painted by Gauguin, Van Gogh's friend, nemesis and short-term house-mate, and reputed to be the cause of the desperation that led Van Gogh to cut off his own ear. These works are mainly located on the ground floor and 2nd floor, in rooms 9, 60, 70, 71 and 72.

Also on the 2nd floor level are the *Sculpture Terraces*. Walk along these terraces to the end of the train station, then back along the other side, entering as many of the additional painting galleries as time allows.

More sculptures await you at the level of the former train tracks, with yet more galleries off to the sides. You may find yourself adding more artwork to visit than you selected for your "Trail."

Lunch at d'Orsay Museum Restaurant or La Frégate

 TIME TARGET: Aim for lunch by 1:30 pm.

Museum Restaurant. (0)1-45-49-47-03
Open: 11:45 am to 5:30 pm Tuesday, Wednesday, Friday, Saturday, Sunday. Open Thursday from 11:45 am to 2:45 pm and 7 pm to 9.30 pm.
La Frégate. 1 rue du Bac. (0)1-42-61-23-77.
Open: 7:00 am – 11:30 pm

You will dine in style in the opulent dining room housed in the restaurant of the former *d'Orsay Hotel*. As an alternative, walk down to, then along, the river to eat outdoors at *La Fregate*. You already will have made your choice for the day and called in your reservations.

Lunch at the d'Orsay Restaurant

The *Museum Restaurant*, now listed as a *Historic Monument*, is still as magnificent as when it first opened to welcome the attendees of the 1900 World's Fair. The painted and gilded ceilings... The huge mirrors at either end... The dazzling chandeliers... The elegant sculptures and décor... Everything about this majestic dining room takes you back in time to the Golden Age.

Food and service at the restaurant are excellent, and the cost is reasonable for such lavish surroundings. "Menus" are great values—€22 for Starter + Main or Starter + Desert, and under €32 for all three (Starter + Main + Desert). For a lighter meal, order a bowl of the cream of mushroom soup, with some fresh bread and a glass of wine.

Lunch at La Frégate, Near d'Orsay

From *Musée d'Orsay*, walk one block back along the Seine to *Pont Royal* and sit outside at *La Fregate*. Named after the frigate that docked under *Pont Royal* during the 1870's Commune era, *La Fregate* is a traditional bistro in true Parisian style, with frescoed ceilings and painted pillars—a pleasure, both for the atmosphere and the food.

You may decide to return here later to dine on sea bass or oyster and shrimp risotto, followed by cheese cake or crème brulée, sitting outside with a view or inside, surrounded by elegance.

Walk Through St. Germain, Away From the River

Now it is time to head in from the river to wander through the high fashion *St-Germain-des-Prés* neighborhood, browsing the fashion boutiques and galleries, with their creative window displays. Later you will walk the winding old cobble-stoned streets of the adjoining *Latin Quarter*, where the environment will shift dramatically from elegant to bohemian, with bookshops and quirky boutiques, cafés and theaters, jazz clubs and bars. These two distinctly different neighborhoods are the "quintessential Paris."

Once a small market village, centered around the historic abbey of *Saint-Germain-des-Prés*, *St-Germain* is one of Paris' most charming neighborhoods, bursting with fine food shops, restaurants, markets and picturesque streets lined with cafés. Wandering down the quiet and quaint side streets is considered by many to be Paris at its best!

Saint-Germain-des-Prés Abbey, with its Romanesque bell tower, was a powerful ecclesiastical complex during the Middle Ages. It stands today as the oldest church in Paris, and a well-known landmark.

Your Walk Begins...

 TIME TARGET: Plan to arrive at the *Cluny Museum* by 4 pm at the latest.

As you leave *d'Orsay*, turn left for a leisurely walk, winding your way over to the *Cluny Museum*, your next stop. Once you have established your sense of direction, feel free to take liberties and meander at will, walking up and down the streets, looking into shop windows, and perhaps pausing here and there in search of treasures.

When you are confident that you know where you are and where you are going, you may wish to separate from your travel companion so that each of you can follow your own interests and pace. Plan to meet up at the *Cluny* at an appointed hour, preferably by around 4:00 pm, to allow you time to enjoy the *Cluny*, and still have time to reach *Luxemburg Gardens* before it closes at dusk.

To ensure you do not become disoriented, always walk *away* from the river and in an up river direction (to your left as you stand with your back to the river) until you reach *Boulevard Saint-Germain,* where your destination is located. By following this general trajectory, you will be able to wander at will and still end up at the *Cluny Museum.* Use the old church, *St-Germain-des-Prés*, as a landmark to keep yourself on track.

Trajectory for Your Walk Toward the Cluny

> ➢ LEFT from the museum to *Rue de Lille.*
>
> ➢ LEFT on *rue de Lille,* passing *Galerie Carole Decombe* and *Arums Gallerie.*
>
> ➢ RIGHT on *rue des Saints-Pères.*

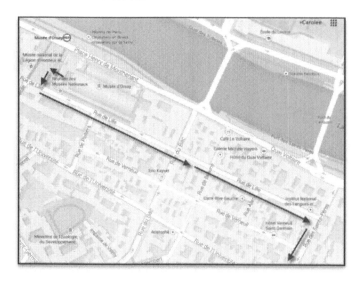

> ➢ LEFT on *rue de l'Université.* Pass *Galerie Seydoux.*
>
> ➢ RIGHT on *rue Bonaparte.* Pass *Chocolat Richart.*
>
> ➢ LEFT on *rue de l'Abbaye.*

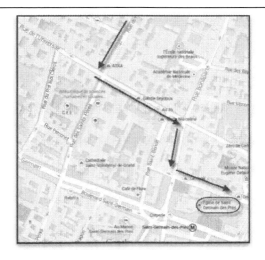

> LEFT on *rue de Buci*. Cross over *rue de Seine*. Pass by *Café Jade*, *Delice Buci*, *Droguerie Thanner*, *Boutique Aqarelle* (flowers) and *Chevignon*.

> RIGHT on *rue de l'Ancienne Comedie*.

> LEFT on *Boulevard Saint-Germain*.

> *Cluny* is on your RIGHT. Turn on *Boulevard Saint-Michel* to walk around the block to the entrance.

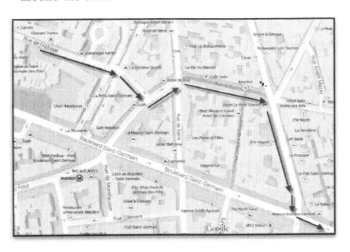

Buci Market & Antiques Shopping

While you are on *rue de Buci*, check out *Buci Market* (open daily, 9 am to 7 pm), a traditional street market in the chic *St-Germain* district. Word has it that *rue de Buci* is where Pablo Picasso did his daily shopping. *Rue de Buci* is lined with specialty food shops (cheese, wine, pastry), as well as places to buy regional fare and prepared Italian dishes.

Explore the Cluny Museum of the Middle Ages

Cluny Museum: Place Paul Painlevé; www.musee-moyenage.fr

Closed Tuesday**

Open: Wednesday—Monday: 9:15 am to 5:45 pm.

Note: Ticket office closes at 5:15 pm

Hotel de Cluny was once home to the powerful Abbots of Cluny, and later owned by Alexandre du Sommerard, an avid collector of medieval art. The back corner of the mansion is built around the remains of a 3rd-century *Roman Bath, Thermes de Cluny*.

The museum holds an unusual combination of collections spanning 15 centuries of Parisian history. These include one of the world's finest assemblies of medieval arts and crafts, the original heads that were loped off the statues of kings above the door of *Notre-Dame,* the remarkable *Lady and the Unicorn* tapestries, and medieval stained glass from *Sainte-Chapelle* (*http://www.therosewindow.com/pilot/Paris-Musee-Cluny/Cluny-Frame.htm*).

Heads of the Notre Dame Kings

One of the highlights of the museum collection, from a historical point of view as well as artistic, is the series of twenty-one (of the original twenty-eight) heads from the *Kings of Judah* statuary above the doors of *Notre Dame*. Decapitated by mobs during the Revolution, who mistook these statues for French kings, the heads were rediscovered in 1977, buried as part of the foundations of a building that was being renovated.

Roman Frigidarium

The surviving section of the *frigidarium*, with its Roman vaults and ribs intact, and fragments of the original decorative wall paintings and mosaics, is about 1/3 the size of the massive 3rd-century *Roman Bath* complex that once stood here. The full complex had a *caldarium* (hot water bath), a *tepidarium* (warm water bath), a *frigidarium* (cold water bath) and a *gymnasium*. The former *gymnasium* is now part of Gallery 9, where the *Notre Dame* heads are on display. Ruins from the *caldarium* and the *tepidarium* are outside, on the museum's grounds.

To Roman men (women were not allowed), the daily bath was a social occasion, a place of comradery, and a lifeline to the news of the day. This was where important matters and business were discussed, and deals were made. These spectacular structures were a version of today's country clubs.

Lady & the Unicorn Tapestries

These exquisite tapestries, woven around the year 1500, are rich and colorful, and evocative of another age. Five of the six tapestries represent the five senses: touch, taste, smell, hearing, and sight. The sixth tapestry remains a puzzle, bearing the inscription: "To my only desire." Possibly this refers to the "desire" for free will.

Walk (or Bike) to Luxemburg Gardens

Instead of continuing to walk, you may be about ready to switch to a rented *Vélib* bicycle to save your feet and move along more quickly. The full loop you are about to make—from the *Cluny* to *Luxembourg Gardens*, then past the *Pantheon* and back to *Shakespeare & Company* near the river—will involve a total of 27 minutes of walking, or a much abbreviated time if you go by bike. So you may prefer to opt for a bike at this point, and glide along instead.

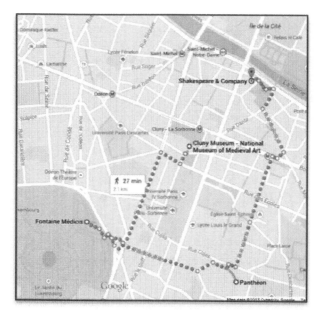

There is a *Vélib* station outside the *Cluny* where you will be able to pick up a bike to ride over to the *Luxemburg Gardens*. Once you enter the park, you will need to walk your bike until you leave the park again. Bikes are free for the first 30 minutes, and purchasing a *Vélib Pass* is a real bargain— €1.70 for a one-day pass; €8 for a seven-day pass. You can purchase passes online, or by using a credit card *with a chip* at one of the *Vélib* Stations.

By using the *Vélib* self-service bike system, you will be able to pick up a bike from any of the 1800 self-service bike stations around Paris and surrounding cities, and return the bike at any of the other locations. *Vélib* stations are located throughout the city, no more than 300 meters apart.

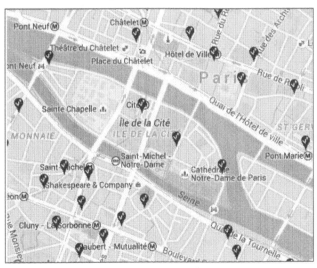

When you return a bike at any of the other locations, the key is to make sure that it is *fully locked* back into a bike post, and that you receive a printed receipt to confirm that the locking process has been successful. Otherwise, as far as the system knows, the bike is still in your possession and you will be held accountable for it. For more information about how to use the *Vélib* bike system, visit *http://en.velib.paris.fr/How-it-works*.

To walk or bike to *Luxemburg Gardens,* follow *Boulevard Saint-Michel* to the entrance gate.

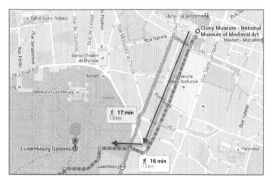

History of Luxembourg Palace and Gardens

As you leave the frenzy of the city streets, you will enter the opulent and peaceful haven that was designed and built in 1612 by *Marie de' Medici,* second wife and widow of *Henri IV.* What surrounds you in this hideaway in the middle of Paris, is Marie's attempt to duplicate the *Pitti Palace* and *Boboli Gardens* of her native Florence, Italy.

It was in *Palais du Luxembourg* that Marie displayed the 24 paintings of herself and her family that she commissioned to be painted by the master artist, *Rubens,* himself. Twenty-one of these paintings depict Marie's own struggles and triumphs in life. The remaining three are portraits of herself and her parents. Some of these self-celebrating paintings are now on display at the Louvre, where you will see them tomorrow.

The *Paris Peace Conference* was held at *Luxembourg Palace* in 1946. Now it is home to the French Senate. Tours of its interior are by appointment only. But the gardens are open to the public.

The *Jardin du Luxembourg* is a favorite garden oasis and rendezvous spot for Parisians and visitors alike. These beautiful and peaceful gardens are designed in the formal French style, featuring broad avenues lined with precisely planted trees and trimmed hedges, immaculate lawns, statues, pools and fountains.

Octagonal Pool, with Toy Sailboats

Visit the ever-popular octagonal pool, with the splendid palace as a backdrop. Generally you will find it filled with toy sailboats, available for rent.

This is a lovely place to pause for a while. And, if you so desire, rent yourself a boat and join the Parisian children (and adults!) in this idyllic pastime.

Medici Fountains

In the gardens you also will find the queen's romantic *Fontaine de Medici*, a shady and peaceful spot overlooking a pond filled with fish.

After wandering the gardens, pause to sit on a quiet bench beside the *Medici Fountains*, and think of Florence, as Marie did when she sat here all those years ago.

Walk (or Bike) Past the Pantheon

Now walk (or bike) to the vast, ornate, architecturally astounding *Pantheon*, modeled after the Pantheon in Rome. This grand edifice was built by Louis XV to fulfill his vow to build a church if he was cured from a serious illness.

After the French Revolution, the Revolutionist government converted the church to a mausoleum where exceptional Frenchmen who had sacrificed their lives for their country or done something great for France would be buried. Among the luminaries buried here are Voltaire, Émile Zola, Victor Hugo, Marie Curie and Jean-Jacques Rousseau.

Walk Through the Maze of the Latin Quarter

Nestled between the Seine and the *Luxembourg Gardens*, the *Latin Quarter* has been the center of learning in Paris for more than 700 years. This charming neighborhood, associated with artists and intellectuals since the Middle Ages, gained its name from the ancient language, Latin, that was spoken by the many generations of students, writers, philosophers and artists who walked these streets and attended the schools and universities nearby, including the Sorbonne.

The streets here are too narrow for a bicycle. So find a station where you can turn in your Vélib bike, then walk the neighborhood unencumbered.

Pause at Shakespeare & Company

> ### Shakespeare & Company
>
> *37 rue de la Bucherie.* (0)1-43-25-40-93
>
> Open 7 days a week, 10am to 11pm

The original *Shakespeare & Company* bookshop was opened in 1919, in a different *Left Bank* location, by Sylvia Beach, an American expatriate from

New Jersey, who used as her only capital $3000 from her mother. The shop doubled as a lending library, publishing house, and boarding house for aspiring writers. And it became the Parisian center of Anglo-American literary culture.

Attracting both readers and writers, the bookshop was a favorite gathering spot for writers and artists of the "Lost Generation," including Ezra Pound, Ernest Hemingway, F. Scott Fitzgerald, Gertrude Stein, D. H. Lawrence, T. S. Eliot, Thornton Wilder, André Gide, James Joyce and many others. Sylvia offered hospitality and encouragement to their authors as well as selling their books. In 1922, she bankrolled and published James Joyce's' controversial book, *Ulysses*, a book that had been banned in the United States and Britain. After his book was launched, Joyce signed on with another publisher, leaving Sylvia with sizeable debts from this daring venture.

The original *Shakespeare & Company* bookshop was forced to close during the German occupation of World War II, then "personally liberated" by Hemingway himself. But he never reopened the shop for business.

George Whitman launched his own English-language bookstore, called *Le Mistral*, in 1951, in the current *rue de la Bucherie* location near the Seine, modeling his shop after Sylvia Beach's original. He later renamed his shop *Shakespeare & Company* as a tribute to Sylvia's enterprise after she died. Whitman's daughter, Sylvia (named after Sylvia Beach), has run the shop since her father's death in 2011, at age 98.

In front of the shop, bookstands surround an ornate 19th century drinking fountain that was erected in the to service the area's poor. When you have had your fill of perusing the outdoor stands, wander inside for an even more extensive stock of second-hand books, stacked floor to ceiling, and everywhere in between.

With your finds from *Shakespeare & Company* in hand, walk over to the nearby *Café Procope (13 rue de l'Ancienne Comédie. (0)1-40-46-79-00)* for a well-earned pause. Find a table on the terrace overlooking the street.

Café Procope was once the haunt of Voltaire and Rousseau, as well as Benjamin Franklin and Thomas Jefferson. Its walls are adorned by author-signed title pages.

Dinner at Le Jardin du Roy in the Latin Quarter

Le Jardin du Roy
28 rue de la Huchette; 01 40 79 56 01

You have made reservations at *Le Jardin du Roy* on the walking street, *rue de la Huchette*, in the heart of the *Latin Quarter*, surrounded by jazz cellars, terrace cafés and restaurants of every nationality. *Le Jardin du Roy* is the restaurant of *Hotel du Mont Blanc*, the hotel where Hemingway stayed when he was not booked at the Ritz. This restaurant is known for its history and location, and also for its reasonable prices and excellent food, with set three-course menus at €14, and total bills, including wine, around €45.

Now for Some Music

SO now here you are in the heart of the *Latin Quarter*. Wander the narrow streets of the *Latin Quarter* and find a piano bar, joining with the locals who have come to enjoy the music.

See the Lights Along the River from a Bridge

As you stroll back "home" along the river, walk partway across a bridge and stand at the rail looking up and down the river at the lights. After all, Paris is the "City of Lights," and here you are in the heart of it. Make note of this moment as an unforgettable reminder of Paris in all its loveliness.

Day 14 (Friday): Art & Gardens, Arches & Towers

> **Before You Set Off for the Day:** Make dinner reservations at an outdoor table for an 8:30 pm at *Beaurepaire Café* near the river (*1 rue de la Bucherie*; (0)1-43-29-73-57).
>
> OR make online reservations for the 6:30 pm or the 9:00 pm seating at *58 tour Eiffel http://www.restaurants-toureiffel.com*).

Today you will visit some of the iconic sights of Paris, including the *Louvre*, the *Champs-Élysées*, the *Arc de Triomphe*, and the *Eiffel Tower*. Be sure to wear comfortable shoes and take along a bottle of water, an umbrella, and your camera. Also bring your *Batobus Pass, Museum Pass,* and Eiffel Tower tickets.

Batobus to the Louvre

 TIME TARGET: Aim to catch the 10 am boat.

Yesterday you purchased a 2-day *Batobus Pass.* Today you will save some time by catching the Batobus at the *Hôtel de Ville* stop. Walk across *Ile de la Cité* on *rue d'Arcole*, passing in front of Notre Dame, then cross the river to the *Right Bank* on *Pont d'Arcole*. The boat landing is on your left after you cross the bridge. Watch for it as you cross the bridge. You will remember this stop from your ride yesterday.

You will be hopping on and off the Batobus all day, in this order:

- Hop on at the *Hôtel de Ville* stop.

- Hop off at the *Louvre stop*.

- Hop back on at the *Champs-Élysées* stop.

- Hop off at the *Eiffel Tower* stop.

- Hop back on at the *Eiffel Tower* stop.

- Cruise "home" to the *Notre Dame* stop.

Spend the Morning at the Louvre

As you visit the phenomenal *Louvre Museum*, housing what is considered to be the most stunning collection of artwork in the world, use your *Museum Pass* to skip the line and enter through the priority entrance.

The building in which this artwork is displayed is the former palace of the kings and emperors of France, spanning from the Middle Ages through Napoleon. So the building is as much an experience as the art that is displayed within its walls. Grand staircases. Opulent rooms, with painted ceilings and luxuriant floors. Expansive courtyards.

You will be able to see only a fraction of the palace and its collections today. The best approach is to focus on having the full experience of the part of the museum you are able to see today, and to know that someday you will return. Each time you visit the Louvre will be an entirely different encounter.

The famous, heavily-visited masterpieces may be at the top of your list for today, starting with *Winged Victory* and da Vinci's *Mona Lisa*. But there is much… much more.

Some History of the Louvre as a Palace

In its first incarnation, the *Louvre* was a medieval wartime stronghold, built shortly after 1190 by *King Philippe Auguste*. During the 1300s, *Charles V* transformed the fortress into a "fairy tale castle"—a splendid royal residence meant to impress his peers.

In the 1500s, *François I*, the king who invited *da Vinci* to live out his life in Amboise as "first painter of France and engineer and architect of the king," refashioned the *Louvre* into a grand renaissance palace. Consuming much of the country's riches for this, and his many other, ambitious building projects, *François* also was a passionate lover and patron of the arts, filling each of his palaces with lavish collections of art and sculpture.

The palace continued to expand over the ages. After *Henri II*, son of *François I*, was killed by a lance that pierced his helmet during a tournament, his widow, *Catherine de Medici*, commissioned a new palace for herself in front of *Louvre Palace*, in the area called *Tuileries*, where the tile ("tuileries") factories had once stood. Catherine lived in *Tuileries Palace* as Queen mother during the successive reigns of three of her sons—*Francis II*, *Charles IX* and *Henri III*—a time of carnage and massacre from the religious warring between Catholics and Protestants.

Catherine's *Tuileries Palace* is gone now, torched in 1871 during the Paris Commune. The 12 men who started the fire used petroleum, liquid tar and turpentine, and set off such a conflagration that it burned its way across the river to Queen Margot's d'*Orsay Palace* on the opposite bank. The fire brigade fought the blaze for two full days. By the time they got it under control, both *Tuileries* and d'*Orsay* palaces had been completely gutted.

During the 1600s, *Henri IV*, the visionary peacemaker who had a wife on each side of the river, connected *Louvre Palace* with *Tuileries Palace* by building the *Grand Gallery*. *Louis XIV*, the *Sun King*, later added the *Galerie d'Apolion* (Apollo Gallery), awash in sun imagery, above the *Petite Galerie* and *Cour Carrée* (Square Court), but then moved his royal court in 1678 to the even grander country palace of *Versailles*.

Throughout the times of expansion, *Louvre Palace* was home to the royal art collection, a lavish display that by the end of the reign of *Louis XIV* numbered 1,478 paintings, making it one of the largest collections of the time. During these centuries, the royal art collection was for royal and noble eyes only.

After *Louis XIV* moved to Versailles, *Louvre Palace* stood abandoned and neglected for over a century, used as storage space for surplus paintings and sculpture. The royal art collection was first opened up to public display in 1750, at an exhibition in *Luxemburg Palace*.

This marked the beginning of an intermittent movement toward making the collection accessible to the public permanently, and culminated with *Louvre Palace* being converted to a national art museum that displays over 70,000 pieces of art, spread across more than 650,000 square feet of gallery space.

Your "Journey" Through History & Art of the Louvre

As you explore this incomparable museum, remember to look up at the ceilings, and down at the floors. Observe the grandeur of the staircases, and views from the windows. You will be walking in the footsteps of long-ago kings, who wandered among these masterpieces of art and sculpture that then were reserved for their eyes only. Feel free to stride among these masterpieces as though you yourself were royalty, roving the lavish rooms of your palace.

Enter Through the Pyramid
You will be entering through the controversial pyramid, designed by I. M. Pei, in the central courtyard of the *Louvre*.

Before you enter the museum, orient yourself to the vast building surrounding you. As you stand at the pyramid, the medieval section, the *Sully Wing*, is straight ahead of you, the *Denon Wing* to your right, along the river, and the *Richelieu Wing* to your left. You will be visiting all three of these areas today, starting with the *Medieval Louvre* in the *Sully Wing*.

You will be able to skip the line using your *Paris Museum Pass*. Once you are inside the pyramid, pick up a full-sized map and study it, standing with your back to the entrance. As you would expect from your orientation efforts before entering, access to the *Sully Wing* is by the escalator straight ahead. *Denon Access* is to your right. *Richelieu Access* is to your left.

Keep this basic grid in mind as you immerse yourself in the museum, and move from wing to wing. This will help you get back on track should you become disoriented or confused. But, if all else fails, you can always take yourself back to the pyramid and start fresh.

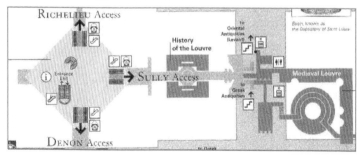

Follow a Path Sequence: → *Sully* → *Denon* → *Richelieu*
This path will take you through the Louvre on a 12-point treasure hunt, from its medieval beginnings, through its 800 years of history. Completing

this circuit will you take around 2 hours, plus the time for a break at *Café Mollien* (in the *Denon Wing*), a lovely museum café on the landing of one of the grand stairways.

Feel free to vary your path and timing according to your interests and stamina. You may want to split off from your travel companion at some point, then meet at *Café Mollien* at an appointed time. If you do go off in separate directions, plan to share your peak discoveries when you reunite. Describe your favorites to each other during your break at the Café. Then possibly take time for a "show and tell," leading each other straight to your best finds.

Begin Your 12-point Exploration

From the Pyramid, take the escalator toward the Sully Wing and follow signs to the Medieval Louvre on the lower floor.

1. Medieval Louvre

View the remains from *King Philippe's* 12th-century fortress, including a massive cylindrical tower. To view the scope of the original site, study the model beside the entrance to the former moats of the fortress.

Walk up the Henri II Staircase from the lower to the ground floor.

2. Salle des Caryatides

Explore the *Louvre's* collection of Roman copies of Hellenistic Greek sculptures. At one end of the room are the *Caryatids*, four large sculpted female figures, supporting a musicians' gallery on their heads.

Look through the east-facing windows for a view over the enclosed *Cour Carrée*.

Leave the sculpture room by the door to the right of the fireplace, and turn right toward the Rotonde de Mars.

3. Anne of Austria's Summer Apartments

If you wish, take time out to find the *Venus du Milo* by turning left and walking through the rooms of Greek antiquities before you head back the other way to the *Rotonde de Mars*.

From the *Rotonde de Mars,* enter the apartments to your left. You are now in the *Denon Wing,* with windows that face the river. These six rooms, sumptuously decorated, were once the apartment of *Louis XIV's* mother, *Anne of Austria.* They now house collections of Etruscan and Roman antiquities.

> *Walk through the second series of rooms that overlook the Seine. Enter the glass-roofed courtyard.*

4. Cour du Sphinx

View the magnificent mosaic from a 4th-century Roman villa in the ancient city of Antioch, and the ancient Greek and Roman monuments.

> *Walk through the west gallery bordering the courtyard. Climb the Escalier Daru.*

5. Escalier Daru

This magnificent staircase, lit from the cupolas above, brilliantly displays the statue of *Winged Victory.*

> *Pass to the left of Winged Victory. Cross the Rotunda to the entrance to the Gallery of Apollo.*

6. Rotonde and Galerie d'Apollon

The rotunda and the *Gallery of Apollo* were formerly the audience chamber for *Louis XIV*—the Sun King. These spaces are overflowing with sun allegories.

Begin your hunt for sun metaphors in the rotunda by studying the painting on the ceiling that depicts the *Fall of Icarus,* a consequence of flying too close to the sun. In the *Gallery of Apollo* look for paintings that map the path of the sun. On the Gallery's vaulted ceiling are allegorical images of *Apollo Vanquishing the Python.*

> *From the Gallery of Apollo, turn left through the Rotunda and pass the stairs. Turn left to walk through Room 4 and 5 of the Grande Gallery.*

7. Grande Galerie

Meander the *Grande Gallery,* pausing briefly, at will, to view Italian paintings from the 1300s to 1500s.

> *Turn right into Room 6, the Salle des États. If the Mona Lisa has been temporarily moved, look for signs.*

8. Mona Lisa

Edge forward to study the small but incomparable painting that *Leonardo da Vinci* himself carried across the Alps in 1515 as a gift for his patron and friend, *François I.*

> *Browse through Salon Denon (Room 76) and Salle Mollien (Room 77). Then find Café Mollien on the landing of the Mollien Staircase, with a terrace that overlooks Cour Napoléon and the Pyramid.*

9. Le Café Mollien, for a Break

Experience this unique perspective on the museum while relaxing with a light snack, surrounded by ornately carved caryatids, and with Charles-Louis Müller's *"Glory distributing Palms and Crowns"* overhead.

In a couple of hours you will be feasting on a late lunch at *Pizza Pino* on the *Champs-Élysées*. So order accordingly.

> *Walk down the Escalier Mollien back to the ground floor to Michelangelo Gallery.*

10. Michelangelo Gallery

Modeled after the *Salle des Caryatides*, complete with marble floors, the *Michelangelo Gallery* houses Italian sculptures, including Michelangelo's remarkable *Rebellious Slave* and *Dying Slave.*

Among the many other lovely sculptures, take a moment to spot *Psyche and Cupid* by *Canova*, with Psyche placing a butterfly in Cupid's palm, symbolic of her innocently offering him her soul.

> *Retrace your steps to the Escalier Mollien, then walk down to the Lower Ground Floor. Cross over from the Denon Wing to the Richelieu Wing.*

11. Cour Puget & Cour Marly

Enter the glass-roofed *Cour Puget* on your right, with impressive statuary from the 17th, 18th and 19th centuries. In the small court farther on, view the remains of the *Palace of Sargon* in ancient Khorsabad.

Cross through the Crypte Girardon (Room 20), to the glass-roofed *Cour Marly* across the way. Here you will find statues from the park at *Marly*, *Louis XIV's* favorite residence, displayed on terraces and bathed in constant natural light. Find for the incomparable Marly horses.

> *Climb to the 2nd floor of the Richelieu wing and locate the Galerie Médicis (Room 18).*

12. Galerie Médici

The twenty-four monumental canvases displayed here were painted by master painter *Rubens* himself between 1622 and 1625. Italian-born French queen *Marie de' Medici* commissioned these huge paintings to depict her struggles and triumphs in life, magnified by gods from ancient mythology. These massive paintings were originally housed in Luxembourg palace, home of Queen Marie. You will be visiting the gardens of this palace later today.

An example from Rubens' paintings immortalizing the life of *Marie de' Medici* is the portrayal of *King Henry IV* gazing in delight at a portrait of Marie, his bride-to-be, and falling hopelessly in love.

Enough for Now!!??

If you return again another day, check the museum website for guidance: *http://www.louvre.fr/en/routes/palace-museum*. The key to fully enjoying the Louvre is to stop before you are totally exhausted.

Take a quick browse through the gift shop before you leave for reasonably-priced replicas of the masterpieces you have seen today. Then head for the exit.

Arc de Triomphe du Carrousel

As you exit the *Louvre* through the pyramid, walk toward the *Arc de Triomphe du Carrousel*, topped by a horse-drawn chariot… the smaller version of the much larger *Arc de Triomphe de l'Etoile* you will be visiting later today. These two celebratory arches, standing at the other end of the *Voie Triomphale* ("Triumphal View"), were designed by Napoleon I in 1806 to commemorate his victories and grandeur.

Look through the central arch of *Arc du Carrousel*, past *Tuileries Gardens* and the *Obélisque*, to the *Arc de Triomphe de l'Etoile* at the western end of the *Champs-Elysées*. Later today you will be standing beside or atop the larger arch, looking back this way toward this smaller one.

Arc du Carrousel is half the size of the *Arc de l'Etoile*. Originally the horses on top were the famous bronze horses from *Saint Mark's Cathedral* in Venice, pillaged by Napoleon in 1798. The originals were returned to Venice in 1815 so what you see now are copies.

This smaller arch was completed in 1808, during Napoleon's lifetime. The larger arch was finished 30 years later (1836), 21 years after Napoleon's 1815 defeat at Waterloo, and 15 years after his death in 1821.

Visit Tuileries Gardens

Now walk through *Tuileries Gardens* toward *Place de la Concorde*, meandering up and down the various pathways as well as walking the *Grande Allée*. *Catherine de Medici* created these Italian Renaissance gardens in 1564, modeled after the gardens in her native Florence, with fountains, a labyrinth, lawns, flower beds, statuary and clusters of trees.

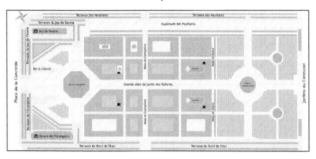

Henry IV later planted the corridor of mulberry trees in hopes of cultivating silkworms to start a silk industry in France. *Louis XIII* used the gardens as his own enormous playground, with a menagerie of wild animals. *Louis XIV* added the *Grand Allée*—the beds of flowers, bordered by boxwood hedges, with three ponds and fountains.

Most of the statues in the eastern part of the *Tuileries Gardens* were added later during the 19th century. Encircling the large round basin are statues, alternating between violent and serene poses, on the themes of antiquity, allegory and ancient mythology. Look for *Diana the Huntress*, *Tiger Overwhelming a Crocodile*, *Tigress Bringing a Peacock to its Young*, *Misery*, *The Good Samaritan*, and *Theseus Fighting the Minotaur*.

These gardens have been open to the public since 1667, and became a public park after the French Revolution. The gardens of today are preserved in their historical layout, maintained by 20 gardeners and protected by 17 security officers. Twice yearly, in spring and fall, the 7,000 square meters of the Grand Carré are planted with 70,000 plants and bulbs, designed to create an interplay of colors and a flowering period that extends from May through October.

Bask in the Sun at the Pond

Comfortable chairs surround the large octagonal basin just before you exit the Gardens. If you spot some empty chairs, pause to bask in the sun alongside the many comfortably relaxing Parisians.

Stop Briefly at l'Orangerie to See Monet's Murals

Up the hill to the left of the basin is *l'Orangerie Museum*, where the murals of *Monet's* water lilies are showcased. *Monet* donated his lily paintings as a monument to the end of World War I, in hopes that, after the horrors of the war, his work would provide a haven for peaceful meditation.

Your *Paris Museum Pass* will allow you to bypass the line and enter immediately, so take advantage of this opportunity to experience these phenomenal murals, however briefly. Photographs of these displays do not come close to the experience you will have standing in the middle of the room, with the lilies surrounding you.

L'Orangerie was originally built in 1852 to shelter the orange trees of *Tuileries Gardens. Monet* himself specified the design for the two oval rooms that were created to display his work. At Monet's direction, the rooms incorporated natural light and white walls, and were sparsely decorated. When the rooms were ready for the panels to be installed in 1923, Monet found himself unable to relinquish them during his lifetime, keeping them until his death three years later in 1926. If you have the time or energy for more art, *l'Orangerie Museum* also contains works by Cézanne, Matisse, Picasso, Renoir, Rousseau, and Modigliani.

Visit the Obelisk in Place de la Concorde

As you exit the gates of the gardens, you will be in *Place de la Concorde*. This is where the guillotine that executed *Louis XVI* was set up in 1793. Other important figures guillotined here, before audiences of cheering crowds, included *Marie Antoinette* and *Princess Elisabeth of France*.

Cross over for a closer look at the 3300 year-old Egyptian *Luxor Obelisk*, popularly called *Cleopatra's Needle*, although it had no connection with the Queen. This obelisk originally marked the entrance to *Luxor Temple in* Egypt, where its twin still remains. *Muhammed Ali Pasha*, self-declared Khedive of the *Ottoman Empire*, and founder of the modern state of Egypt, shipped the obelisk to Paris in 1833 in exchange for France's latest technological marvel, a highly accurate clock. The Khedive had the clock installed in *Mohammed Ali Mosque Square,* but to his (and Egypt's) misfortune, the clock never worked.

Look closely at the hieroglyphs on the obelisk. These symbols exalt the reign of the pharaoh *Ramesses II.* The impressive gold-leafed, pyramid-shaped cap on the top was added by the French government in 1998 to replace the original golden cap that is believed to have been stolen in the 6th century BC. There are two other well-known *Cleopatra's Needles* in the world. One stands in the heart of London, along the Thames, and the other in New York City, in Central Park.

Hire a Bike Taxi from the Obelisk to Champs-Élysées

Before you cross the street from the center of the square, look to the left of the gate to the gardens for pedal cabs. Negotiate a price with one of the drivers for the ride down the considerable remaining length of *Avenue des Champs-Élysées* to *Banana Republic,* where the shops begin. Then hop aboard to be whisked along in comfort to *Pizza Pino* for lunch.

Late Lunch at Pizza Pino Overlooking Champs-Élysées

Pizza Pino

31-33 Avenue des Champs-Élysées. (0)1-40-74-01-12

After your long morning of art, sculpture and gardens, you will be ready for lunch. Hop off your pedal cab, and cross the street to the red awnings of *Pizza Pino.*

Since timing has been somewhat unpredictable today, you will not have made reservations, and so you will be taking your chances securing a table. But because you will be arriving at an odd hour for lunch, your chances will be very good. Request a table along the sidewalk, or upstairs, with a view out over the engaging parade of humanity on the *Champs-Élysées*.

Browse the Shops Along the Champs-Élysées

Boulevard Champs-Élysées may not be the place to find a bargain, but window shopping is free. All the high-end stores are here, from *Louis Vuitton* to *Gucci* to *Swarovski* to *Montblanc* to *Cartier*.

While high-end shops are the draw in this neighborhood, you also can shop in popular favorites that you would see in the US, like the *Gap*, *Benetton*, *Disney Store* and *Levi's*.

Check the small boutiques for finds that are more uniquely French. If you happen upon a sale, you may find stylish treasures that will not break the bank. But save part of your shopping budget for tomorrow in *Montmartre* and the *Marais*.

Since shopping is a personalized activity, this would be a good time to separate from your travel partner, with a plan to meet later, perhaps at the stairs to the tunnel under the traffic to the *Arc de Triomphe*. If it starts to rain, consider this to be a "sign," and take shelter in a shop where the selections look particularly appealing.

Visit the Arc de Triomphe

In 1806 *Napoleon I* ordered that this larger arch be built to honor the *French Grande Armée*, that had, by that time, conquered most of Europe and was thought to be invincible. He did not see it completed during his lifetime.

The *Arc de Triomphe* is said to be the largest triumphal arch in the world and cost 9.3 million French francs to build, a virtual fortune at that time. The opening of the arch is so large that a pilot flew his biplane through the center of it during the Paris victory parade after the World War I. Recorded on the walls under the vault are the 128 battles that were fought by the *Grande Armée,* and the names of the 558 generals who led the army to victory.

At the base of the arch stands the eternal flame, first lit in 1920 to recall the sacrifice of an unknown French soldier who gave his life during *World War I.* The torch is relit every evening at twilight. When President and Jacqueline Kennedy visited here to pay their respects, Jacqueline was so moved that she used this as the model for the eternal flame she established in honor of her husband.

Take the tunnel on the right side of *Champs-Élysées* to cross under the craziness of traffic that surrounds the arch. Do NOT attempt to get to the Arc by crossing at street level. Signs point to the stairs down to the tunnel. There is no charge.

Your *Paris Museum Pass* allows you to go to the top of the *Arc de Triomphe.* From here, you will have a breathtaking 360° view of Paris, with the *Eiffel Tower* in one direction, *the Louvre* in another, and *Sacré Coeur Basilica* in *Montmartre,* perched high up on its hill.

To get to the top of the Arc, climb the 284 steps of the small, spiral one-way staircase. There is another staircase to come back down. The steps are solid, so you will not have the additional dizzying challenge of looking down through the stairs to the bottom as you climb. There is an elevator to the top, but it stops one flight short of the viewing area, and is meant for use by the disabled.

Despite the steps, it may be worth it to you to make the effort to reach the top. If you need to avail yourself of the elevator to save your knees, it will not hurt to ask. From the terrace on top, soak in the unique panoramic view over the *Champs-Élysées,* and celebrate your own victories, including the considerable triumph of getting up here.

Taxi to the Petit Palais

Now back through the tunnel, and across the *Champs-Élysées* to the other side, to hail a taxi to the *Petit Palais*, near the *Alexandre III Bridge*, where you will catch the *Batobus* to the *Eiffel Tower*. If you are running late for your tickets up the *Eiffel Tower*, ask your driver to take you straight to the tower.

Ask your driver to drop you off at the *Petit Palais*, and plan to walk to the river from there. As you drive down *Avenue Winston Churchill*, you will see a vast glass building on your right and an exquisite smaller building on your left. These are the *Grand Palais* ("Large Palace") and the *Petit Palais* ("Small Palace"), both constructed in 1900 for the *Paris Exposition Universelle*.

The *Petit Palais* was designed to exhibit the exquisite grandeur of an actual French palace. It has a pillared façade and grand porch, with wrought iron entrances and elaborate cupolas, all topped by a dome. If you have the time, walk into the lovely semicircular courtyard and garden of the palace. Your Museum Pass allows you access for free.

Catch the Batobus to the Eiffel Tower

To find the *Batobus* stop, walk to the left of *Pont Alexander III*, with its lavishly gilded statues, and descend the stairs to the dock. As you board the *Batobus*, you will be able to spot the *Eiffel Tower* across the river, beyond the bridge.

From the Batobus, watch again for the scale model of the *Statue of Liberty* on *Swan Island*, standing within the shadow of the tower.

Visit the Eiffel Tower from Multiple Viewpoints

 TIME TARGET: Arrive at the *Eiffel Tower* by 4:30 pm to use your 5:30 pm tickets. If you are splurging on a 6:30 pm dinner at *58 Tour Eiffel*, arrive by 5:30 pm.

Cost: **€17.** Purchase tickets online for a specified time at: *http://ticket.toureiffel.fr*.

Lift tickets to the 1st level are included if you booked dinner. Pick up tickets at the welcome desk between the north and east pillars.

You have seen the *Eiffel Tower* twice from the river, brilliantly lit on your first night, and from the *Batobus* yesterday on your way to *d'Orsay*. Although the tower is impressive when viewed in its entirety from the river, this has not fully prepared you for what you will experience now as you stand beside it, walk beneath it, and ride the elevator up to the top.

A Little Background About the Tower

The *Eiffel Tower* was built as the entrance to the *1889 World's Fair* in Paris, and to celebrate the 100th anniversary of the fall of the Bastille that launched the French revolution. Standing 984 feet tall, the tower far surpassed the height of the 555-foot *Washington Monument* that had been the world's tallest structure up to that time. The *Eiffel Tower* remained the tallest man-made structure in the world for the next 41 years, when it was surpassed by the 1046-foot *Chrysler Building* in New York City.

Many Parisians at the time the *Eiffel Tower* was built called it "monstrous." Artists and intellectuals led the vigorous public outcry against the tower, publishing a manifesto, with 300 signatures, that voiced their objections.

"We, writers, painters, sculptors, architects, passionate lovers of the beauty, until now intact, of Paris, hereby protest with all our might, with all our indignation, in the name of French taste gone unrecognized, in the name of French art and history under threat, against the construction, in the very heart of our capital, of the useless and monstrous Eiffel Tower."

The original plan was for the tower to be dismantled after 20 years. But by then it had proved itself valuable as a radio communications tower, so it was allowed to stay. During World War I, the tower was used to spot enemy zeppelins, and during World War II, to intercept messages transmitted by the Nazis.

Today the *Eiffel Tower* is considered to be an architectural masterpiece and an icon of Paris. It is one of the best-known structures in the world, and has inspired more than 30 similar towers around the world.

The tower is repainted every seven years to protect it from rust. Initially painted reddish-brown, and later yellow, it now is colored "*Eiffel Tower* brown," painted in three progressively lighter shades, from bottom to top, to augment its visual impact against the sky.

View the Tower from its Feet to its Peak

When you disembark at the tower, walk up to its massive legs, oriented with the four points of the compass. Then walk under it, as visitors to the *1889 World's Fair* would have done when they entered the exposition. Look up into the intricate geometry of the tower's angles and braces, a total of 18,038 pieces, joined together by 2½ million rivets. Take many photographs to capture the gossamer weave of this phenomenal iron lattice structure.

You will be able to avoid the daunting lines at the *Eiffel Tower* (as long as 2 to 4 hours), because you already will have purchased your tickets well in advance of your trip. Your tickets will be for the specific time slot you selected, either the final daytime slot at 5:30 pm, or the first evening slot at 7:30 or 8:00 pm. It is essential that you arrive ahead of your designated time. If you are more than 30 minutes late, your tickets may be voided and you will not be allowed entry.

Pre-booked tickets will give you priority access to the 1st and 2nd floors, and from there to the summit. Once inside, you will be free to spend as long as you like, anywhere you like, on the tower. The final lift down from the top leaves at 11 pm.

If you have opted to splurge on dinner at *58 Tour Eiffel*, your lift ticket is included. Pick it up at the welcome desk between the north and east pillars. Again, arrive early.

At your designated time of entry, board the elevator and get off at the 1st level. Walk out onto the glass floor to look down, if you dare. If you are able to accomplish this walking on air, suspended above the ground, have your picture taken as proof of yet another moment of triumph.

Take the stairs or lift to the 2nd level and walk the circumference, enjoying all the views. Then catch the lift to the summit. Buy yourself a glass of champagne from the *Champagne Bar* that is tucked into the structure of the tower, your pick of pink or white bubbly, served perfectly chilled. Celebrate this moment as you survey all of Paris below you, from your birds eye view.

Take the Batobus "Home"

If your dinner plans are at *Beaurepaire Café*, it is now time to take the *Batobus* "home" along the Seine. From April to September, boats continue to run until 9:30 pm. If you will be staying at the *Eiffel Tower* for dinner, and miss the final boat, just take a taxi home.

On this ride along river from the *Eiffel Tower* to *Notre Dame*, check to see how many bridges you can identify. *Pont Alexander III* (gilded statues). *Pont Royal* (stone arches). *Pont Neuf* (bearded heads). Add one more bridge to your list... *Pont des Arts*.

You already may have noted *Pont des Arts*, the seven-arch metal pedestrian bridge, supported by sturdy stone pillars. This bridge was once covered in almost one million "love locks." Romantic couples attached these locks to the bridge, then threw the key into the Seine, as a symbol of the strength of their everlasting commitment.

By 2015, an estimated 45 tons of locks had been bolted to the bridge, overwhelming the historic iron grillwork, breaking off sections of the bridge, and endangering boats passing below. These locks were removed in 2015, with great difficulty, to preserve the bridge. But the millions of matching keys still lie at the bottom of the river.

Dinner at Beaurepaire Café

> *Beaurepaire Café*
>
> *1 rue de la Bucherie.* (0)1-45-49-47-03

If you are dining this evening at the charming *Beaurepaire Café*, near the river, you will enjoy outstanding food and wine, made from fresh, regionally-grown products. *Beaurepaire* is open without interruption Tuesday to Sunday from Noon to 10:30 pm.

This is a small and very popular restaurant, so hopefully you will have made reservations earlier in the day, and your table will be waiting.

OR Dine Elegantly at 58 Tour Eiffel

If you have decided to dine atop the *Eiffel Tower*, this big splurge will be an experience of a lifetime. You will have made your reservations well in advance of leaving for your trip on the website: *http://www.restaurants-toureiffel.com*. There are many people hoping to dine here, and seating is extremely limited.

When you make your reservations, you also will make your choice among three options for dinner: "Tentation" ("temptation") for €85 each, "Plaisir" ("pleasure") for €99 each, or "Emotion" ("emotion") for €119 each.

All three options include a lift ticket, a glass of champagne as an aperitif, and a 3-course dinner, with appetizer, main course, and dessert. The "Plaisir" option also includes one bottle of wine for every 3 people, as well as mineral water and coffee.

The "Emotion" offers all of the above, but also guarantees a window seat with a stunning view of the *Tracadéro* across the Seine.

Day 15 (Saturday): Montmartre & the Marais

> **Before You Set Off:** Make reservations for a 1 pm lunch at *l'Eté en Pente Douce* in *Montmartre* (*23 rue Muller*. (0)1-42-64-02-67).
>
> Make dinner 7:30 or 8:00 pm dinner reservations at *Bistrot Beaubourg*, near the *Pompidou Center* (*25 rue Quincampoix*; (0)1-42-77-48-02).

Today you will experience two additional neighborhoods of Paris, village-like *Montmartre*, and the eclectic *Marais*. Before you head up to Montmartre, you will have a chance to stop by *Maubert Market* again. In *Montmartre* you will admire the works-in-progress of sidewalk artists and visit the stunning *Sacré-Coeur Basilica*, then lunch outdoors at *l'Eté en Pente Douce*.

After you descend once more to the level of the river, you will wander the twisting streets of the *Marais*, pausing at will in search of vintage and fashion clothing to bring home with you as mementos of the classical Parisian sense of style. When you wear these finds after your return home, you will be transported back to this, your final day in Paris.

Revisit Maubert Market

If you are following the recommended schedule, today is Saturday, and it is Market Day again at *Maubert Market* (open Tuesdays, Thursdays and Saturdays, 7:00 am to 2:30 pm). So start your day with breakfast near *Maubert Market* on *Boulevard Saint-Germain* at *rue des Carmes*. This will put you next to the *Maubert-Mutualité Métro Station*, where you will catch the Metro to *Montmartre*.

As a temporary Parisian, you may have come to love street markets as they do. With their color and charm, their clothing, jewelry, hats, and wine, and their fresh foods and flowers, these markets are great fun. You may have discovered the fun of connecting with local vendors and artisans, and possibly doing a bit of bartering when you purchase multiples.

Stop for breakfast at *Metro Café* across the street from the market. Try a mushroom and cheese omelet, with a croissant and café au lait.

After breakfast, take a final spin through the market in search of treasures. Choose a treat or a bottle of wine to carry with you and enjoy later, sitting on the steps of *Sacré Coeur*, looking down over Paris.

Take the Metro (or a Taxi) to Montmartre

Board the Metro to *Montmartre* at the *Maubert-Mutualité Métro Station,* next to *Maubert Market.* Purchase a *Single-Use Ticket* (€1.80) for central Paris, Zones 1 & 2.

➤ Take *Train 10* toward *Boulogne–Pont Saint-Cloud* for 4 minutes (4 stops).

➤ Get off at *Sèvres-Babylone.*

➤ Change to *Train 12* toward *Front Populaire* for 15 minutes (11 stops).

➤ Get off at *Abbesses.*

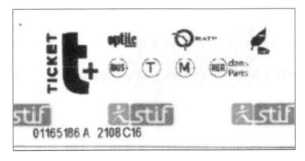

A one-day pass costs €7, so you will not be traveling enough today to get your money's worth. Your ticket will give you access to all 16 lines of the Paris Metro system for a single continuous journey of any length, including changes to other lines.   *ticket*

You will be able to purchase your Metro from a ticket window inside the station, or through vending machines. At either the ticket windows or the machines you will need a *smart-chip credit card*. If you are not carrying a smart-chip card, make sure you have sufficient Euro cash or coins.

To print the Paris Metro map you before you leave home, go to:

http://parisbytrain.com/wp-content/uploads/2014/01/paris-metro-map-2014.pdf

As an alternative to traveling by Metro, catch a taxi straight to *Gare Basse* of the *Funiculaire*.

A Little About Montmartre

Montmartre is one of the most historic and interesting neighborhoods in Paris, a unique village perched on a 427-foot high hill. Known as a creative breeding ground, as well as for its bohemian lifestyle, *Montmartre* has been home to many famous artists, including Salvador Dali, Amedeo Modigliani, Claude Monet, Pablo Picasso, Camille Pissarro and Vincent Van Gogh.

Sacré-Coeur Basilica, and the artist's square, *Place du Tertre*, are the chief well-known attractions, as well as the famous nightclubs, like the *Moulin Rouge*. But beyond these, the charm of this area is in its village-like feel.

You will be able to wander this area with the confidence, knowing that you are unlikely to get lost, at least not for long. With *Sacre-Coeur* sitting on the crest of the hill as a landmark, you will always be able to find your way just by looking up. So feel free to immerse yourself in the steep, cobbled streets and wander at will.

When You Reach Montmartre

From the *Abbesses* Metro stop, walk 6 minutes along *rue Yvonne le Tac*, that becomes *rue Tardieu*, then look up to your left toward the Basilica to spot the lower station, *Gare Basse*, of the *Funiculaire*.

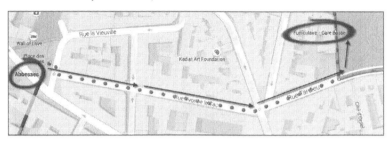

Climb the Steps or Take the Funicular to the Top

To get up to the Basilica, climb the 220 steps. Or take the *Funiculaire* from *Gare Basse* ("*Low Station*") to *Gare Haute* ("*High Station*") to be carried up to the summit in 1½ minutes, with your lungs still intact.

The *Funiculaire* opened in 1900 in time for the *Paris Exposition*—the event for which *d'Orsay Train Station* & *Grand Hotel* were built.

Watch the Sidewalk Artists on Place Tetre

When you reach the top of the steps, head off to your left toward the old town square, *Place du Tertre*, located about 200 meters from *Sacré Coeur*. Opened in 1635, this vibrant square is considered to be the heart of the village. Later you will walk back to *Sacré Coeur*, then over to *l'Eté en Pente Douce* for lunch.

265

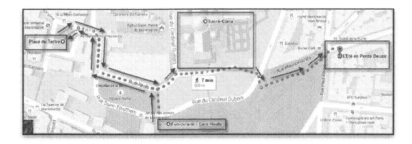

Famous throughout the world for its painters, portraitists and caricaturists, *Place du Tertre* is the perfect place to linger, watching the artists at work, as well as the colorful parade of people. The square is now divided into 149 one-square-meter spaces, each shared by two artists who rotate in and out, working in relay. Artists are licensed concession owners, allowing them to set up their easels and to showcase their work in the square. The standard waiting period for artists who wish to apply to work in the *Place du Tertre* is about 10 years.

These 300 total painters, portraitists and caricaturists line in the square year-round, poised and ready to sell you their work, or to paint your picture on the spot. Prices range from €25 to in excess of €100.

If you do decide to have your portrait painted, first walk around watching the artists at work, then select an artist whose actual work is as good as his/her samples. And always arrive at a price before the artist begins. A common tourist trap is for an artist to begin work before you have agreed on a price, setting you up to be exploited.

Stand on the Basilica Steps & Look Out Over Paris

Now head back to *Sacré Coeur*. Construction of the Basilica began in 1875, as a "guilt offering" and to "cure France's misfortunes" after it suffered defeat by Prussia in the Franco-Prussian war, followed by the bloody 1871 Commune. The Rom- anesque-Byzantine style Basilica was built out of travertine, a stone that naturally bleaches brighter and whiter as it ages. Above the triple-arched portico are bronze equestrian statues of France's national saints, *Joan of Arc* and *King Saint-Louis IX.*

The view from the Basilica steps is one of the most spectacular in Paris—made even more impressive at night. Pick a spot on the steps to sit and see Paris spread out beneath your feet. Enjoy the treat or wine you brought with you from *Maubert Market,* and possibly the street musicians who often set up to perform, using the steps as an amphitheater. If you happen upon a bridal party out to shoot photos, as we did, move aside to give them a clear shot, if need be.

Step Inside Sacré Coeur

Sacré Coeur Basilica

Open: Daily from 6:00 am to 10:30 pm. Entrance is free.

Mass: Monday to Thursday: 7 am, 11:15 am, 6:30 pm and 10 pm. Friday: 7:00 am, 11:15 am, 3 pm, 6:30 pm and 10 pm.

Step inside the Basilica and take a seat near the front. In contrast to the brilliant exterior, the interior of *Sacré Coeur* is dim and somewhat gloomy, brightened only by the 475-square-meter golden mosaic of *Christ in Glory* over the altar, one of the largest mosaics in the world.

The mosaic represents the risen Christ, clothed in white, with arms extended and a golden heart, surrounded by the saints who protect France—Virgin Mary, Saint Michael, and Saint Joan of Arc. The grand pipe organ, built in 1898, is considered one of the most remarkable in Paris, France and Europe. It is the most widely-heard pipe organ in the world after that in *Notre Dame.*

Lunch at l'Eté en Pente Douce

l'Eté en Pente Douce (reservations at 1 pm)

23 rue Muller. (0)1-42-64-02-67)

Walk down and away from the crowds that surround the Basilica in time for your 1:00 pm lunch reservations at the friendly and charming *l'Eté en Pente Douce*. This delightful restaurant is a find, although it does takes a bit of seeking out.

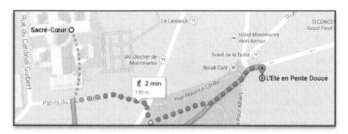

With your back to the Basilica, walk to your left and across the street to the steep staircases that descend the hill to the tree-shaded terrace of *l'Eté en Pente Douce*, where you have 1 pm reservations for lunch (23 Rue Muller, 75018 Paris, France; (0)1-42-64-02-67).

When you reach the charming little square at the bottom of the stairs, you will be able to spot the multi-colored outdoor tables of this lively, tucked away restaurant. Order quiche and a salad, and some of the very nice house wine. Their bread is highly praised, as are their apple tarts, if you have room for desert.

Metro or Taxi to the Marais for Some Vintage Shopping

To catch the Metro to the Marais after lunch, walk 5 minutes along *rue Muller*, then right on *rue de Clingnancourt* and left on *rue Poulet* to the *Château Rouge* Metro stop. Or catch a taxi from the restaurant directly to *Bis Boutique Solidaire* at 7 Boulevard du Temple in the Marais area.

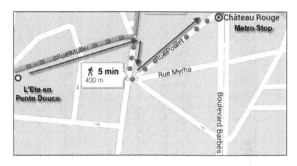

If you are going by Metro:

> Take *Train 4* toward *Mairie de Montrouge* for 6 minutes (5 stops).

> Get off at *Strasbourg-Saint-Denis.*

> Change to *Train 8* toward *Creteil–Pointe du Lac* for 3 minutes (2 stops).

> Get off at the *Filles du Calvaire* Metro stop.

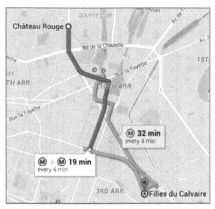

This may sound complicated, but your route will be well marked and relatively easy to follow. And it will be a part of the adventure.

Browse the Marais for Vintage Clothing & Fashions

If you love vintage shopping, you will do well in the Marais. Even if you are not a shopper, you will have plenty to see. Just agree to wander while your partner searches for treasures, and plan to meet up later at *Le Relais de l'hôtel de Ville at 50 rue de Rivoli (0)1-48-04-77-37*, where you can enjoy a glass of wine and great people-watching while you wait.

Another option in this area for the non-shoppers is the fascinating *Carnavalet Museum*, at 16 Rue des Francs Bourgeois (0)1-44-59-58-58. The *Carnavalet* occupies two neighboring mansions, and is dedicated to the story of Paris from its bygone days (a 4600 BC dugout canoe) to the present day. Exhibits illustrate the private lives of famous Parisians and developments in Parisian design, and immerse visitors in revolutionary history from the French Revolution to the Paris Commune.

Your *Marais Vintage Walk* will take you along *boulevard du Temple* to *rue des Rosiers* to *rue de Rivoli*, then to *rue du Roi de Sicile* and *rue de la Verrerie*, targeting five shops:

- *Bis Boutique Solidaire*,

- *Vintage Désir*,

- *Free 'P' Star*,

- *Mam'zelle Swing* and

- the *Kilo Shop*.

You will be walking through an eclectic historic neighborhood. Stop at will along the way to explore other shops that look interesting.

First Stop: Bis Boutique Solidaire

> *Bis Boutique. 7 boulevard du Temple. (0)1-44-78-11-08.*
>
> *Tuesday to Saturday, 10 am–7 pm*

As you exit the *Filles au Calvaire* Metro stop, your first vintage boutique, *Bis Boutique Solidaire*, will be only a 1-minute walk away.

➢ Head left from the station.

➢ Turn left on *Boulevard du Temple*.

➢ *Bis Boutique Solidaire* will be on your left at *7 Boulevard du Temple*.

Bis Boutique offers reasonably priced used clothing in a chic and contemporary setting. Browse for bargain designer pieces on two levels. A *Guy Laroche* jacket for €55. A pair of *Zadig & Voltaire* jeans for €12. *Gelati* pumps for €30. Dozens of other items for men, women and children. Think of this as a treasure hunt.

Next Stop: Vintage Désir

> *Vintage Désir. 32 rue des Rosiers. (0)1-40-27-04-98.*
>
> *Open daily, 11:30 am–9 pm*

➤ Walk to the right, back along *Boulevard du Temple* to the Metro stop.

➤ Turn right on *rue des Filles du Calvaire.*

➤ Continue onto *rue Vielle du Temple.*

➤ Turn left on *rue des Rosiers* to *Vintage Désir* at *32 rue des Rosiers.*

This shop is in the center of *rue de Rosiers,* one of the busiest streets in le Marais. Although the space is cramped, the clothing is well organized, and if you have time to go through everything, you may find a quality item for a bargain price. You can find lightweight dresses here for €10 and coats for about €20.

Now to Free'P'Star.

> *Free'P'Star. 20 rue de Rivoli. (0)1-42-77-63-43.*
> *http://www.freepstar.com*
> *Monday to Saturday, 11 am–9 pm; Sunday, noon–10:00 pm*

➤ Continue along *rue des Rosiers.*

➤ Turn right on *rue Ferdinand Duval* to *rue de Rivoli.*

➤ Turn right on *rue de Rivoli* to *Free 'P' Star* at *20 rue de Rivoli.*

Brimming with vintage and second-hand clothes and accessories that would be twice as expensive in New York, *Free 'P'Star* "salutes the bargain without compromising its collection." Joyfully cluttered and disorganized, the space is crammed with piles of purses and berets, bins of scarves and ties, and racks of colorful cotton dresses. Find a *Zara* sweater here for €2 or a silk blouse for €5.

Next Stop: Mam'zelle Swing

Mam'zelle Swing. 35 rue du Roi de Sicile. (0)1-48-87-04-06

http://www.mamzelle-swing.com

Monday to Saturday, 2:00 pm–7:00 pm

➢ Continue along *rue de Rivoli.*

➢ Turn right on *rue Vielle du Temple.*

➢ Turn left on *rue du Roi de Sicile* to *Mam'zelle Swing* at *35 rue du Roi de Sicile.*

This shop is easy to spot because of its florescent pink exterior. Inside is even more exciting! This is the perfect place to find one-of-a-kind pieces. Dresses, hats, bathrobes, coats, gloves, jewels, scarves.

No vab

You'll pay slightly more here, but for higher quality garments. Less polyester, fewer shoulder pads, more natural fiber. The shop is not as crowded as the others, and everything is arranged beautifully.

Last Stop: the Kilo Shop

Kilo Shop. 69-71 rue de la Verrerie (0)9-67-13-79-54

Sunday & Monday: 2:00 pm–7:45 pm.

Tuesday to Saturday, 11:00 am–7:45 pm

➢ Continue along *rue du Roi de Sicile* as it becomes *rue de la Verrerie*.

➢ Stop by *The Kilo Shop* at *69-71 rue de la Verrerie*.

The Kilo Shop is a veritable warehouse of vintage clothing, with two floors, menswear on the lower floor, and womenswear upstairs. You will pay for your selections based on weight; each type of garment (jackets, blouses, pants) has a price per kilogram.

Meet Up at Le Relais de l'Hôtel de Ville, 50 Rue de Rivoli

Le Relais de l'hôtel de Ville at 50 rue de Rivoli

(0)1-48-04-77-37

Fully satisfied from shopping, walk back out to *rue de Rivoli* to meet at *Le Relais de l'hôtel de Ville* (across from *Hôtel de Ville* Town Hall) as planned, at an outdoor table.

Depending on how successful you were in your shopping, you will be close enough to stop by and drop off your treasures at "home" before continuing on to *Pompidou Center*.

273

Walk to the Pompidou via Rue du Renard

From your meeting spot at *Le Relais de l'hôtel de Ville*, walk back to *rue du Renard* and turn right (away from the river). You will see the avant-garde *Pompidou Center* up ahead on your left well before you reach it. With the internal skeleton of the building's systems color-coded and exposed on the outside, you will immediately see why an article in *Le Figaro* declared "Paris has its own monster, just like the one in Loch Ness." Green pipes are for plumbing and blue ducts are for climate control. Electrical wiring is encased in yellow, and circulation elements and safety devices are red.

Walk left toward the front entrance of the museum into *Place Georges Pompidou*. Then follow your eyes, ears and interests. This area is alive with activity and people. You will have many options for entertaining yourself until dinner time.

Walk Around Pompidou Fountain

Pause to study the whimsical and colorful *Niki de Saint Phalle* sculptures in the *Stravinsky Fountain*. Find a spot to watch a street performer or observe the progress of a sidewalk artist at work, then toss a coin into the hat.

Wander through the shops that border the concrete "lawn" in front of the Pompidou, where young people actually manage to look comfortable lounging on the unyielding rock beneath them. These are likely places to find a few final treasures and gifts.

Step inside the museum to ride the external escalators to the top, where you will have an expansive view toward *Montmartre* in the distance. With your *Paris Museum Pass,* museum entry will be free. So if you have the interest and inclination, puzzle your way through some of the modern art exhibited inside.

Dinner at the Bistro Beaubourg Near Pompidou

Bistro Beaubourg. 25 rue Quincampoix.

(0)1-42-77-48-02

Your dinner reservations are at *Bistro Beaubourg,* where you can purchase dinner, including wine, for under €20 each—a rarity in Paris. This lively bistro around the corner from the *Pompidou,* is a popular gathering spot with the locals, who crowd together at outdoor tables that almost touch, while waiters weave precariously between them.

The bistro borders a tiny traffic island where neighborhood parents bring their tykes to ride tricycles in the late afternoon.

Back to the River by Foot, Taxi or Bike

Now back to the river, by foot. Or if you are exhausted, just catch a taxi, or pick up a Vélib' bike in the square a few steps from the Bistro. If you decide to walk or bike, take a different bridge "home" to see the river from a new perspective.

> Continue along *rue Quincampoix*.

> Right on *rue de la Reynie*.

> Left on *Boulevard de Sebastopol*, walking toward the river.

> Left onto *rue de Rivoli*.

> Through the gates into the park with *Saint-Jacques Tower*, all that remains from a 16th-century flamboyant gothic church that was demolished during the French Revolution.

> Counterclockwise along the path that cuts across the park, exiting through the gates at the corner of *Avenue Victoria* and *rue Saint-Martin*.

> Follow *rue Saint-Martin* to *Pont Notre Dame*.

> Cross the Seine to *Ile de la Cité*.

Your walk home will end up at the location of the *Flower Market*. Now you know where are, and how to get around. Walk "home" or wherever else you please as your final day in Paris comes to an end.

Find a Boat Bar & Watch the Bridges Light Up

When you have rested, and possibly done some of your packing, make your way back to the river for one last drink at your favorite *Boat Bar* as evening falls and the lights appear. Order a bottle of wine and listen to the music and the sounds along the river.

If you now count yourself among the millions who have fallen in love with Paris, you will return someday. So instead of "goodbye," say "au revoir"— "until I see you again."

NOTE: It will be best to arrange for your taxi to the airport tonight so you can rest assured that you will be on time for your flight tomorrow.

Day 16 (Sunday): Fly home

To Charles de Gaulle Airport by Taxi or Train

Today is a travel day. So it will be challenging. Give yourself the luxury of arranging a taxi in advance to pick you up in ample time for the 1-hour drive to *Charles de Gaulle* airport, arriving 2–3 hours before your plane departs.

If you would prefer, take the RER B line from the *Saint Michel/Notre Dame* RER/Metro station. But be careful to board the right train. Not all RER B trains stop at *CDG* airport.

To determine whether the next RER B train to arrive will take you to CDG, consult the overhead panel above the platform to see if the light is lit next to "*Aéroport Ch. de Gaulle 1*" or "*Aeroport Ch. de Gaulle 2 – TGV.*" Also, all trains with names that start with the letter "E" will stop at *Charles de Gaulle.*

And So... On to Arrangements & Preparations

Now that you have a full picture of your trip, its experiences and encounters, timing and modes of transport, it's time to move on to the practicalities and mechanics of putting your trip together.

SECTION III:

ARRANGEMENTS & PREPARATIONS

CHAPTER 9:
Making Your Trip Arrangements

Are you ready to start planning your trip? Chapter 9 will take you through making your arrangements and adjusting the plan to fit your own schedule, budget and preferences. *How? Where? When?* and *What Will It Cost?* Also this chapter provides you with a model timeline and countdown so that by the time you leave on your trip, you will have everything in place and be ready to fully enjoy your journey.

In Chapter 10, you will work your way through the practicalities, preparing for everything from money to electronics to having along everything you need and packing it efficiently.

You will be formalizing as many of the details and logistics for your trip as possible—planes, trains and accommodations—before you leave, while you still have full access to the Internet, and the ability to print out information, maps, timetables, vouchers, reservations and confirmations.

For those tasks that will best be accomplished in France, you will gather together now all the information you will need to complete them efficiently when you get there. Your *Batobus pass* and *Paris Museum Pass* will be on your list to purchase after you arrive. And you will arrange taxi drivers as you need them.

Arrangements to Make in Advance

By planning and making your arrangements in advance, you will be able to select places to stay that are optimally-located, so that when you walk out your door each day, you will be in the heart of the village, town or city you have come to visit. Establishing the framework of your trip in advance will allow you more latitude to be spontaneous once you arrive—to shift and rearrange, live in the moment, and seek out experiences as they present themselves. To customize your plan as you make arrangements, download and adapt the files at *http://YourGreatTriptoFrance.com/CustomizeYourTrip/*.

In *Amboise*, you will stay in old town, on the river, and at the foot of the castle. In *Mont Saint-Michel*, your room will be on the Mont itself, so that after the tour groups and tourists leave, you will have this mystical place almost to yourself.

Your *Bayeux* lodgings will be near the museum that houses the tapestries, and within a quick walk of the pedestrian street strung with cafés, wine shops and bakeries. In *Paris* you will stay on the *Left Bank*, within a block or two of the bridge across the Seine to *Ile de la Cité* and *Notre Dame*.

Your main mode of transport will be by train, both between your four primary destinations, and when you venture out on day trips. Once you arrive in a location, you will use the most interesting and scenic transportation option available to you there. From Amboise, you will race through the countryside by taxi to reach the Loire Valley châteaux, passing tidy vineyards and charming small villages. From the small medieval town of *Bayeux,* you again will travel by taxi to the *Normandy Beaches* and back.

In Caen, you will master the tram, and also take a spin on the *Petit Train.* In *Paris*, you will get around primarily by Batobus, and take the Metro and funicular up to *Montmartre.*

When you arrive in each location, you will set out on a self-guided "walk-about" of your immediate neighborhood, using a set of small preprinted maps. This will enable you to get well-oriented, and give you the sense that you are starting to know your way around. Then you will make a visit to the local *Tourist Information* (TI) office and pick up a full map of the town in order to expand your range of familiar territory.

Reserve Full Experience Accommodations

In order to book optimum accommodations, it will be best to start planning your trip at least 6-8 months in advance. This will provide you with a broader range of appealing, "full experience," options from which to choose. If you do not have that much lead time, just plan to get started as soon as possible.

To make your selection for each booking, start with a "fly over" of the area for an overview of what is available and where it is located. By using this fly-over method, you will have a clearer perspective of where you want to establish yourself during your visit so that you already will "be there," in the heart of it all, when you venture out for the day.

In the smaller towns, and especially on *Mont St Michel,* the wonderful rooms with views, in well-located, charming, full-experience lodgings, are in short supply and book early. It is essential to book them as far ahead as possible.

Your booking list is:

☐ *Amboise*—four nights, *Days 1–4.*

☐ *Pontorson*—one night, *Day 5*

☐ *Mont Saint-Michel*—two nights, *Days 6–7.*

☐ *Bayeux*—four nights, *Days 8–11.*

☐ *Paris, Left Bank*—four nights, *Days 12–15.*

Survey Your Options First

Using the booking.com website, *www.booking.com*, enter the locale and dates for your first stay—Amboise. Then use *Map View* for a visual overview of all your available options.

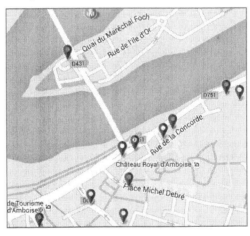

Zoom in and out as you do a "fly over" of the specific part of town where you want to stay, near the river and the castle. Hover your mouse over one pin mark at a time to view the key information about its cost and availability. Then click on any options that look promising to learn more about them.

By using this aerial overview of your options, you will have what you need to locate and select a "full experience" lodging, at a price that will not overtax your travel budget (more about this later). In addition, you will begin to gain a sense of the captivating places you will be visiting. Even this necessary exploration task can become part of the fun and anticipation of your trip.

Book the Accommodation and Room of Your Choice

Once you zero in on your choice of hotel or manor house, you will be able to choose your specific room, making your choice while balancing the cost against the quality of the experience. You also will be able to read the reviews written by other travelers who stayed there. Decide if and when you want to splurge for a room with a view... or possibly even a balcony.

Another decision you may need to make as you select and book your room, is whether or not you are willing to pay extra for "Free Cancellation." The "Free Cancellation" option allows you to make reservations early, while you still have a good range of choices, and yet retain the flexibility to make adjustments to your trip plans later should you need or wish to do so.

Chapters 4–8 have offered suggestions about where to focus your search to find optimum "full experience" lodgings in each of the four home-base locations for your trip—Amboise, Pontorson and Mont Saint-Michel, Bayeux and Paris. Flip back to these earlier chapters and make use of these recommendations to ensure that your trip will be a great one.

Purchase Plane Tickets When the Price is Right

Coming from the USA or Canada, your trip will begin with an overnight flight, arriving at *Charles de Gaulle* early the next morning. To follow the recommended schedule, book flights that depart on a Friday evening, and return on a Sunday. Travelling from Great Britain or continental Europe, fly out on a Saturday morning, and home on a Sunday.

This schedule assumes a two-week vacation from work, leaving on a Friday evening (or Saturday morning) and returning home on a Sunday. If your calendar is more flexible, you will be able to reduce the cost of your plane tickets by flying on less popular days of the week, then making the necessary adjustments to the *Day Plans* for your trip.

The key to making your flight arrangements will be to book the best flight times you can find, with the shortest trip durations, and for the best price. It is best to wait until 2 months from your travel dates to make your reservations. But start earlier to monitor ticket prices, and be prepared to make your move if and when prices dip below $1000 each (or under $200 if flying from Great Britain or Continental Europe).

You may be able to bring these costs down significantly if you are aware of five variables defined by *Rick Seaney* of *Fare Compare*: *www.farecompare.com*.

1. *How far ahead you book.* Don't book too soon or wait too late. For International tickets, book at least 1½ months ahead. For domestic flights, buy tickets at least one month before departure.

2. *If you fly hub to hub.* Check to see if flying out of or into a nearby airport will save you significant money. Larger airports, particularly hubs, often have cheaper fares.

3. *What day you book.* The optimum booking day is Tuesday at around 3 pm, when airlines release their most discounted seats.

4. *What days you fly.* If possible, plan to fly on less popular days, since these are cheaper, classically Tuesdays, Wednesdays or Saturdays. The most expensive days are usually Fridays and Sundays.

5. *How many tickets you book at a time.* Book one ticket at a time, even when there are two or more of you traveling. When you book multiple tickets at the same time, they will be sold at the same price, even if one ticket would have cost a lower price.

Don't Book Too Early or Too Late

Although it will be expensive to delay too long in purchasing your airline tickets, it is also possible to shop too early. Airlines typically have as many as 10 different price points on a single plane. Knowing when to buy and when not to buy is key to saving you money.

Airlines begin actively "managing" prices and systematically releasing cheap seats 3–4 months before departure for domestic travel and 4–5 months before international travel. If you buy earlier than that, chances are you'll pay too much. But also avoid shopping after the two-week window. Most legacy carriers raise their airfare prices dramatically inside the 14-days-to-departure window. This is to take advantage of the last minute business travelers who often don't know their travel schedules in advance and are willing to pay higher prices because they probably are not paying for their tickets themselves anyway.

Since you will be setting up your accommodations well in advance of purchasing your airline tickets, begin tracking prices earlier to establish your itinerary and schedule. In order to track price trends, search *Opodo* (*http://www.opodo.co.uk/*) and *Trip Advisor* for current price deals on multiple airlines, using multiple travel search engines at the same time.

Also set up real-time e-mail alerts on your choice of travel sites—*Travelocity*, *Vayama*, *Priceline*, *FareCompare*—to be notified when an airline drops prices. *FareCompare* tracks prices for over 500 airlines, in real-time, and notifies you *exactly* when lower-priced seats are released so you can make your purchase at an optimum time.

Keep a sheet of paper near your computer to record price fluctuations. When you spot an excellent fare for a good flight, be prepared to make your move immediately. Airlines release only a few lower cost seats at a time, so it is essential that you be first in line to purchase them.

Fly from Hub to Hub

Bigger airports mean more competition, especially for international travel for both U.S. and international airlines. This competition brings ticket prices down. Airlines charge a premium price when you bundle your connecting flights to or from smaller airports in with your international flight from hub to hub. This means you may overpay if you leave from your nearby smaller airport or fly into a smaller European airport.

Once you have arrived in Europe, short flights are inexpensive, and trains are excellent. Your best strategy may be to book your international flight hub to hub, then handle the connections to the smaller airports separately, both coming and going.

Pick the Right Day to Buy

The conventional wisdom is that Tuesday is the best day to buy airline tickets. Hopper's results show Thursday to be the optimum day to buy, for both domestic and international travel. The worst times to buy are on the weekends, with Saturday having the highest prices for domestic travel and Sunday the highest prices for international travel.

	Domestic			International		
	Best	Worst	Savings	Best	Worst	Savings
Buy	Thursday	Saturday	$10	Thursday	Sunday	$25
Depart	Wednesday	Sunday	$40	Wednesday	Sunday	$60
Return	Tuesday	Friday	$45	Wednesday	Friday	$60

Pick the Right Days to Fly

According to a summary of Hopper's data, Wednesday is, in general, the cheapest day to depart on your trip. But the price differences may be small, with savings of around $40 for domestic travel and $60 for international flights. The most expensive day to travel is not Friday or Saturday, but Sunday.

Compare prices by looking at several possible combinations of days to fly that might work for you. Depending on the price differences, adding an extra day in Paris to the end of your trip, and returning on a Monday, or even on a Tuesday, instead of on a Sunday, may partially pay for itself in airfare savings. Oh well!

Shop One Passenger at a Time

Airline reservations systems are required to charge the same ticket price for everyone in your party, even if there are lower-priced seats available for a portion of your group. Being aware of this simple glitch in the reservation system can save you money on trips with two or more passengers.

Split your ticket purchase into multiple transactions, and the savings will be worth the bother. Just complete these transactions at the same time so you will be able to match up flights, and select your seats so you can fly together.

Watch Out for Horrible Connections

As you research your options for flights, pay attention to travel duration as well as travel times and costs. Flight schedules can include some truly horrible connections.

For example, one option for round trip tickets from *Charlotte NC* to *Paris* shows a cost of $1287 for an excellent flight going over—non-stop, with a duration of *8 hours and 10 minutes*. But the return flight has a duration of *21 hours and 23 minutes*! Further investigation reveals an overnight layover at JFK, from 7:45 pm Monday evening until 6:15 am Tuesday morning. And the cost is actually $10 *more* than for the option with nonstop flights going both ways. So read the fine print, including the trip's *duration*, before you select your flights.

Consider "Open Jaw" Flights

On this *Great Trip to France*, you will be flying round trip to *Charles de Gaule* in Paris. But for future reference, or should you decide to add other destinations to this trip, be aware that generally it is no more expensive to fly "open jaw" (into one airport and home from another), than to fly round trip. Flying "open jaw" can save you the precious time and expense of backtracking to your arrival airport.

If you fly into *Paris*, for example, but then cross the *English Channel* on the *Eurostar* to spend a few days in *London*, just fly home from *London*. This will cost you less, all total, than taking the train back to *Paris* to fly home from there. And you will save an entire travel day that you then can put to much better use in *London*.

Check the Specifics for Your Airport

To view a report that is specific to the airports you will be using, visit the site: *http://www.hopper.com*. Hopper reports are based on data drawn from around 10 million flight price queries per day.

As a sample, this report on flights from *Charlotte NC* to *Paris*, shows a wide range of prices, from $720–$1224. At the time of this report, flying out on a Tuesday and returning on a Wednesday would save $91; booking on Wednesday would save $352.

$720 — $1224

Fly out on a **Tuesday**, return on a **Wednesday**, save up to $91.

The best day to buy a roundtrip ticket from Charlotte to Paris is Wednesday, saving up to $352. The best day to depart is Tuesday, saving up to $49. The best day to return is Wednesday, saving up to $41.

Consider Using Airline Points

You may have been collecting airline points through various credit cards and frequent flyer programs. As an example, the AAdvantage card that is offered through American Airlines compiles points from miles traveled as well as for credit card use, and generally offers a large number of bonus points to new card holders. Through this program, it is possible to fly round-trip internationally for 50,000 points, and domestically for 25,000 points.

To see your flight options using points on American Airlines, click to "redeem points" and search for the dates you will be traveling. As you select your flights, you are told how many additional points you will need in order to obtain a ticket. It is possible to purchase additional points should you come up short. Using airline points can save a considerable amount of money on an international ticket, even if you need to pay to supplement your points.

Book Your Trains

You will not be able to book train tickets for your actual dates of travel until the timetable for those dates is released, generally three to six months before your trip. But use the *RailEurope.com* website earlier to research your train arrangements as part of your planning process. Note that you will receive a discount for *two or more traveling together.*

As part of firming up your plan, enter fake dates that mirror the days of the week and the times you will be traveling. Determine what your options will be based on:

1.   Type of train service—regional or city-to-city,

2.   Departure and arrival times,

3.   Duration of the trip,

4.   Number of train changes, and

5.   1st versus 2nd class costs.

6.   Are reservations required?

Use RailEurope to Plan & SNFC to Book

The easiest website to use for planning is *raileurope.com*. Primarily owned by the French and Swiss rail companies, *RailEurope* has been in business for many decades, and provides a robust site that clearly shows you your options, provides needed information, and walks you through the steps to purchase your tickets.

When you actually do book your tickets, you may be able to save money by using the SNFC site, the rail system for France (*http://www.sncf.com*).

Country sites can be confusing, but they generally offer better fares. *RailEurope* charges as much as 20% more for tickets than an individual country rail site. So consider using *RailEurope* for planning, then making your ticket purchases on the country site.

On the *SNCF* site, click the down arrow in the top right-hand corner of the screen, and select "English" for easier navigation. *But when you are asked your country of origin, select "Australia" to avoid being rerouted back to RailEurope.*

When is the Best Time to Book Train Tickets?

You will be able to begin booking your train tickets approximately three months before your trip, depending on the country. Countries vary in how far ahead they firm up their timetables and put train tickets on sale. The *French Rail System* begins selling tickets for regional trains 6 months ahead, 4 months for most other trains, and 3 months for trains to Germany, Netherlands and Belgium.

Fares are cheapest right after they first go on sale, then rise steadily as more seats are sold. Price differences for early versus late purchases can be substantial, especially for long-distance train rides between major cities. As an example, a ticket that costs €130 when purchased on the day of travel can cost €99 when purchased one week ahead or €69 if bought three months early.

Lower fares depend on the number of seats already sold, not on how many days in advance they are purchased. So the rule of thumb is to purchase your train tickets as soon as they go on sale.

Rail Pass or Tickets?

The decision about when to use a *Rail Pass* and when to purchase a ticket depends on the length of each train ride. A ride of less than three hours generally costs less when you purchase a ticket, since a *Rail Pass* averages around $77 per day.

For longer train rides, or for travel days that involve multiple train rides, tickets can total as much as $200, and a *Rail Pass* will save you money.

Rail Passes are issued only for *three* or more days. To determine if you will benefit from a pass, check to see if your tickets will total more than $77 per day on *at least three* of your travel days.

Regional or City-to-City Trains?

The *SNCF* rail system operates 7,500 regional trains daily, servicing 5,000 stations. The prefix for regional trains is *TER* ("Transport Express Regional"). Regional services meet the needs specified by the 22 French regions and their *Regional Councils,* connecting small towns to urban transport hubs where travelers can then access *SCNF's* main *City-to-City* train lines. This makes it possible to catch a train to take you to and from almost anywhere in France.

Train travel between countries in Europe is also economical and efficient, generally using high-speed trains that streak through the countryside at up to 200 miles per hour. Within France, as you already know, the high-speed train is the TGV. Between Paris (or Brussels) and London, the Eurostar will speed you along under the English Channel. Thalys zooms you to Amsterdam, and TGVLyria to Geneva, Switzerland.

As a rule, *City-to-City* trains offer faster service than regional trains, but with fewer stops. *TER* trains are slower and stop at more stations. As you plan your moves from place to place, and make your train selections, note the type of train you are booking, as well as the departure and arrival times, and the number of train changes.

Are Reservations Required?

Some direct city-to-city train routes require that you book a seat reservation (around $7) in addition to purchasing a ticket or using a rail pass. When you board a train with reserved seats, locate your assigned coach and seats before you settle in.

If you miss a train with reserved seats, you will need to go to the ticket window and purchase another set of seat reservations. It will not work just to hop aboard the next train, as you would do with a local train that does not require seat assignments.

For *TER* trains with no assigned seats, you will have the flexibility of shifting to a different train at a different time, so long as it is heading to the town indicated on your ticket.

As you travel around France by train, you will be able to determine which kind of train you are boarding by looking closely at your tickets. For example, the ticket below is for: *TGV train 6193, Car 16 ("Voiture 16"),* and *Seat 47 ("Place Assise 47")*

First Class or Second Class?

French trains are generally clean and pleasant. Either first or second class tickets will provide you with comfortable seats, spectacular views and a smooth ride. Seats in first class are slightly larger, but second class seats are more than adequate. On some older trains, first and second class seats are almost identical. All cars provide restrooms, heat and air conditioning. Refreshments are sometimes available from a dedicated bar car or a trolley service that passes down the aisles, offering drinks and snacks for sale.

With either first or second class tickets, you will be handling your own luggage, including lifting it on and off the train. Rack space to store your luggage will be available, both overhead and at one or both ends of the car.

Some Advice... Write Down Trains & Times

Record on your Day Pages the specifics of your train journey—train numbers, destination stations, departure and arrival times. For TER journeys, these departure and arrival times generally will not be printed on your tickets, so you will be forced to rely on your notes to know when to get to the station, what train to board, when your train will depart, and when to get ready to hop off.

When you need to make connections, your notes will tell you how long you will have to make your train change, what destination you are heading to next, and which train you will be riding.

Also Write Down Alternate Trains & Times

In order to retain flexibility, particularly on day trips, make a habit of noting times for trains that depart before and after those you are planning to use. Since RER (regional) tickets can be used at other times during the day, you may want to know what time to get back to the station should you decide to come home early, or stay later.

Book Train Tickets for Your Trip

You will be booking *seven* trains for your trip, eight if you decide to take the train to the airport on the day you leave *Paris* to fly home. Your booking list is:

1. *Charles de Gaulle* to *Amboise* (one-way): *Day 1.*

2. *Amboise* to *Blois* (round trip): *Day 4.*

3. *Amboise* to *Pontorson* near *Mont Saint-Michel* (one-way): *Day 5.*

4. *Pontorson* to *Bayeux* (one way): *Day 8.*

5. *Bayeux* to *Caen* (round trip): *Day 9.*

6. *Bayeux* to *Caen* (round trip): *Day 11.*

7. *Bayeux* to *Paris* (one-way): *Day 12.*

8. *Paris* to *Charles De Gaulle Airport* (one way): *Day 16* (optional).

Booking 1: CDG to Amboise

For your first train trip, you will leave from *Charles de Gaulle* airport, and speed through the French countryside by TGV for under two hours to reach *Amboise* in the *Loire Valley*, your first home base. You will change to a TER train in Blois or at *St. Pierre des Corps*, outside of *Tours*, for the short ride to *Amboise*.

Booking 2: Amboise to Blois and return

The train for your day trip to *Blois* will be a TER. You will have many options for departure times, both going and coming home.

Booking 3: Amboise to Pontorson

On the day you leave *Amboise* for *Mont Saint-Michel* on the western coast of France, you will take a sequence of trains, with several train changes along the way, probably in either *Tours* and *Rennes* or *Tours* and *Caen*.

Booking 4: Pontorson to Bayeux

The train trip from *Pontorson* to *Bayeux* leaves at *9:16 am* and arrives at 11:03 am. *Be on this train*, or you will have a long wait for the next one! As you can see below, the next train from Pontorson to Bayeux leaves at 5:37 pm in the late afternoon.

FRI 20 MAY	SAT 21 MAY	SUN 22 MAY		
09:16 PONTORSON MONT ST **11:03** BAYEUX		1h 47m Direct		TER
17:37 PONTORSON MONT ST **19:31** BAYEUX		1h 54m Direct		TER

Booking 5 & 6: Bayeux to Caen

For your day trips from *Bayeux* to *Caen*, you will have many options of TER trains, coming and going. The 8:37 am or the 9:20 am morning trains to *Caen* will give you an early enough start to have a good block of time to explore Caen. The 5:29 pm or the 6:03 pm trains back to *Bayeux* are good choices for the return trip.

8:37AM Bayeux	8:53AM Caen	0hr 16min	SNCF Intercités 3302
9:20AM Bayeux	9:38AM Caen	0hr 18min	SNCF TER 52614
5:29PM Caen	5:45PM Bayeux	0hr 16min	SNCF TER 52817
6:03PM Caen	6:19PM Bayeux	0hr 16min	SNCF Intercités 3313

Booking 7: Bayeux to Paris

When you journey from *Bayeux* to *Paris*, plan to leave on the 8:37 am train, arriving at *Paris St. Lazare* at 10:46 am.

8:37AM	10:46AM	2hr	
Bayeux	Paris St	9min	
	Lazare		Intercités 3302

Booking 8 (optional): Paris to CDG

Although a taxi may be less stressful, the cheapest and fastest transportation to Charles de Gaulle (CDG) from central Paris is by taking the 40-minute ride on the RER B (blue line on RER maps). The cost is 10€ one way.

If you elect to take the train to the airport, board the RER B at the *Saint Michel/Notre Dame* RER/Metro station. You will want direction *Aéroport Charles de Gaulle*, with the arrival stations *Aéroport CDG 1* or *Aéroport CDG 2 TGV*. The first train leaves Paris Gare du Nord for CDG at *4:56 am*, arriving at *Terminal 1* at *5:28 am* and at *Terminal 2* at *5:30 am*.

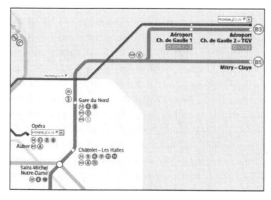

Be careful to board the correct train. Not all RER B trains stop at *CDG* airport. Consult the overhead panel above the platform to determine if the light is lit next to *"Aéroport Ch. de Gaulle 1"* or *"Aeroport Ch. de Gaulle 2–TGV."*

When you arrive at CDG by RER B, the train will make stops at both *Terminal 1* and *Terminal 2*. If your flight will be leaving from *Terminal 1*, you will, in fact, get off the train at *Terminal 3*, then take the CDGVAL shuttle tram to *Terminal 1*. Look for signs on the overhead walkway above the tramline to determine which side of the CDGVAL tram line you need to board to reach *Terminal 1*. As you may remember from your arrival at

CDG 16 days ago, *Terminal 3* is actually located between *Terminal 1* and *Terminal 2*. So you will need to pick the correct direction for *Terminal 1*.

Consult the RER B schedule at: *http://parisbytrain.com/paris-rer-b-schedule-stations-interchanges/*. Allow plenty of time, and plan to arrive at the airport three hours before flight time.

A Quick Review About Traveling by Train

Review the complete description of how to travel by train in *Chapter 5* before you leave on your trip.

To summarize here, follow these eight main steps:

1. Find the "Big Board" to check for your train and track.

2. Pick up sandwiches and drinks for your ride.

3. Locate your track and confirm that this is your train.

4. Validate your ticket prior to boarding.

5. Board the correct car and find your seat.

6. Stow your luggage.

7. Make note of the stop before yours, so you will know when it is almost time to get off.

8. Gather your belongings at the door *before* the train reaches your station.

Local Transport, Museum Cards & Reservations

Although you will probably wait until you arrive in France to purchase your various *Museum Cards* and *Transport Cards*, review your *Day Pages* before your trip so you will know when, where and how to make these purchases once you arrive. These cards and passes will make your travel infinitely more pleasurable.

For the days on which you will be traveling by taxis, including out to the châteaux in the *Loire Valley*, and from *Bayeux* over to the *D-Day Beaches*, the information you will need with you on the days you use drivers is included as part of your trip *Day Pages*.

You do need to complete one local purchase before you leave on your trip—your tickets (and possibly dinner reservations) for the *Eiffel Tower*.

Check the *Day Pages* for all the information you need to make these arrangements in advance.

How Much Will Your Trip Cost?

The proposed budgeting philosophy for your trip will be to balance *splurging* on peak experiences with *conserving* when pleasant lower-cost opportunities present themselves. This strategy will provide you the most for your money, yet enable you to stay within your budget.

The model budget below estimates costs for accommodations, airfare, trains, taxis, local transportation, food, entry fees, treasures and gifts, breaking these main trip costs into three basic categories:

1. Necessary costs *in advance* of your trip—accommodation deposits, airfares and train tickets. These costs you will know in advance and can be controlled by finding the lowest prices.

2. Necessary costs *during* your trip—accommodation balances, food, local transportation, entrance passes. These can be balanced between splurges and economies.

3. Optional costs for treasures and gifts.

Costs in Advance of Your Trip

A reasonable transportation cost estimate for this trip would be around $1200 each for airfare if you are flying from the US or Canada, and around $200 if traveling from Great Britain or continental Europe. Add to this $300 each for train tickets. This equates to around $1500 each, or *$3000* for two. Of course, airfare will be considerably less expensive if you are traveling to France from Great Britain or continental Europe.

These known upfront costs are a main source of the "sticker shock" of European travel. The good news is that once you cross the Atlantic and arrive, you will be spending the same, or possibly less, than you would if you were traveling in the United States.

To control your accommodation costs, keep to a $200 per night average by balancing your choices, spending less in one place when you spend more in another. *Paris* accommodations will most certainly be more expensive than those in *Amboise*. *Mont Saint-Michel* will cost more than your night in *Pontorson*, near the train station, or your nights in *Bayeux*. If you follow the model of averaging out your accommodation expenses to $200 a night, your total for 15 nights will be another *$3000* for two.

Some accommodations will require a deposit to hold your reservation. Assuming an average of $200/night for your hotels, and approximate deposits of 20%, this adds another $600 to the advance costs for your trip.

Costs During Your Trip

Next come the costs *while* you are on your trip, namely your per diem costs—your daily budget for meals, transportation, and entry fees. To calculate your per diem costs, again use the philosophy of balancing out splurges with economizing, anticipating an average of around $200 a day for two ($100 each). This daily allowance is likely to work out well, and will give you many fine options throughout your trip.

If your budget gets skewed by a day of spending either too little or too much, rebalance it by arranging meals that are priced in the opposite direction. Balance elegant dining with picnics in the park. Both will be fun.

And remember that even if you had stayed at home, you would have spent money for groceries and entertainment. So subtract $250 per week ($500 for the duration) from your per diem total before you add it to your full trip budget. With a per diem of around $200 a day, and subtracting $500 for what you would have spent in two weeks at home, the total per diem cost equates to $2500 for two ($1250 each).

The Grand Total for Your Trip

The grand total, then, for your great trip to France is around $8500, or $4250 each. With any luck, you may be able to trim another $500 from this total by finding airline tickets for under $1000 each and discounted train tickets. This could easily bring your total down to $8000 for two, or $4000 each, for a two-week trip. Traveling from Great Britain or continental Europe, airfare will come in at around $200 each, give or take. All this can be adjusted up and down, of course, according to your preferences, but this model budget will give you an idea.

Your Great Trip to France: Estimated Budget		
Airfare	*For 2*	*$2,400*
Trains	*For 2*	*$ 600*
Accommodations	*For 15 nights*	*$3,000*

Per Diem	For 15 nights	$2,500
	TOTAL:	$8,500
	EACH:	$4,250

So… the bottom line is that if you can manage $4250 each, you can take your 2-week dream vacation to France from the US or Canada. If you cut back to a 1-week version of the trip (visiting your choice of two of the destinations), your costs will be reduced to around $3150 each. From the UK or Europe, reduce this cost to around $3250 each for a 2-week trip, and $2150 each for a 1-week trip.

Optional Costs for Treasures and Gifts

The third category of costs, treasures and gifts to bring home, is entirely optional. You may decide on an upper limit. But it is also wise to establish a lower limit, so you will not come home empty-handed.

One approach to trip purchases is to bring home items you will use—a lightweight coat, a soft leather portfolio, cloth placemats and napkins. Useful items brought from abroad are an excellent means to preserve the memories of the days and special moments of your trip. Every time you wear that scarf, or those sandals, or that hat, or that pendant, you will be transported back to this time of intense experiences and discoveries.

Strategies to Come Up With Travel Money

Where do you find the money to take your great trip? Here are some ideas. Only some ideas will apply to you, but this will get you started.

Make Travel a Priority

First, shift your lifestyle in ways that make travel a priority. Place travel at the top of your list when you make choices. Money spent on travel is money spent well. Travel is one of the few expenditures that will "pay you back" more than you spend—in experiences and learning, as well as in pleasure. Yes your Honda dealer is offering you a good trade in for your car for the latest model. Then there's your Starbucks coffee on the way to work every morning. And your lunch out.

That stack of catalogs in your mailbox offers many temptations. And those big sales at the mall readily lead to buying something.

Granted it is easier to pick up consumable items, such as gift bags, Ziplocs, birthday cards, and hand soaps during one of your regular stops at the grocery store or Target instead of making a monthly run to the *Dollar Store*, where these and other disposable items cost $1 each instead of $4–$5. And what about those "money leaks" from monthly subscriptions that seem just to accumulate, and then automatically renew year after year?

Turn each buying decision into a question.

- Would I rather buy a new car this year or take a great trip to France?

- Would I rather stop by Starbucks each morning, or wait to sip coffee in a French café?

- Do I really want or need to eat lunch out every day, or would I be willing to pack lunch 2–3 times a week, and bank my savings to spend in Paris, dining at the restaurant on the *Eiffel Tower*?

- Would I rather buy more clothes from catalogs and the Mall, or travel to France and purchase them at a weekly market or at a vintage shop in Paris?

- Would it be worth it to me to make a monthly stop by the *Dollar Store* to stock up on gift bags, Ziplocs, birthday cards, and hand soaps and add to my trip account the $3–$4 per item that I save?

- Are there any monthly subscriptions that I could live without, or possibly even that I don't know I still have?

The table below estimates potential savings, based on these first few moves you could make. These add up to more than the $8,000 you will need in your trip account to cover the basic costs for your trip, with enough left over to buy many treasures to bring home.

Categories	$ Saved	Per Year
Keep my car another year	$400/month car payment	$4,800
Cut back catalog & Mall shopping	$200/month	$2,400
Skip the Starbucks	$125/month	$1,500
Pack lunch twice a week	$125/month	$1,500

Purchase 35 items/month at the Dollar Store	$125/month	$1,500
Cancel 2 monthly subscriptions	$40/month	$480
	TOTAL:	$12,180

Capture Your Travel Funds in a Separate Account

To ensure that your trip savings plan proceeds on schedule, set up a separate account designated *for that purpose and that purpose only*. Then fund this account with a specific amount on a regular basis. Be firm in your resolve that this money will only be used for travel.

If you held off on purchasing a car, and cut back on catalog and Mall shopping by $200 per month, add $600 to your travel account monthly. If you skipped Starbucks and packed your lunch twice a week, put away another $250, plus $165 from your *Dollar Store* and your monthly subscription savings. This totals $1015 per month. But even if you set aside $750 per month, you will have enough for your trip, with $500 for treasures.

Use a "Day Page" System After Customizing Your Trip

This guide provides you with the connect-the-dots framework for your trip, along with detailed *"Day Pages"* in Chapters 4–9. If you follow these plans, you will know how to move from place to place, and what to do, day-by-day, to accomplish a superb version of your trip. You will know why what you are doing is special, and how to make the most of it. And you will know some of the juicy parts of the history that surrounds you.

Make Adjustments & Adapt the Trip "Day Pages"

Make adjustments to the framework for your trip according to your own particular interests and energies. Then adjust based on your changes. As you arrange your accommodations, air and train travel, add your own details to your version of the *Day Pages*. Use the downloadable *Day Page* file from *http://YourGreatTriptoFrance.com/CustomizeYourTrip/*, then adjust:

- All critical information.

- Orienteering Notes.

- Markets & Events.

302

Adjust Critical Information

Replace the sample accommodation notes with the places where you have arranged to stay. Include all contact information: address, phone, email address and website. Copy/paste key information from the accommodation's website, along with photos, history, what's nearby, room descriptions, and reviewer notes about favorite neighborhood restaurants, cafés and markets.

Adjust Orienteering Notes

Your first hour or so in each new location will be devoted to getting yourself oriented by walking out your door to learn the streets around you and where to locate your neighborhood markets, ATM, pharmacy, cafés and restaurants. Since the orienteering notes and maps in this book are based on sample accommodations, you will need to adapt your orientation walk to fit your actual neighborhood.

Adjust for Markets & Events

French *Market Days* are always interesting and memorable. It is well worth making adjustments to your trip *Day Pages* to include any opportunities you may have to visit them while you are in each locale. If you follow the proposed trip schedule in this guide, you will, at a minimum, be able to attend the *Sunday Market* in *Amboise*, the *Saturday Market* in *Bayeux*, the *Sunday Market* in *Caen*, and the *Maubert Market* and the *Flower Market* in *Paris*. If you end up with a different travel schedule, add your own markets.

Finalize Day Pages to Print & Take Along

Download the files to customize your *Day Pages* with your own specific information at *http://YourGreatTriptoFrance.com/CustomizeYourTrip/*. Print out your personalized version to take with you. As you set out each day during your trip, take along the *Day Pages* for that day so that you will have ready access to everything you need for the day to go smoothly. If you make mid-trip adjustments because you get tired or it rains or you happen upon something too wonderful to miss, you will be free to switch around some of the days. As long as you have your *Day Pages* with you, you will know where to go, what to do, and how. You will be able to travel about with confidence.

Trip Arrangements Countdown

If you have the option, begin planning your trip at least six to eight months in advance, and follow the countdown outlined below. This is the ideal, and will improve your chances of booking accommodations that are in ideal locations. Also this timeline spaces out the larger expenses to make the trip more doable financially, as well as time-wise and logistically.

If it turns out that you have less than six months to plan and arrange your trip, speed up this timeline based on your realities. But begin booking your accommodations as soon as you know your basic travel schedule. And even if you are following a condensed timeline, *do* include all the steps.

Throughout the planning period, spend time thinking and imagining, reading through the *Day Page* chapters of this guide, and discussing "must do" hopes and expectations, both yours and your travel partner's. To further prepare for your adventure, watch movies and read novels that are set in France.

Timeline Summary

- *6 months ahead: Itinerary, accommodations & passports.*

- *5 months ahead: Maps & language learning.*

- *4 months ahead: Trip-related purchases.*

- *3 months ahead: Airline & train tickets.*

- *2 months ahead: Any remaining pre-trip arrangements—passes, tickets, drivers, reservations.*

- *1 month ahead: Starting cash. Set things up at home.*

- *Final week before: Prep and pack (twice!).*

- *First tasks on arrival.*

6 Months Prior to Trip

☐ Establish timeline for trip.

☐ Make any desired changes to trip itinerary.

☐ Make and adjust bookings.

☐ Create initial budget; add actual accommodation costs.

☐ Start *Day Pages*. Add info and maps for bookings.

☐ Obtain or renew passport, if needed.

5 Months Prior to Trip

☐ Order map of France, with a blow-up of the Loire region and of Paris.

☐ Remap orientation "walk-about"s based on bookings.

☐ Order *"French at a Glance"* phrase book. Consider ordering *Pimsler French* CDs or *Instant Immersion French*.

☐ Start language learning.

4 Months Prior to Trip

☐ Make trip-related purchases to address the *10 Priorities* for comfortable, safe, organized, engaged, connected travel (more about this in Chapter 10).

☐ Start tracking air fares.

☐ Start planning train travel.

3 Months Prior to Trip

☐ Make plane reservations.

☐ Book trains.

☐ Add plane and train information to *Day Pages*.

☐ Update trip budget.

2 Months Prior to Trip

☐ Purchase pre-trip passes, cruise tickets or concert tickets.

☐ Make any needed pre-trip reservations.

☐ Book drivers in advance, if needed.

☐ Add pass, ticket, reservation & driver info to *Day Pages*.

1 Month Prior to Trip

☐ Obtain starting cash.

☐ Finalize & print *Day Pages*.

☐ Shift funds to travel accounts.

☐ Make arrangements for home responsibilities.

☐ Personalize and print out packing list.

FINAL WEEK Prior to Trip

☐ Pack checked bags, carry-ons, and personal items.

☐ Check items off on personalized packing list to ensure that nothing essential is missed.

☐ Unpack and eliminate 15% of what you're taking, then repack.

☐ Review your trip documents to ensure that you have connected all the dots and that everything you will need is organized and readily accessible.

And So... On to Preparing for Your Trip

Now that you have a full picture of how you will plan your trip, its experiences and encounters, timing and modes of transport, it's time to focus on how to prepare yourself for your journey, and what to do immediately after you arrive.

So now, onward to getting yourself prepared.

Chapter 10:

Preparing for Your Great Trip

Next we will focus on how to prepare yourself for your journey. What do you need to take with you? How should you organize and pack it? How will you handle your money matters? How will you find your way around? What electronics will you need and how will you manage them? How will you connect with the locals through language readiness and cultural adaptation?

Make Your List: What to Take Along & Why

Understanding how to pack for your trip and optimize your suitcase can make a big difference in how smoothly your whole trip goes. Pack too much and you'll be struggling with a heavy suitcase getting on and off trains and in and out of hotels. Pack too little and you'll find yourself wearing the same clothes over and over again and shopping for essentials in unfamiliar stores. Finding the right balance is essential.

Since you will be carrying around and living out of a suitcase for several weeks, the challenge is to strike a balance. On the one hand, you will need to bring along all your "must have" necessities. On the other hand, it is essential that your suitcases are light enough to be manageable as you lift them on and off trains and up and down stairways. Doing a good job with your trip preparations will ensure that your days of travel will be comfortable and hassle-free.

So what should you plan to take with you? A good way to think this through is to anticipate the various life-needs, functional needs and contingencies to be prepared to handle during your trip. You will need to be prepared to:

1. *Select the right suitcases* that meet airline standards, are very light-weight when empty, and pull along on 360° spinner wheels.

2. *Use a packing system* to maximize space, minimize repacking time during your trip and prevent wrinkles.

3. *Dress comfortably* for warm and cool, sunny and rainy weather, and to walk miles each day up and down hills and across cobblestones.

4. *Manage and handle your money.*

5. *Carry and readily access your trip documents,* including passport, plane and train tickets, accommodation phone numbers and addresses, reservations and *Day Pages.*

6. *Use phones and electronics abroad.*

7. *Safely carry* passports, credit and debit cards and cash.

8. *Set out* each day, ready for anything.

9. *Stay healthy* for the duration of your trip, ready to handle a variety of possible physical challenges without lost days.

10. *Interact and relate* with the locals.

11. *Bring home* treasures and gifts.

12. *Capture* your trip so you will be able to revisit it in the future.

We will start with your suitcases, then move to packing to meet airline restrictions, as well as to optimize space and ease of access. From there we will build a complete list to address each of these ten critical functions, and carry everything around safely. For a customizable digital version of your packing list, visit: *http://YourGreatTriptoFrance.com/CustomizeYourTrip/*

Select Your Suitcases Well

Your approach to what suitcases you will bring is a matter of personal choice. There are advantages and disadvantages that need to be weighed depending on your style of travel and your physical strength.

In this section we'll cover:

- Airline-enforced baggage and security restrictions,

- How best to distribute what you take among your two suitcases and your personal item,

- How to choose the right suitcases, and

- How to use a packing system to optimize space, stay organized, and prevent wrinkles.

Baggage Restrictions: What Airlines Will Allow

Airport security restrictions and airline baggage limitations have become stricter over time. Understanding some of these basic restrictions can save you time at the airline check-in counter and help facilitate getting you through the security screening process with minimum hassle.

What you will have to work with for the duration of your trip parallels what the airlines will allow:

- one checked suitcase (free for international travel),

- a carry-on, and

- a personal item (e.g., a purse or book bag).

We firmly recommend that you bring all three, and plan your packing accordingly. Some highly experienced travelers have fine-tuned their packing regimens over time, and take pride in being able to fit everything they need for several weeks into a single carry-on. But there's no reason to push yourself this hard, or to limit yourself this severely, just starting out. You can refine your packing style bit by bit with every trip you take, and gradually adjust your packing style to suit your own preferences.

The key is to keep your checked suitcase as light as possible. You will be rolling it around, hoisting it on and off train cars, and lugging it up and down stairs (when no elevator is available). So it needs to be manageable.

Your Checked Suitcase

Checking your first suitcase is typically free for international travel, so you should take advantage of this by checking one bag. Checked bags can be no larger than 62 inches total (length, plus width, plus height). As an example, a bag that is 27"L by 21"W by 14"H would add up to a total of 62 inches (27+21+14=62).

The weight limit for checked bags is 50 pounds. Any bag that exceeds these limits will incur steep "overage" fees. Standards may vary slightly between airlines, so confirm the luggage size and weight restrictions for your airline after you book your tickets.

Your Carry-On Suitcase

Carry-on suitcases can be no larger than 45 inches total (length, plus width, plus height). As an example, a bag that is 22"L by 14"W by 9"H totals 45 inches (22+14+9=45). Most airlines post a 50 pound weight limit for carry-on bags, but they typically don't weigh these bags to enforce the limit.

When looking to purchase a carry-on suitcase, look for the words "carry-on" in the suitcase description, or use that as part of your Google search to ensure that its dimensions comply with airline size restrictions.

Restrictions on liquids
Airport security in both the USA and Europe, TSA in the US and the EU in Europe, restrict the quantity of liquids, aerosols, gels, creams and pastes you are allowed to carry into the cabin in your carry-on bag (or your personal item). The cutoff is 100 ml, equivalent to 3.4 ounces. All liquids must be contained in a clear quart-sized Ziploc bag to allow the contents to be easily screened, and to prevent leakage.

Duty-free liquids are an exception to this limitation so long as they remain sealed inside a security bag along with the receipt. Medications and baby food may be exempt from the volume restriction. Check the TSA and EU websites for more information about exceptions to the volume limit.

Other restricted items
There are a number of items you will not be allowed to bring into the cabin in your carry-on luggage at all. These include any sharp object that could be used as a weapon, including corkscrews, scissors, pocket knives, nail files and clippers. Weapons, explosives and inflammable items, are forbidden, as well. Basically anything that can cause harm to other people is prohibited in the cabin of the plane. Check the TSA and EU websites for more information about restricted items.

What to pack in your carry-on
Pack into your carry-on suitcase any items that you can't be without if your main, checked suitcase is delayed or lost in transit and that you will not need access to during your flight. This includes any required medications, a few days of clothes, an extra pair of shoes, an umbrella or rain poncho, electronics and chargers and even some toiletries and cosmetics that you can't be without (so long as they are under the 3.4 ounce liquid limitation). Your goal is to have everything you need to travel comfortably for one or two days, if your checked suitcase is delayed or lost.

Opening your carry-on during flight may be tricky, so pack anything you would like to access during your flight in your personal item instead.

Distribute the weight

Another use of your carry-on is to distribute the weight from your checked suitcase and make it easier to handle. Distributing the weight between your checked and carry-on suitcases in this way will help make transporting both suitcases much easier, and also will protect against weight overage fees. Heavier items such as books and shoes are good candidates to shift into your carry-on for weight distribution purposes.

If you're traveling as a couple, or with a friend, factor in you and your travel partner's strength, and how much weight each person traveling can comfortably handle. Make your weight distribution decisions accordingly. On train travel days, the stronger of you will likely end up managing the two larger bags, and the weaker the two carry-ons. You may consider sharing a single carry-on, although this will make the bag twice as heavy to lift up into trains and carry up and down stairs.

One additional note… Since you will have a carry-on, you may opt to bring a medium-sized suitcase as your checked bag rather than a large one. Again, this depends on your packing style, and what you intend to bring with you.

Your Personal Item

You are also allowed to bring a book bag, large purse, or large satchel as a personal item onto the plane, and keep it under the seat in front of you. Use this bag for items you may need to be able to access before, during and immediately after your flight such as:

- [ ] passport and driver's license,

- [ ] credit and ATM cards and starter Euros,

- [ ] frequent flyer info, tickets, E-tickets and vouchers,

- [ ] prescriptions and medical information,

- [ ] insurance information (both trip and personal),

- [ ] hotel reservations and *Day Pages*,

- [ ] cell phone and battery charger,

- [ ] tablet or computer, and

- [ ] *Your Great Trip to France* guidebook.

Other items you may want to use during your long flight include:

- ☐ book or magazines,

- ☐ special medications and Melatonin (to prevent jetlag),

- ☐ lightweight sweater or jacket,

- ☐ inflatable neck pillow, eye mask, and earplugs (for overnight flights),

- ☐ personal earphones (to listen to music or watch movies), and

- ☐ toothbrush, toothpaste, floss, mouthwash, deodorant, brush or comb, and possibly an electric razor, to freshen up.

You may even consider a travel-sized dry shampoo to reduce oil, and eliminate airplane hair. You will have lots of time on the plane, you might as well feel fresh, confident and ready to tackle your first day in France!

Choose the Right Suitcases

For this trip, you will be traveling for 15 days, so one large suitcase (under 62 total inches), plus one carry-on (no larger than 45 inches total), and one personal item should provide ample room. Both checked bag and carry-on need to have wheels, preferably 360° spinner wheels, and should be very light weight.

If you limit your clothing to only one week's worth, to be washed mid-trip (we'll cover how to wash your clothes during your trip later in this chapter), your suitcase will remain relatively light, especially if you purchase a lightweight suitcase to begin with. You will have ample room for your toiletries, electronics, planning materials, books and miscellaneous items, and still have space left over to add treasures along the way.

As you consider choosing a suitcase, think through what your suitcase will represent while you are traveling. Your suitcase will be more than just your closet. It also will be your logistical hub, your medicine cabinet, your home office, and your communication center. Take everything you need. But make sure each item you take passes the "do I need it enough to want to carry it?" test.

In this section we cover choosing your suitcases and packing them to optimize space. This will enable you to bring all your essentials without being overwhelmed by overly heavy or disorderly suitcases.

Hard-sided versus Soft-Sided

Hard-sided luggage can be slightly lighter then soft-sided luggage and protects fragile items better. However, it lacks flexibility when you attempt to fit it into an overhead compartment. Soft-sided luggage can be compacted and absorbs shock better. And it typically has more expandable pockets to help accommodate additional items. But many soft-sided bags do not have wheels, and some cheaper luggage can tear.

360° Spinner Wheels versus Inline Wheels

The 2-wheel or inline-wheel suitcase rolls forwards and backwards, and can be easier to maneuver on uneven surfaces like cobblestones. However the awkward pulling motion of dragging the bag behind you can strain your wrists and shoulders. Also these bags are prone to tipping over when the front pockets are loaded.

The 4-wheel-spinner bag has become popular because it improves mobility and makes maneuvering fairly easy. It is very stable, and can rotate 360 degrees, allowing you to roll the bag at your side, push it in front of you, or pull it behind you. This flexibility of movement can reduce the strain on your wrists and arms. *If you do not own a 4-wheel-spinner bag, we strongly recommend that you treat yourself and purchase one to take on this trip, even if you think you could eke by with your current luggage.*

How to Save Money When Shopping for Your Suitcases

Lightweight luggage with 360°-spinner wheels can be pricey, but it is possible to find options for under $200—even for 2- or 3-piece luggage sets. Visit *http://YourGreatTriptoFrance.com/CustomizeYourTrip/* for lists and links to current value options.

A second option is to conduct a Google search for "lightweight spinner luggage," and add the word "discontinued," "clearance," "sale," or "closeout." Many sites offer filters to narrow down your options to only the types of bags you're interested in.

Search *amazon.com, travelsmith.com, zappos.com, ebags.com, macys.com, target.com, belk.com,* and even *newegg.com* and *overstock.com.* You'll find brand names like *TravelPro, IT Luggage, Samsonite,* and *Delsey*. All of these make high-quality suitcases, with lightweight options that aren't overly expensive. Focus on lightweight bags with 360°-spinner wheels.

Use a Packing System to Stay Organized & Unwrinkled

Now for some tips and guidelines on wrinkle-free packing & maximizing space. You're going to be living out of your suitcase for several weeks in a number of different cities, packing and unpacking your suitcase everywhere you go. In order to really maximize the real estate you have available to you in your suitcase, and to save you a good deal of time maintaining your suitcase, we suggest that you take a modular approach to packing.

A modular approach involves separating your gear into separate modules and kits. Modules can be sorted into similar items, like shirts, socks and underwear, pants and shorts. Kits can be organized by function—laundry kit, grooming kit, electronics kit, outdoor kit, and so on. This type of order may seem to be too much of a bother before you leave on your trip. But once you are on your way, you will thank yourself many times over for setting up your suitcases to keep all your belongings more organized.

Pre-trip organizing will make it simpler for you to get to what you need as you pack and unpack in each city, without pulling your whole suitcase apart. When you arrive in each location, just quickly unpack your modules and kits into the drawers and closets. Then refill and pack them quickly back into your suitcases when you are ready to move on to the next place.

There are a number of modular packing approaches to stay organized, make best use of limited space, speed up packing and unpacking in each city, prevent your clothes from wrinkling, and isolate dirty or wet clothing. Our favorite methods, used in combination, are:

1. packing folders, cubes and sacs,
2. clothes-rolling,
3. bundle-wrapping, and
4. space-saver bags.

Use Garment Folders, Packing Cubes and Packing Sacs

The core of your modular packing efforts will come from garment folders, packing cubes and packing sacs. These will significantly speed up your packing and unpacking, and are a great way to stack and compress clothing of the same type, as well as to organize odds and ends that otherwise will fall to the bottom of your suitcase and be difficult to find again when you need them.

While packing folders, cubes and sacs are available from a number of different manufacturers, we like *TravelSmith*, and also *Eagle Creek*, because their products are well-designed for ease of use, with a variety of sizes and colors, consistent quality, positive reviews and 100% guarantees (*Eagle Creek* also has lifetime warranties).

Garment folders have Velcro closures so multiple items can be folded and stacked, then compressed. They work well for larger items, like shirts, pants, skirts, sweaters and pajamas, and come with a folding board. By holding folded clothing tightly together so it does not move about freely, these envelopes keep wrinkles and creases to a minimum.

Packing cubes are zippered, with mesh tops so you can easily see what's in each. They are perfect for smaller clothing items like socks, belts, ties, or undergarments. When nestled together and zipped up in a packing cube, your rolled clothing will stay put even without the rubber bands or ball bungees that would be needed otherwise to keep your rolled clothes from unraveling.

Packing sacs are moisture proof and made of a see-through plastic so you can see what's inside. The smallest size can organize earbuds, cables and chargers for your electronics.

Use medium-sizes for your plane toiletry kit, or makeup kit. And the large size organizes and protects your trusty guidebook, maps and French phrase-books.

Both *TravelSmith* and *Eagle Creek* have toiletry bags in all sorts of shapes and sizes. Just make sure to get one with a hook, so you can hang it up wherever you go.

All of these items come in a range of colors. So you may want to add color coding to your packing strategy for additional efficiency.

If you still have some mild wrinkling and creasing of your clothing, take along and use a product like *Downy's Wrinkle Releaser* to relax fabric fibers so wrinkles can be smoothed out with your hand. *Wrinkle Releaser* is safe for most fabrics. Just spray it on your rumpled clothing, tug, smooth and wear. It comes in a three-ounce bottle, which is perfect even to be packed in your carry on.

Roll Up Your Clothes

The majority opinion from experienced travelers is that folding your clothes into rectangles and stacking them is by far the worst way to approach packing a suitcase, although many people use this method to fold and store clothes at home. Unfortunately, folding your clothes in your suitcase this way creates creases and wrinkles, unless you use garment folders as discussed above.

Also, folded items do not fill up the entire height and width of your suitcase, thus wasting space. Rolled clothing can be stacked together more tightly, better utilizing the full dimensions of your suitcase (refer to the clothes rolling guide below). Also, rolling up your pants, skirts, shirts and coats will help prevent wrinkling.

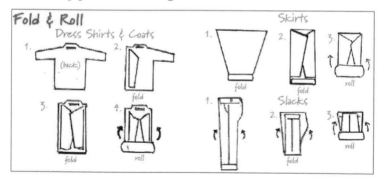

After rolling your clothes, place the opening of the roll against the bottom of the suitcase so it will not unroll and get wrinkled. In order to prevent your rolled clothing from unrolling when it is unpacked and repacked in each city you visit, use rubber bands, or small ball bungees (easily found at any hardware store) to keep each item neatly secured.

When rolling larger garments, skip folding them in half first before rolling them up to avoid a hard crease-line.

Bundle-Wrap Your Clothes

Another effective wrinkle-preventing packing method is to bundle- wrap larger items around a core of soft clothing. The idea here is that wrapping clothes around a central core object helps to avoid folds that cause creases. Also, the wrapping process anchors your clothing in place, creating a slight bit of tension on the fabric, that reduces wrinkling.

Create a soft "core" by tightly wrapping underwear, socks, pajamas or bathing suits in a t-shirt. The ideal dimensions for your core is around 11" by 16" (30cm by 40cm). Button all jackets and shirts, and zip all zippers.

The best place to bundle-wrap your clothing is on a large flat surface, such as a bed. Work from your most tailored and wrinkle-prone clothing to your least. Wrapping your clothes in this order will put your more wrinkle-prone clothing on the outside of the bundle, where the larger radius of curvature will reduce wrinkling.

Lay your jackets flat (this is the only item that faces downward). Then add skirts, dresses and long-sleeved shirts (with their sleeves out flat), oriented vertically, alternating direction so that the top one third of each item overlaps what lies beneath it. Allow room to insert the core later.

Continue to layer items on top, including short-sleeved shirts, pants, sweaters, shorts, and finally T-shirts, smoothing out wrinkles as you go.

Once all your clothes are in place, add the core. Now wrap the last item placed in the stack around the core, then the next item and so on, until all of your clothes are wrapped around the core. When wrapping shirts, wrap the sleeves around the core first, then the body. Again, be careful to smooth out wrinkles as you go.

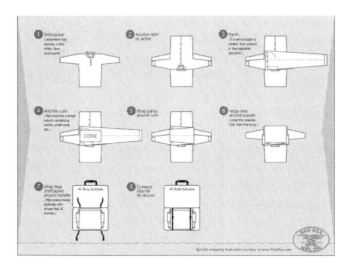

One disadvantage to bundle-wrapping is that you will need to unwrap the entire bundle to get to a particular item. This method typically works best if you plan to unpack everything when you arrive at your destination, and hang it all in the closet.

Use Space Saver Bags

Space-saver roll-up bags can more than double your available space for clothing by removing extra air. They are very easy take along, then use as needed. Consider using several small to medium sized bags, rather than one large bag, so you can stay better organized. Like packing cubes, space-saver bags work great with clothing that's less likely to wrinkle, such as T-shirts, socks, undergarments, sweaters, sweats, and pajamas. If you're assembling entire outfits beforehand, you could even include wrinkle-proof shorts, skirts, or lightweight slacks.

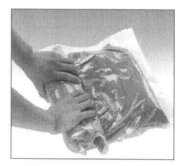

Load the bag with neatly folded or rolled clothes and seal the bag with the double zipper. Then, starting at the zipper, roll up the bag to compress it, forcing out the air through the one-way valve at the bottom of the bag (see below). Congratulations, you have just reduced the space for your clothes by 50%!

Using sealable bags is a great way to isolate dirty, or wet clothes from everything else and to prevent clothes from getting soaked if your luggage gets exposed to rain while traveling.

Also, as with packing cubes, using space-saver bags makes unpacking quick and easy in each city by simply choosing the storage bag with the type of clothes you will need there, and placing the entire bag into your hotel dresser drawer. When you're ready to pack up again, reseal and compress each bag, place it back in your suitcase, and off you go.

Blend Modular Packing Methods Together

Combine these various packing strategies into a packing system that works best for you. For clothing, bundle-wrap blazers, jackets, dress shifts and other wrinkle-prone items. Use clothing folders and the rolling method for the rest. And take along a wrinkle-releaser spray.

Use a packing cube for each category of smaller items and odds and ends, or a packing sac for items that must stay dry. Take along space-saver bags to be ready to compress and isolate the dirty laundry, or clothes that you no longer plan to use.

Now that you understand how modular packing works, mix and match these methods to best suit your travel style, speed up packing and unpacking, minimize wrinkling, and stay organized.

Take the Right Clothes

Pack light, but well. While on your trip, you will want to feel good about how you look. But you do not need or want to carry along so many clothes that lifting your suitcases into the train will be a strain.

One good approach to selecting what to take along on a 15-day trip is to coordinate five, or six outfits, then plan to rotate as well as mix and match them. Here are some rules-of-thumb.

Take Non-Wrinkle Cotton Clothing

Select textured or blended cotton clothing that doesn't wrinkle, if possible. Cotton or blends will be comfortable in buildings with no air conditioning. Visit *http://YourGreatTriptoFrance.com/CustomizeYourTrip/* for some good options and links where you can find them.

319

An excellent source of affordable, wearable, comfortable and stylish women's clothes is http://www.theeccentriccat.com.

Take Your Favorites, Including Colors

No need to stick entirely with neutrals. If you take solid navy or denim bottoms, you can vary your outfits by combining them with different colors of tops. For women, a few extra scarves can create even more variety without increasing the weight of your load.

Take Layers for All Climates

You may encounter variations in temperature, and you most certainly will encounter rain. Pack layers that will be comfortable in the cool of morning, then can be rolled up and put in your day bag when the day turns warmer, and donned again as evening falls.

Have a Shoe Swapping Plan

Traveling can tire out your feet, with all the walking over rough surfaces and up and down hills and steps. Take along multiple pairs of comfortable walking shoes to keep your feet happy for the duration of your trip. Happy feet make for a happy trip!

Spend the money for very comfortable shoes, with memory foam to ensure an equal distribution of pressure to the feet. and an anatomically-shaped foot bed to eliminate pressure and friction. You may need to add insoles or even custom orthotics to your own shoes to adjust their support elements. Proper arch and heel support go a long way toward preventing sore feet, especially if you are walking on uneven surfaces. Plan to alternate shoes to vary the pressure points on your feet. Be sure to break in any new shoes long before you leave.

Visit the Dr. Scholl's website *(https://www.drscholls.com/)*, or your favorite drugstore, before your trip to pick up insoles and any other foot comfort products you anticipate needing to keep your feet in good condition. And plan to take along foot powder to cool and sooth your feet, and to decrease skin irritation from rubbing.

Some Clothing Tips for Men

- ☐ A polo shirt is dressier than a tee and is easily layered.

- ☐ Dark colors look clean longer than light colors.

- ☐ Pack at least 2 pairs of *comfortable* shoes.

- ☐ Put shoes in a cloth or plastic bag to protect your clothes.

- ☐ Stuff items inside your shoes to consolidate space.

- ☐ Bring moleskin, second skin, or other blister treatments.

- ☐ Pack a small daypack to hold everything you may need for the day when you set out each morning.

- ☐ Bring an umbrella so you will not be stopped when it rains.

Some Clothing Tips for Women

- ☐ Start with navy pants and skirts.

- ☐ Bring a variety of cotton non-wrinkle tops in different colors.

- ☐ Put in a few scarves, or plan to purchase them at the markets.

- ☐ Pack 2–3 pairs of *comfortable* shoes.

- ☐ Bring a sweater, vest and jacket for layering.

- ☐ Pack a Daypack and a market bag.

- ☐ Remember to bring an umbrella and a sunhat.

Pack Your "Wash-Ery" to Wash Your Clothes Mid-Trip

The key to being able to cut the clothes you bring in half is to plan to do a load of wash mid-trip. When it's time to wash clothes, you have several options—wash small items in the sink or bathtub, pay your hotel to wash your clothes, or visit a laundromat. Many laundromats offer a drop-off and pickup service, but this service comes at a price.

To keep it simple, bring along your own "wash-ery" that contains: 1) a small container of dish detergent and 2) a portable clothesline. Designate a packing cube to make these items easy to locate in your suitcase.

One tried and true method to wash a full load of cloths in record time is to put them all in a bathtub filled with water and the dish detergent you brought from home. When the tub is filled with clothes and around 6 inches of water, climb in barefoot and proceed to stomp and swish everything around for several minutes. Picture vineyard workers stomping grapes and you'll get the idea.

Follow the soap cycle with a rinse cycle. Then roll each item in a towel to press out most of the water, and hang your wash on the shower rod, the drying rack, or the portable clothes line you brought along.

If you're lucky enough to have a washer or dryer available at any of the locations where you are staying, make sure to ask the owner how to use them. European appliances operate differently, and can be tricky to figure out on your own. Also, these appliances tend to be smaller, so avoid the temptation to overload them.

Plan and Set Up Your System for Handling Money.

When traveling in France, you will be using the Euro for everything. With a little bit of preplanning and by following a few simple tips, you can avoid common pitfalls and save hundreds of dollars in bank fees and costly foreign currency exchange rates when exchanging US dollars for Euros or making point-of-sale (POS) purchases from merchants.

Bring Startup Euros with You

Some travelers may feel more comfortable with some startup Euros in their hand before they even board the plane. Euros will cover initial travel expenses like food and drinks in the airport, and your first taxi ride. However, keep your startup Euros at a minimum. To maximize your savings, it's better to take advantage of the more favorable bank-to-bank exchange rates at any ATM machine in France. There are 25 ATM machines within Charles de Gaulle airport, located in the terminals and after passport control.

Use a Coin Purse to Manage Euro Change

The euro system uses coins for anything smaller than a 5€ note. So almost immediately you will find your pockets getting heavier and heavier with 1 euro and 2 euro coins. A small change purse is a necessity to make it easier to manage and carry all the extra change you will receive every day.

Your natural impulse may be to reach for paper euro notes to pay for low-cost items. Instead, check your change purse first. But make sure to hold onto a few 1 euro coins. Some public restrooms charge up to 1 euro per visit. In restrooms without attendants, your only way in will be by having the correct coins.

ATMs and Bank Withdrawal Limits

The best plan for getting cash as you travel is to use ATMs. But be aware that your bank may impose a daily ATM withdrawal limit. So it is a good idea to keep a comfortable supply of cash by stopping at ATMs before you get too close to running short.

The *best* currency exchange rate that you can get is an interbank rate offered by foreign bank ATM machines when you use your bank ATM debit card to withdraw foreign currency. While there are often bank fees assessed by your bank each time you use an ATM machine, at the end of the day you will still get more euros for dollars than any other method, despite the fees (in the following pages we will discuss how to greatly reduce, or eliminate most, or all bank transaction fees).

Call the numbers on the backs of all the debit and credit cards you will be using to let them know you will be traveling abroad. While you have them on the phone, you may be able to have them increase the daily limits for withdrawals on your debit cards so you can have access to more euros at any one point in time.

The ATM machines themselves often have their own daily withdrawal limit, ranging widely between €150 – €450 (some may be higher, depending on where you are). You may discover that you can only withdraw a small number of euros in high traffic areas such as train stations, airports and during weekends, when ATM machines are not serviced.

When an ATM will not give you the amount that you request, incrementally reduce your withdrawal amount until the transaction does go through. Then try to make additional withdrawal transactions at the same ATM machine using a different card, or at a different bank's ATM machine, until you reach your bank's daily withdrawal limit.

If you're worried about security using a foreign ATM machine, don't be. But do take the normal precaution of covering the keypad when you enter your pin code (more about travel safety later in this chapter).

Use the Best Money Exchange Method

Here are a number of ways to exchange dollars into Euros, including how much money you can expect to spend to exchange money using each method, from worst to best. The first four options are rip-offs. Use the fifth type of exchange whenever possible.

Rip-off Level 5: Foreign Exchange Companies

Avoid these at all costs. Foreign exchange desks can be found at airports, city centers, hotels, and tourist sites. These are some of the worst exchange rates you could get, sometimes as high as 20%.

Rip-off Level 4: Travelers' Checks & Prepaid Credit Cards

Travelers' checks used to be a popular method for exchanging currency, but are no longer a good option. You will need to find a place that exchanges checks for local currency. And when you do, the fees that you will pay can add up to $9 per check.

Prepaid credit cards through foreign exchange companies like Travelex can be preloaded with euros to spend, then used just like credit or debit cards at ATM machines or for point-of-sale purchases. But they are laden with fees (for withdrawals, inactivity, to close the card, etc.)

Rip-off Level 3: Buying Cash Online or Through Your Bank

Websites like oanda.com, and travelex.com will sell you euros online and mail them to you, or give you the option to pick them up at one of their stores. This is less costly than the preceding two options for obtaining euros, but still involves fees and the cost of mailing. If you are a member of AAA, the exchange and mailing fees are lower than most other online options.

Your bank likely will offer the service of exchanging euros for dollars. But if you think just because you have a relationship with your bank they will give you a good exchange rate on foreign currency, think again. And, of course, these methods will only work for your supply of "start-up" euros.

Rip-off Level 2: Independent ATM Machines Like Travelex and Euronet

Independent ATM machines are sometimes located right next to bank ATM machines, but have much higher fees. They may present hype about "dynamic currency conversion" (DCC), or offers to "lock-in," or "guarantee" your conversion rate. These promotions are misleading. You will still be charged higher rates.

When you do use an independent ATM, you may come to a prompt that asks if you want to be charged in dollars or in euros. Always choose the local euro currency. Also, be wary of merchants who promote dynamic currency conversion or offer to convert their prices to dollars before running your credit card. These are not offers that will benefit you.

The Best Option: Bank ATM Machines

The *best* currency exchange rate is an interbank rate offered at foreign bank ATM machines, using your bank ATM debit card. While your bank will still assess fees each time you use an ATM, at the end of the day you will still get more euros for dollars than by using any other method.

How to Save Even More Money at the ATM

Now that you know the most favorable exchange method, the focus shifts to comparing the typical debit card point of sale (POS) and ATM bank fees. In the following pages we will discuss how to greatly reduce, or even eliminate, bank transaction fees, as well as a few other tips.

Debit Card Bank Fees

Many banks charge a fixed fee per transaction ($2-$5) plus an international transaction fee of 1%–3%. These fees apply for using your debit card at ATMs, as well as for point-of-sale transactions. To see comparisons of bank transaction fees, refer to the table below. If your bank is not listed, check their website, or give them a call, to learn about their ATM and POS fee structures.

Foreign Transaction Fees by Institution

Institution	Fee Structure	
	ATM Withdrawal	POS Purchase
Banks		
Ally Bank	1% of amount	1% of purchase
Bank of America	$5 + 3% of amount	3% of purchase
BB&T	$5 + 3% of amount	3% of purchase
BBVA Compass	$2 + 1% of amount	3% of purchase
BMO Harris Bank	$2.50 + 3% of amount	3% of purchase
Charles Schwab Bank	N/A	N/A
Chase	$5 + 3% of amount	3% of purchase
Citibank	$2.50 + 3% of amount	3% of purchase
Citizens Bank	$3 + 3% of amount	3% of purchase
Comerica	$5 + 3% of amount	3% of purchase
EverBank	1% of amount	1% of purchase
Fifth Third	$5 + 3% of amount	3% of purchase
HSBC	$2.50 + 3% of amount	3% of purchase
Capital One 360	N/A	N/A
KeyBank	$2.50 + 1% of amount	1% of amount
M&T Bank	Greater of $5 or 3% of amount	3% of purchase
PNC	$5	3% of purchase
Regions	$5	3% of purchase
SunTrust	$5 + 3% of amount	3% of purchase
TD Bank	$3	N/A
TIAA Direct	$2 + 2% of amount	2% of purchase
USAA	$0* + 1% of amount *Up to $15 of other banks' charges refunded each month. No USAA fee for the first 10 withdrawals each month. $2 USAA fee applies to subsequent withdrawals.	1% of purchase
US Bank	$2.50 + 3% of amount	3% of purchase
Wells Fargo	$5	3% of purchase

http://www.nerdwallet.com/blog/banking/debit-card-foreign-transaction-international-atm-fees/

Opening a New Account to Avoid Banking Fees

To avoid fees entirely, consider opening a new checking account. *Capital One 360, USAA* and *Charles Schwab* offer free checking accounts with no international currency exchange fees, no ATM fees, and no minimum balance, or monthly service fees. Most credit unions, and a handful of other banks, offer reduced fees as well.

Setting up a new checking account to get a low or no fee debit card is quick and easy, and can save you hundreds of dollars in fees on a single trip.

Use Credit Cards with Chips

While magnetic-stripe cards are commonplace in the US, microchip cards have been the preferred European technology for nearly a decade. Magnetic-strip cards are accepted by most human agents in stores, restaurants, and hotels.

But be aware that newer vending machines, train and Metro ticket machines, pay-at-the-pump gas stations, and even Vélib' bikes (Paris' bike-share program) require a microchip card.

Many credit card companies are in the process of changing to microchip cards. Even banks with magnetic-stripe cards may offer special travel credit cards with microchip technology.

Keep in mind that Visa and MasterCard are the most widely accepted credit cards in Europe, although American Express is often accepted by businesses that cater to tourists and business travelers. Discover Card is generally *not* accepted.

Street and outdoor market vendors are unlikely to accept any credit cards at all. Small cafés and restaurants, and many businesses, will accept credit cards only for larger purchases (e.g., over 20 €).

Maintain Your Financial Security

If you plan to rely on your debit card to withdraw money throughout your trip, carry a backup card just in case. It's a good idea to keep your backup card in a safe place that is separate from your main card (possibly tucked into a plastic bag in the lining of your suitcase) in case your primary card gets lost or stolen.

Make photocopies of your cards, front and back, with the customer service number on the back clearly legible, so you can immediately report any theft or loss of your cards. Keep these paper copies in a separate place from your cards. If you're traveling with someone else, give your companion a copy of your card information as additional backup.

Keep Trip Docs and Day Pages Readily Accessible

It is essential that you keep your important trip documents organized, secure and at your fingertips when you need them. Your passport, tickets, credit cards and important documents each need to be assigned their own safe, known location, and kept there at all times. Nothing can rain on a vacation like misplacing one of these items! What a nightmare to be rifling through your suitcase on the platform as your train is about to leave, desperately searching for your train tickets. Important documents, critical trip-related papers, *Day Pages* and organizational tools top the list.

Important Travel Documents & Trip-Related Papers

Keeping your trip documents and papers well organized and readily accessible will greatly reduce your stress and be a significant factor in helping to make this a great trip! A starting checklist to use for planning and packing includes:

- ☐ Passport,
- ☐ Itinerary,
- ☐ Flight information,
- ☐ Confirmations for accommodations,
- ☐ Train numbers and times (some tickets will not show this critical information),
- ☐ Train tickets,
- ☐ Vouchers and passes,
- ☐ *Day Pages*,
- ☐ Trip budget,
- ☐ Maps, and
- ☐ Copies of credit and debit cards.

Trip "Day Pages"

Your *Day Pages* will be your "ace in the hole"—an essential ingredient to having a great trip. They will give structure to your trip and optimize how you navigate through each day, always knowing what's coming next.

You will have addresses, telephone numbers, and closing times at your fingertips to call ahead for reservations, to handle whatever comes up, and to stay on schedule when timing is important—catching the train, arriving before closing hours, getting to restaurants in time for your reservations.

And as you make your way, you will have as well a little background and history of the places you will be visiting.

In your revised the *Day Pages*, you also will have your *Orienteering Instructions*—Google map walk-arounds that start at the door of your hotel or flat, and help you get your bearings and become better acquainted with your own neighborhood in each city.

Office Supplies to Keep Your Trip Docs Organized

Assign your main travel tickets, vouchers and documents to their own designated cases or folders. Keeping all your travel documents organized, accessible and safe is essential for stress-free travel. A passport wallet for your passport, plane and train tickets and back-up credit cards is an excellent choice.

For your trip papers, plastic expanding accordion file folders are a great, waterproof tool for staying organized. Designate different folders and pouches for each type of document, for example: Carry heavily-used pages, such as itinerary, maps and schedules in clear sheet protectors to save them from rain and other forms of wear and tear.

- Clear plastic sleeves for itinerary and accommodation information, with next needed information visible on top,

- One portfolio for each destination's *Day Pages,*

- A separate portfolio for completed days,

- A plastic sleeve or portfolio to carry the current day's *Day Pages* with you in your day pack,

- An accordion coupon holder for receipts and a small journal to keep track of them.

These office supplies can be found at office supply stores like *Staples, Office Depot* or *Office Max,* or more inexpensively at *Walmart* or even the *Dollar Store.*

Expandable Folder   Sheet Protectors   Plastic Portfolio

Be Prepared to Use Phones and Electronics Locally

You will need to plan how you will manage your phones and electronics before you leave on your trip. For certain you will need:

☐ Cell phones that will work in France.

☐ Network service with coverage in France.

☐ Power converters to plug in your electronics, since Europe uses 220-volt power, not 110-volt as is used in the USA.

☐ Extra outlets to recharge phones and other rechargeable items.

☐ A laptop or tablet for web access (optional).

Cell Phones That Work in France

To make your whole trip go smoothly it is essential that each member of your travel party carries a cell phone that will work in France. It is critical that you be able to communicate with your travel companions when you get separated or decide to head in different directions. Also you will need to call ahead to hotels, make reservations for restaurants and tours, and call taxis while on the go.

Navigating cell phone usage in a foreign country can unfortunately seem complicated and potentially costly. We've distilled down the critical information to just a few key points, so make sure to pay close attention to this section. There are several things to consider that can save you a tremendous amount of wasted time and headache, as well as a considerable amount of money.

You will have three primary options:

• Unlock your smartphone and purchase your French SIM card before your trip.

- Purchase a simple phone with French SIM card online before your trip, or when you arrive in France.

- Use your own carrier's International service from France.

If you use an unlocked smart phone, and add a data plan to the French SIM card you purchase, you also will be able to access Google maps to navigate while walking, browse the Internet when you need to do research, and consult French language training apps like the free *Duolingo,* or direct translation apps like *Google Translate,* to overcome the language barrier.

The advantage of making your purchases and plans before your trip is that you will have your phone with you, and once your French SIM card is activated you can start using it to call ahead, summon taxis or handle any challenges that should arise.

Unlock Your Smartphone & Purchase a France SIM Card Before Your Trip

Unlocking your smartphone before you leave on your trip may be the best option *if and only if:* 1) your current provider will allow it, and 2) your phone is capable of picking up the frequencies used in France (900 MHz and 1800 MHz).

Once your phone is unlocked, you will be able to switch out your existing SIM card to a prepaid SIM card (with data plan, if you so choose), purchased from one of the French wireless carriers on a *pay-as-you-go basis, with no contract.*

The SIM card you purchase will come pre-cut in three formats to fit standard-chip, micro-chip, or Nano-chip phones. Just break off the required chip size to insert into your phone.

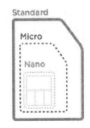

Once you have your French SIM card installed, you will be able to add talk time as you need it. To add talk time, stop at a café, supermarket or tobacco shop, and purchase a "carte recharge" (recharge voucher). Then enter the code printed on your voucher into your phone, following the instructions from your service provider, and, voilà, you will have added minutes of call credit.

Check with your wireless carrier to determine if you are eligible for unlocking your phone. Some carriers require that your phone is no longer under contract before they will allow you to unlock it.

To determine whether or not your smartphone can receive French frequencies, 900 MHz and 1800 MHz (GSM-900 and GSM-1800), do a Google search for your phone's make and model. Not all US cell phones will work in France.

Purchase a Simple Phone & SIM Card in France

If instead of unlocking your smartphone, you decide to purchase a simple phone you will be able to do this online before you leave on your trip. Or you may opt to wait until after you get to France to buy your phone and SIM card. This is easily accomplished at any of the service providers, including *Orange, SFR, Telefonica,* and *Bouygues Telecom.*

Select a *quad-band GSM phone* if you will be making additional overseas trips in the future. *Quad-band phones will work in over 200 countries around the world by simply inserting the appropriate SIM card.*

Use Your Own Phone and Network Service

You will, of course, also have the option of using your own phone and your regular carrier's international service. But this is a very bad idea. Usage charges can be prohibitively expensive, upwards of *$1 per minute* for calls, both incoming and outgoing.

Choose a Network Service with Coverage in France

As you might expect, France has a range of cell phone network service providers. *Orange* (by France Telecom) and *SFR* (by Numericable) are two of the largest, with 99% coverage. Network service resellers like *Lebara* and *Lycamobile* rent cell tower bandwidth from the major providers. These can save you considerable money for short-duration prepaid plans on a *pay-as-you-go basis, with no contract.*

International SIM cards, including 30-day cards, are available from:

* *Lebara (http://www.lebara.fr)*

* *LeFrench Mobile (http://www.lefrenchmobile.com/en.html)*

* *Orange (http://store.orange.com/us/)*

These sites are in both French and English, making it easy to order, activate and purchase more minutes, as needed, online.

The best possible SIM card deal available at the time of publication is from *Lebara*, with *unlimited* text and voice, and 4 gig of internet data, for 25€.. For this deal, Lebara will not ship outside of France. So you would need to have your SIM card shipped to your first accommodations in Amboise.

Another Lebara offer that *can* be delivered Internationally, with the same unlimited voice and texts, but with 2 gigs of data, is available for under 45€. For details about this, and any additional offers that develop at a later date, consult *http://YourGreatTriptoFrance.com/CustomizeYourTrip/* for updates, details, and purchasing instructions. Also, you can refer to this same link for a short, step-by-step video to walk you through how to sign up for these Lebara deals and activate your phone. This Lebara tip alone can save you up to 100€—twice that for two cell phones—as compared to plans where you will pay by the minute.

If you decide to wait to set up your phone service after you get to France, possibly at the *Orange* store in Amboise, you will have assistance from the sales clerk to ensure that the French SIM card and network service are installed and activated properly. *Remember to bring your passport with you to the Orange store.* A photo ID is required to have your SIM card and cell phone service activated.

To install your French SIM card yourself, wait until you arrive in Europe where the SIM card will automatically connect to the network. You will need the little key that opens the SIM card tray of your smartphone to swap out the card.

Keep in mind that technology moves quickly, so this cell phone information will evolve and change over time. To learn about updated options, do a Google search to find out what the current landscape is for French SIM cards, or consult *http://YourGreatTriptoFrance.com/CustomizeYourTrip/*.

How to Dial Using Your French SIM Card Cell Phone

You will have a new cell phone number once your French SIM card has been activated. Immediately place calls to each other in order to capture these numbers, and also write them down in a readily accessible place.

To dial within France, first dial "0." This is the *trunk code*. Then dial the area code and the local number.

To dial the Internationally, dial 00 first. This is the *exit code* to leave the French network. Then dial your country code (e.g., the country code for the US is "1"). Next dial the area code and the local number you are trying to reach. Go to *http://www.countrycallingcodes.com/* for more instructions on dialing country to country.

Using Electronics Abroad

Power adaptors, converters, charging cables, extension cords and multi socket extension plugs are easy items to overlook. But they are essential to managing your electronics while you are in France.

Power Adaptors

You will need a power *adapter* to plug in all your electronics while you are abroad. If you are coming from the United States, you are accustomed to a 110 Volt power supply. But, France and other parts of Europe and the world use a 220 Volt power supply. This means that without a power adapter you will be unable to plug in or recharge any of your electronics during your trip.

Fortunately, a simple adapter will work for most common electronics. Adapters that will work in European countries can be purchased online individually, or in packs of 5 or more, for just a few U.S. dollars (pictured on the left below). Alternatively, you could use a universal adapter (pictured on the right below) that will work in most countries around the world. But this device will be more expensive and bulky. Some adapters even include USB ports to charge multiple devices at the same time.

Current devices, including laptops, tablets, smartphones, e-readers, MP3 players, cameras, and USB battery chargers, typically are built to handle a range of voltages. For example a device marked 110-240 V or 110/240 V (with a dash or slash separating the 2 voltages), can handle input voltages from 110 to 240. Newer hairdryers, electric razors, toothbrushes and irons typically also are dual voltage, as shown by the voltage range printed on the device or its transformer block.

Power Converters

You probably will not need to take a power *converter* on your trip. Converters are needed only for older hairdryers and irons that were not designed to handle dual-voltage input. These are marked with ranges of 110–120 V (to allow for small power fluctuations). Just leave these single-voltage devices at home. When you plug a 110 V device into a 220 V wall socket, the device will heat up from drawing too much current and quickly burn out.

If for some reason you must bring along a single-voltage device, you will need to purchase and pack a *step-down power converter* to convert the 220 V power from the wall socket to the 110 V input limit of the device. Power *converters* are more expensive, heavier, and bulkier.

Charging Cables

The typical charging cords that you may need are for cell phones, computers, tablets, cameras, razors, toothbrushes, and your portable USB battery charger. Think through other items of yours that may require a charging cable and add it to your packing inventory master list.

Portable USB Power Bank

Another handy take-along item is a portable power bank to take along in your daypack or pocket as a backup charger. These can be real life savers when you are out all day and need to recharge your cell phone, camera, or tablet after heavy usage.

They come in a variety of shapes, charging capabilities and sizes that can fit in a pants or jacket pocket, and can be purchased for under $10.

Extension Cords and Multi socket Extension Plugs

Wall sockets in France can be limited, and are sometimes inconveniently located, especially in some of the historic buildings where you will be staying. Be prepared to set up additional plug-in points to be able to handle all of your electronics.

By bringing along an extension cord and a multi-socket extension plug, you will be ready to set yourself up regardless of what you find. But be careful not to overload the extension by plugging in too many devices. Check the current rating marked on the extension lead before plugging devices into it. Most are rated at 13 Amps, but some are rated at only 10 Amps or even less. This means that when you add together the current used by all the items you have plugged in, the total cannot exceed 13 (or 10) Amps. Even when you have space to plug in four devices, this does not mean it is always safe to do so.

Devices like cell phones and laptops use only small amounts of current, so can be plugged into the same outlet. But a hair dryer and an iron, or a coffee pot and a lamp, plugged into the same socket can quickly cause the plug to overheat and even start a fire.

Web-Access Devices

You may consider bringing along a netbook, tablet, or light-weight laptop to have the ability to check bank balances, move money, send and receive emails, refer to trip information, write journal entries, Skype with family and friends, and search the Internet.

Most hotels, and even some restaurants, offer Wi-Fi. Or you can use your unlocked cell phone with data plan to create your own Wi-Fi hotspot, and use it for your other devices.

Alternatively, you may elect to rely on an unlocked smartphone for your internet access. If so, set up before you leave all the apps you might need to handle necessary computer tasks while you are away.

If you do decide to rely completely on your smartphone for web access, you may consider bringing along a travel-sized Bluetooth keyboard. These can be purchased for around $20 and weigh just over half a pound. They can be very handy, allowing you to write emails and journal entries in a fraction of the time it would take using the keyboard interface on your smartphone.

Safely Carry Passports, Credit and Debit Cards & Cash

France is a fairly safe country, but there are pickpockets and several scams that you should at least be aware of to stay safe during your trip. Big cities like Paris, with large concentrations of tourists tend to attract pickpockets. Fortunately, it's relatively easy to avoid becoming a pickpocketing victim. This will be very unlikely, if you follow our simple tips. Ultimately, the best security is just being aware of your surroundings and taking a few simple precautions.

Pickpockets tend to travel in groups, and target densely populated areas such as tourist sites, train and Metro stations, restaurants, and museums. Surprisingly, many pickpockets are children or adolescents, since it is extremely difficult to jail minors in France.

Ladies, make sure to carry a purse that zips and wear it across your body to make it more difficult for someone to snatch it and run. If you have a backpack-type purse, swing it around toward the front, resting it at your side. Always keep your purse where you can see it. In restaurants, keep it where you can feel it, like between your feet or in your lap.

Men, as an extra precaution, keep your wallet in your front pocket. One clever strategy is to wrap your wallet in a rubber band. This will make it extremely difficult for someone to pull it out of your pocket without you knowing.

When You Go Out, Take Along Only the Bare Essentials

As a general rule, leave most of your valuables in a safe at the hotel or apartment where you're staying, or hidden in your suitcases. It's not necessary to bring your passport or other items of value with you. Instead, carry with you an alternative form of identification and a copy of the key pages of your passport. Keep a second photocopy of your important documentation in your luggage. This will make it easier for these items to be replaced, if something gets lost or stolen.

Carry with you only the cash you will need for that day so as to limit your losses if you do get pickpocketed. Split up your cash between you and your travel partner, and among multiple locations on your person and in your daypack or purse.

The Option of Wearing a Money Belt

One of the best ways to keep your important documents, cards, tickets and large bills safe is to use a money belt, which will allow you to hide these items under your clothing and out of sight of would-be pickpockets.

Money belts come in several different designs:

- Around your waist, tucked into your pants (front or back).

- Around your neck or shoulder in a holster, with the strap crossed over the shoulder, and the wallet under your arm.

- Around your leg, when wearing long pants.

- With a belt loop through your belt, tucked into your pants (against your thigh, or hip).

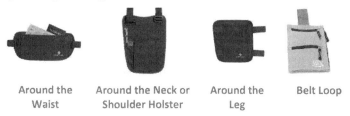

| Around the Waist | Around the Neck or Shoulder Holster | Around the Leg | Belt Loop |

Here are a few tips when using a money belt:

- *Don't keep all your money in your money belt.* Carry enough cash for the day in your pocket, purse, or wallet so you won't need to remove your money belt in public (go somewhere private to do this, like the restroom).

- *Select a comfortable design.* Around-the-waist, and leg designs can get uncomfortable in hot climates. Around-the-neck or shoulder and the belt-loop designs work just as well, but are cooler and can be more comfortable.

- *Select a lightweight, breathable material.*

- Some money belts have additional features like lightweight stainless steel wire to prevent slicing through the lanyard straps. These are not needed when your wallet is hidden under your clothing.

Expert Traveling Tips for Smarter and Safer Travel

Here are some additional guidelines for traveling safely...

Use Inside Compartments & Wear Your Bags Properly

Transfer valuables like cash or cellphones to an inside compartment of your bag or a deep front pocket. Never wear your purse or bag on one shoulder—this makes it an easy target to be snatched, especially in crowded conditions where you're less likely to feel the strap being cut.

Instead, sling your bag over your chest in crisscross style, and keep it close to you and visible. If you wear a backpack, do not keep valuables in outside zipper compartments. You may think you'll feel someone opening a backpack pocket, but pickpockets are experts at being surreptitious, and they often work in groups.

Beware of ATM and Cashpoint Scams

Stay extremely vigilant when withdrawing cash from ATM machines. These can be favorite spots for potential scammers and pickpockets. Do not agree to help anyone who asks to learn how to use the machine, and do not accept "help" or advice on how to use it yourself. Type in your code in total privacy, and ask anyone lingering too close to back off. Do not be drawn into conversation while you are entering your pin code.

Beware of Crowding and Distractions

In crowded places, like the Paris metro or around popular tourist attractions, pickpockets often work in groups and take advantage of the confusion. One member of a "team" may attempt to distract you by engaging you in conversation, asking for money, or showing you a small trinket, while another goes for your pockets or bag.

When you are standing in line, or in very crowded conditions, make sure your valuables are safely stored in a money belt or an inside compartment of your bag. Hold your bag close to you, preferably where you can see and feel it. At restaurants, especially at outdoor tables, keep your bag between your feet. And in the metro, it may be best to avoid sitting or standing close to the doors, since some pickpockets adopt the strategy of grabbing bags or valuables and exiting the metro car just as the doors are closing.

Here are a few pickpocket tricks and scams to watch for in major tourist locations:

339

- **Help with your bag.** Some Metro stations have lots of stairs. Watch out for people who attempt to "help" you carry your suitcase up the stairs. While you're taken off guard, their accomplice may seize the opportunity to pickpocket you.

- **"Charity" workers with clipboards.** Young girls with clipboards may approach you, signaling that they are deaf or mute, then indicating they want you to sign a petition and make a donation to their charity. While you read and sign the petition, an accomplice is trying to pickpocket you.

- **Metro grab.** Be wary of small groups of people crowding you before the Metro doors shut. They may be setting the stage to grab your purse, then hop off the train as the doors begin to close. And be careful using your cell phone if you're standing near the door of a subway car. Thieves can reach in to snatch your phone just as the doors are closing. Also, be wary of anyone who stands very close to you unnecessarily, when it isn't crowded. They too could be up to no good.

- **The "found" gold ring scam.** This con involves someone "finding" a gold ring near where you are standing. When they see that you have noticed the ring too, they pick it up and point to the hallmark inside indicating that the ring is made of 18K gold. They then offer to "share" the find with you, and sell you "their half" of it at a vastly exaggerated estimate of what it is worth. If you fall for this, you later may discover the ring is worthless costume jewelry made of brass.

- **The "friendship" bracelet.** This scam starts with one of the "string men" (an apparent jewelry vendor, carrying string bracelets) who engages you in innocent conversation, saying that he would like some help with a "demonstration," or that he wants to show you a magic trick. Before you know it, he grabs your wrist, quickly ties a homemade bracelet of colored string around it, then demands a ridiculous sum of money, like 20€, as payment. You will find that you can't easily remove the bracelet yourself. If you refuse to pay, the con man doggedly follows you around until you pay him just to get rid of him.

- **Change-making scams.** In this scam, a cashier counts out your change, and pauses their count in the middle to see if you prematurely grab up your bills and leave. Keep your own count, and make sure you receive all the change you are due.

- **Bill dropping scam.** In this con, a cab driver pretends to drop the large bill you hand them, then switches it for a smaller bill before giving you your change.

These scam artists prey on rushed tourists who aren't paying attention. Always be very alert when dealing with money. When paying for an item or service, it is a good idea to note out loud the bill denomination you are handing them, and wait for confirmation, before you let go of it.

You get the general idea. If someone bumps into you, take a quick inventory of your belongings. If people crowd around you on public transportation, or on an escalator, again be aware that pickpockets might take advantage of the confusion. If someone drops something in front of you (like a gold ring, or a bunch of items that need to be picked up), keep your valuables close at hand, if you decide to help them. If someone thrusts a newspaper or map in your face, there may be hands underneath reaching for your belongings. Be focused and deliberate when using ATM machines.

A little diligence will make you a better, more aware traveler, and protect you from being taken advantage of by potential pickpockets and scam artists. Remember that this isn't your hometown, so you do need to give some attention to your personal safety and the security of your belongings. A little extra awareness and diligence can prevent a ruined vacation when you're traveling.

All of this said, it is essential that you do not allow caution to become paranoia. Most people you meet on your trip will be perfectly honest. In the hundreds of days we have traveled in Europe, we have had only one incident of theft, and that was a car break-in at night, outside Mont Saint-Michel. We have experienced the "making change scam" twice, and the "gold ring scam" once. But we didn't fall for any of these. Now you won't either.

Report any Incident of Pickpocketing

The *US Embassy* recommends that if you do fall prey to theft or pickpocketing, call for the police immediately. The French equivalent of 911 is **112.** Memorize this single number in case you ever need it, and your call will be redirected as needed. If help does not arrive promptly, go to the nearest police station to file a report. Then report the loss of any important valuables to your embassy or consulate.

Be Prepared to Set Out Each Day Ready for Anything

Take along everything you will need to set off each morning fully equipped for the day, prepared for anything so you can last all day. Be ready for rain. Be prepared to stop at the market to pick up items to carry home. Have all the information you will need that day by carrying your *Day Pages*. Bring along all the passes, vouchers and tickets you will be using before you return home tonight.

Follow the *Day Prep* list below every day as you set out. On days that you plan to have a picnic for lunch, add to what you normally carry along the items on the *"Picnic-ery list."*

Day Prep List

- ☐ Sun protection
- ☐ Sun glasses and hat
- ☐ Umbrellas
- ☐ Water
- ☐ Shopping bags
- ☐ *Day Pages*
- ☐ Passes, vouchers & tickets

Picnic-ery List

- ☐ Plastic cups (or wine glasses) and plates
- ☐ Paper or cloth napkins
- ☐ Light-weight utensils and corkscrew
- ☐ Ziploc bags
- ☐ Bread, cheese, wine and thou…

Stay Healthy

Traveling can be strenuous. You may develop blisters or aches and pains or even sniffles. Pack a selection of items to handle various contingencies, working from this *Pharmacy List*. Hopefully you will not need any of it, but you will have it with you just in case to prevent small complaints from slowing you down.

Pharmacy List

☐ Band-Aids and antibacterial cream.

☐ Cold-eeze and decongestants.

☐ Vitamin C packets.

☐ Melatonin (to overcome jetlag or other sleep irregularities).

☐ Tums and Excedrin.

Prepare to Communicate, Interact and Relate

We talked before about smiling and laughing, and the positive affect they have on other people. Now we will go into more detail about how to set the stage and prepare in advance to make fun connections with the French during your trip.

Language Readiness: The *Dozen Essential Phrases*

To manage well in France, and to make connections with the ever interesting locals, it is essential that you engage in two key practices. First, do make an effort to speak at least some French—the beautiful language of the country. This is a matter of being considerate and well mannered. A few phrases will go a long way.

Here's why. As a language French is very different from English, both in vocabulary and in the order in which words are combined into sentences. This makes French a bit difficult for English-speaking people to master. But it also makes English difficult for French-speaking people. If you put words in the correct order for English, they are in the wrong order for French, and vice versa.

So when you interact with French people, assume that they are just as uncomfortable speaking English as you are speaking French. The best practice is to meet part way. When you make an earnest attempt to speak to them in French, this opens the way for them to risk attempting to speak to you in English. In general, you will find the French people to be friendly and helpful once they are past the potential embarrassment of speaking imperfect English.

The second critical practice is to recognize that the French are extremely formal and polite in their language and in their dealings, with each other and with you. You may cause offense without meaning to, or even come across as rude, if you do not recognize and practice their basic formal courtesies.

For example, it is customary to say hello to the shopkeeper when you enter a shop, then say thank you and goodbye as you leave. It is always essential to say "excuse me," as well as "please" and "thank you." And each statement must be accompanied by the appropriate honorific— monsieur, madame or mademoiselle (for a man, a woman or a young girl or woman, respectively).

Here are *12 Essential Phrases* to carry with you, and use regularly during your trip. These will give you a good start at coming across as the polite and considerate guest you certainly intend to be.

12 ESSENTIAL PHRASES
Greetings
1.   Bonjour, madame. Bonjour, monsieur. (Hello). Ça va? (How are you doing?) Au revoir, madame/monsieur. (Goodbye).
Starting up communications
2   Parlez-vous anglais? (Do you speak English?)
Good manners
3.   Excusez-moi, s'il vous plaît. (Excuse me, please).
4.   Merci, madame. Merci, monsieur. (Thank you sir/ma'am).
Necessary
5.   Où sont les toilettes? (Where are the restrooms?)
Getting Directions
6.   Où dois-je valider mon billet de train? (Where do I validate my train ticket?)
7.   Dans quelle direction est Notre Dame? (In what direction is Notre Dame?)
At the Market
8.   Combien pour ça? (How much for this?)
At the Restaurant
9.   Une table pour deux près de la fenêtre. (A table for two next to the window.)

> 10. Quelle est votre recommandation entre ces deux? (What is your recommendation between these two?)
>
> 11. Je voudrais vin blanc (rouge, rosé) s'il vous plait (white, red or rosé wine). Je voudrais de l'eau gazeuse (de l'eau sans gaz) s'il vous plaît (bottled sparkling water or bottled still water). Je voudrais une carafe d'eau (a free pitcher of tap water).
>
> 12. L'addition, s'il vous plait. (The bill, please).
>
> *NOTE:* Follow each of the above with please (s'il vous plait) and the correct honorific (monsieur, madame or mademoiselle).

Plan to Add Three New Phrases Per Day

If there are other particular needs that you anticipate having while you travel, add additional phrases to this preliminary list. Then go to *Google Translate* (*https://translate.google.com*), set the left box to English and the right hand box to French, type in your needed phrase in the left box, and click the "Translate" button.

Print out and carry with you your *Essential Dozen* phrases, plus any others you have added. Go to *www.YourGreatTriptoFrance.com/CustomizeYourTrip* For a digital copy of these phrases, and to access additional language resources. By having these phrases ready, you will be able to overcome the feelings of awkwardness as you begin to connect and relate.

Continue to carry and refer to this *Phrase Sheet* until you have all the phrases mastered. Once you have fully mastered your preliminary list of phrases, consult your *Phrase Book* to select three new phrases to learn each day, selecting phrases that you will be able to put to immediate use.

If you are using your smartphone, you can download a free app called *Duo Lingo* (also available at *www.duolingo.com*). This app will give you daily word and phrase lessons. Or you may consider being an early owner of a Pilot, the world's first smart earpiece that translates between users speaking different languages *as they speak* (http://www.waverlylabs.com/).

This small bit of preparation and effort will make a huge difference in the quality of your trip and in your ability to connect with and communicate with the French. As you adapt, the French will respond to you with warmth and interest.

Bring Home Treasures

As you add treasures to your suitcase, you will not want to be limited. And you certainly will not want to carry around extra weight. But you can have it both ways.

Purchase what you want to purchase, then periodically pack up a box to mail home. This moderate expense is well worth it. You will maintain your freedom to shop as you like, yet still be able to heft your luggage into the train. Equally importantly, your luggage will not be overweight when you check in for your flight home.

To be prepared to "mail home the weight," take along a small pouch that contains the items on this *Mail-ery List*.

Mail-ery List:

☐ Wide tape
☐ Scissors
☐ Marking pen

Capture Your Trip to Revisit It in the Future

Aside from finding treasures to bring home, nothing will recall fond memories and feelings of nostalgia from a great trip more than looking through the pictures you captured along the way. Here are some tips about bringing your trip home with you.

Take Lots of Pictures

Digital cameras have made it easy to take an unlimited number of pictures, so there really is no reason not to make daily photo taking a habit. Some travelers opt to just use their cell phone cameras, while others prefer to have a dedicated camera with extra features. Most cameras and cell phones come equipped with a megapixel rating that is high enough to meet just about anybody's needs and to deliver beautiful, high-resolution images.

Digital cameras offer a bevy of automatic features that make it simple and easy even for photography novices to take great shots. Features like Zoom allow you to focus in on the elements you want to highlight in your shot. You also will have flash and no flash options readily available to you. This is useful since many museums will allow indoor photos so long as you turn off your flash.

Whatever camera you choose to use, make sure that it is one that you will be willing to carry with you and use everywhere you go. Some of the best pictures we've ever taken were unplanned experiences that we were able to capture because we just happened to have our cameras or cell phones handy.

You have seen some of these shots. The Frenchman throwing his arm around Barry on the Boat bar in Paris. The women offering wine tasting in the wine shop carved into the wall that encircles Amboise Castle. The stylish scarf vendor on market day.

Here are a few tips when taking photos to bring home:

- Manage storage space on your camera or phone by offloading your pictures to another device (or to the cloud) mid-trip to free up space. Bring along the connecting cables you will need for these uploads.

- Consider bringing additional memory cards for your camera. If your camera is battery operated, bring extra batteries.

- Bring an inexpensive portable USB charger to keep your cell phone or rechargeable camera charged while you are out and about all day, away from electrical outlets.

- Get in the habit of charging your cell phone, camera and USB charger every night to start each day with a full charge.

- If you use your cell phone as a camera, turn off Wi-Fi, and Bluetooth when you are not using them to conserve your battery. When you don't need to be connected to the cell network, put your phone in airplane mode to save even more battery life and extend your photo-taking ability. Note: You can use a free app like "Battery Doctor" to free up additional memory on your cell phone to extend battery life even further.

- Use your camera or phone when you are exploring and getting oriented in each new area. Take pictures of street signs and cross streets at each turn, then use them like breadcrumbs as you retrace your steps.

And So... Now You Are Off...

So, are you ready now to take your great trip to France? You know what is possible and now you also have a plan. You know exactly *what* to do, *why* you would want to do it, and *how* to do it, every step of the way. And you have envisioned your trip in vivid detail so you can enjoy looking forward to it.

You know how much money your trip will cost, and what trade-offs and choices you will be making in order to get the most out of your travel budget. You have clear guidance that will take you through the process of making the arrangements, then preparing yourself well for a successful journey,

You will not be traveling in a group. But you will not be alone out there on your own either. We have taken this trip ourselves, so we know how much fun you are going to have, and that the quality of your experience will significantly surpass that of any group or ad hoc trip you've taken in the past, or heard about from family or friends.

You will be embarking on a style of travel that will immerse and absorb you so completely, you will return home already planning where you would like to travel next. We hope that you feel inspired, well-guided, confident, empowered and ready to set off on your own travel odyssey.

Bon Voyage!!

INDEX

M

N

260, 267, 276, 277, 282, 296, 344

353

265

V

W

Thank you for Reading...

Dear Reader...

We appreciate your taking the time to read *Your Great Trip to France: Loire Chateaux, Mont-Saint-Michel, Normandy and Paris!* We hope you have enjoyed envisioning your trip in detail, and that you will apply what you have learned to take your own Great Trip when you are ready.

Visit YourGreatTriptoFrance.com/CustomizeYourTrip/ (or, the shortened link bit.ly/1pZ9T1y), to access your exclusive insiders' bonus content that includes all the resources you will need to adapt your trip to the specifics of your own final travel arrangements. Here you will be able to download your customizable *2-week Trip Calendar, Day Pages, Itinerary, Budget* and *Packing Checklist* (accessible through Microsoft Office, or the free, cloud-based Google Docs), as well as two options for a 1-week trip, should your travel time be more limited. When you have customized your trip, print out your *Day Pages*. Then separate and staple each day into its own transportable packet to carry with you in your daypack when you set off each morning.

You will also find the authors' *trip photo gallery, short videos detailing a variety of how-to tips (including a ninja travel tactic that will make setting up your overseas communications drop dead simple, while potentially saving 100€ on your SIM card and cell phone connection service), as well as additional future travel resources that we will continue to add over time.*

Finally, we would like to ask you a favor. If you are so inclined, we would greatly appreciate your writing an Amazon review for *Your Great Trip to France.* Reviews are tough to come by these days, but are essential to the life of a book. You, the reader, have the power to make or break a book. We highly value your honest feedback, both positive and negative. Your comments and responses will help us to improve future editions and books in the *Your Great Trip Book Series* to provide our readers with the very best travel experiences. Please visit Carolee's Amazon.com author page on at amzn.to/26R7yaN, then click on the *Your Great Trip to France* book thumbnail image, then *Customer Reviews,* to post your review.

Best wishes, and happy travels...

Carolee Duckworth & Brian Lane

Complete Pre-planned Trip & Guide to Smart Travel

YOUR *Great* TRIP TO ITALY

FLORENCE ★ VENICE ★ CINQUE TERRE ★ TUSCANY

An Unforgettable Dream Vacation for Independent Travelers

CAROLEE DUCKWORTH & BRIAN LANE

Ignite Your Passion for Travel!

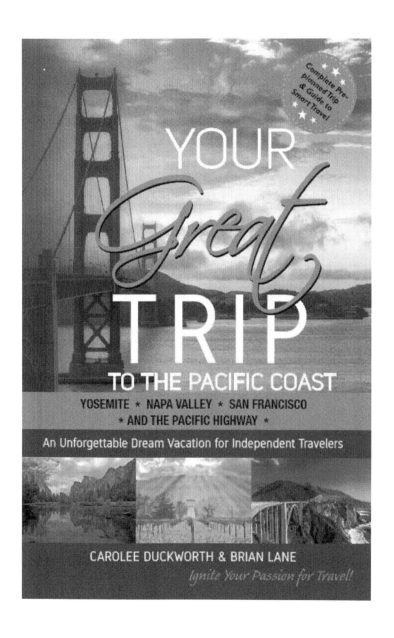

Complete Pre-planned Trip & Guide to Smart Travel

YOUR
Great
TRIP
TO THE PACIFIC COAST

YOSEMITE ★ NAPA VALLEY ★ SAN FRANCISCO
★ AND THE PACIFIC HIGHWAY ★

An Unforgettable Dream Vacation for Independent Travelers

CAROLEE DUCKWORTH & BRIAN LANE

Ignite Your Passion for Travel!

Your Great Trip Series

Coming Soon...

http://YourGreatTrip.com

Your Great Trip to France Series

Provence, the Cote d'Azur & the French Alps

Beyond Paris: Giverny, Fontainebleau, Versailles & Angers

Encircling the Mediterranean: from French to Italian Riviera

Your Great Trip to Italy Series

Florence, Venice, Cinque Terre & Tuscany

Sorrento, Capris, the Amalfi Coast & Rome

Swiss and Italian Lakes and Alps by Train: Geneva to Lake Como

Your Great Trip in the USA Series

The Pacific Coast: Yosemite, Napa Valley, San Francisco & the Pacific Highway

Florida, South: Ft Lauderdale, Miami South Beach, the Keys & Key West

Rocks & Oases: Sedona, Las Vegas & the Grand Canyon

Your Great Trip to Canada Series

Victoria & Vancouver by way of Seattle

From Niagara Falls to Quebec City, with Montreal

32441501R00200

Made in the USA
Middletown, DE
04 June 2016